Y0-BDU-998

THE ABORIGINAL TRIBES OF INDIA

The Aboriginal Tribes of India

Stephen Fuchs

ST. MARTIN'S PRESS NEW YORK

St. Martin's Press, Inc., 175 Fifth Avenue, New York, N.Y. 10010
Printed in India
Library of Congress Catalog Card Number: 76–27186
First Published in India in 1973
First Published in Great Britain in 1977
First Published in the United States of America in 1977

Preface

It is strange that up to the present time no anthropologist has attempted a complete survey and description of the aboriginal population of India. Certainly, there is A. Baines' *Ethnography* (Strasbourg, 1912). But this book includes also the nonaboriginal peoples of India, and the author's description of the individual tribes and peoples is too short to present their proper characterisation. Further, he devotes thirty-one pages to the so-called 'hill-tribes'. Moreover, since the book was published in 1912 a revision of its data would anyhow be long overdue. More than anything else, India's attainment of independence has changed the whole policy regarding the aboriginal tribes. Finally, the book is long out of print and not easily available.

H. Risley's *The People of India* (Calcutta, 1915), recently republished, does not, as the title suggests, consider all the races of the Indian sub-continent and is, moreover, mainly concerned with the problems of caste.

G.S. Ghurye's *The Scheduled Tribes* (Bombay, 1959) restricts itself to certain features and problems of the Indian tribals. And it contains some theories of the author which have not been generally accepted by anthropologists.

N. K. Bose's *Tribal Life in India* (New Delhi, 1971) is more a popular description of the tribals for the general reader. The same may be said of *Tribal India* by K. L. Bhomick, *et al.,* and *Indian Tribes* by Chakravorti and Mukherjee.

This author therefore hopes that his present book fills a real need and will prove useful to students of Indian tribal life who want a concise, but comprehensive and reliable, description of the tribal population of India (and Pakistan).

After going through the first two chapters of the book, the reader will realise how difficult it was to group the Indian tribes systematically. An arrangement of the tribes according to their standard or culture or occupation or racial origin proved impossible. The author finally decided to group them geographically. Even that could not be followed too rigidly.

Another problem presented itself when the description of the individual tribes was attempted. A full portrayal of each tribe would have resulted in a tiresome repetition of the cultural features which many tribes have in common. It was found advisable to give first in each chapter a presentation of the general situation of the tribes in a region and then to point out the special features found in individual tribes.

The author found it expedient to start by giving, as a kind of basic introduction, a concise description of the work which prehistorians and archaeologists have carried out so far to bring light into the cultural and racial history of India. This is followed by an anthropological survey of the living races and peoples of India, though for want of reliable information it is still incomplete and often based on mere conjectures.

The reader may find that the author has often been harsh in his criticism of the treatment which the more civilised peoples of India have meted out to the aboriginal tribes. To counterbalance this criticism the author has included a final chapter in which he describes the various efforts of the Indian Government towards the economic and social uplift of the aboriginal tribes and their complete integration in the national life of India as fully-fledged citizens with equal rights and opportunities. It is quite natural that experts in the field of Indian ethnology will find many gaps and mistakes in this first attempt at classification and scientific presentation of the Indian tribes. The author will be grateful if they are pointed out to him. An eventual second edition, in case there is a need for it, will then make the necessary corrections and fill the gaps left in this first attempt.

Bombay STEPHEN FUCHS
26 January 1973

Contents

	Preface	v
I.	The Prchistoric Races of India	1
II.	The Aboriginal Races of India	22
III.	The Aboriginal Tribes of Northern India	78
IV.	Nomadic Tribes in the Plains of Northern India	105
V.	The Tribes in the Central Area	134
VI.	The Tribes in Eastern India	197
VII.	The Tribes in South India	238
VIII.	Tribal Welfare in India	288
	Index of Subjects	299
	Index of Authors	302
	Index of Tribes	305

CHAPTER I

The Prehistoric Races of India

FOR THE prehistorian and anthropologist it is a very difficult task to arrange the peoples and cultures of India in the chronological sequence of their appearance on this subcontinent. Even their subsequent history well up to the Aryan invasion is shrouded in obscurity. Though stone implements of prehistoric man have been found in various sites dating back to the Lower Palaeolithic period, so far no skeletal finds have been made of these earlier times. And the human fossil finds of later periods are too few and insignificant to enable us to draw any definite conclusions as to the racial history of India in prehistoric times.

In the last twenty years or so prehistoric research in Asia and especially in Africa has progressed considerably. A better knowledge of these prehistoric areas has, however, shown that the European Stone Age sequence and chronology are not always applicable to Asia and Africa. Even terms such as 'Lower, Middle and Upper Palaeolithic' lose their meaning to some extent when applied outside Europe.

The reasons responsible for this situation are: Firstly, new types and forms of implements make their appearance which differ from those found in Europe; secondly, the Ice Age affected only the mountainous northern parts of India, while the rest of the subcontinent had alternatively a Pluvial and a Dry Period; thirdly, the fauna was not always contemporary in different regions—it appeared and disappeared at different times in different regions;* and, finally, prehistoric stone cul-

*Stegodon, a primitive elephant, for instance, died out in China in the

tures of the same type need not be contemporaneous in Asia and Europe. It is well-known that stone tools of a Palaeolithic type survived in India and Africa even into modern times. Bottle glass, for instance, was used even till recent times by tribal peoples in Africa and India to fashion microliths. A.P. Khatri [(1964), p. 767] reports microliths fashioned of glass (which consequently cannot be of great antiquity) found at Adamgarh near Hoshangabad in Central India. It is stated that Bushmen in South Africa used to buy bottles of perfume, not for the perfume which they contained, but for the glass which broke in such a manner as to make the kind of microliths which they preferred to use as implements [cf. J.D. Clerk (1959), p. 26].

Definite correlations will therefore have to wait until the combined research of geologists, palaeontologists, biologists and prehistorians establishes more reliably the sub-divisions of the Pleistocene taking into consideration the continents outside Europe, or until more exact methods of absolute chronology have been worked out [cf. S.C. Malik (1964), p. 205]. Still, a preliminary survey may be attempted here, subject to future revision, when new finds warrant such a revision.

The Races of the Early Stone Age

The existence of pre-Pleistocene *Ramapithecus,* a hominid ancestral form of man, between fourteen and eight million years ago in the Nagri Zone of the Siwalik hills in north-western India, would suggest the possibility of hominisation in India. However, no traces of specimens of the subsequent phases of evolution towards the human species, nor any fossils of the earliest definitely human forms have so far been found in India. Neither *Australopithecine* nor *Anthropus erectus* remains are in evidence from this area. Rumours are that such finds had indeed been made in various places, but as their significance was not recognised, they were reburied or disappeared in some other manner. But there is still a good chance that similar finds will one day be made, especially after a systematic search for them.

Lower Pleistocene, in India in the Middle Pleistocene, and in Indonesia at the close of the Pleistocene.

Even though fossil evidence is lacking, the existence of man in India in early Palaeolithic times is proved by the tools which he manufactured, used and left behind. The earliest indication of the existence of tool-making man in Pleistocene India is found in the last phase of the second glaciation or at the beginning of the second interglacial period. In deposits of this geological age crude, heavy stone-axes and pebble chopping tools* were found in the upper terraces of the Soan, Beas and Banganga rivers, and the tributaries of the Indus in north-western India. In the lower terraces the hand-axes become smaller and more finely worked. There are also cleavers, discoidal cores,† flakes, and still a high proportion of choppers (pebble tools). The diversity of artefact types warrants the division of this industry into pre-Soan, Early-, and Late-Soan periods.

Another site of Early Stone Age tools has been discovered at Adamgarh (near Hoshangabad in Madhya Pradesh) in the Narbada valley. Here, too, hand-axes, chopping tools, ovates, and a few cleavers were found.** The proportion of hand-axes and choppers decreases in the upper layers of this industry, while cleavers become more numerous, are of greater variety and more finely made. In a still later phase they change into flake tools, even to scrapers and pointed flakes. They resemble the Acheulian and post-Acheulian types of European industries.

The site at Adamgarh was discovered and described by R.V. Joshi in 1964, while the finds in the Soan valley were made in 1939 by H. De Terra and T.T. Paterson; those in the Beas river valley were made by B.B. Lal in 1956.

Early Stone Age industries were also found around Madras (at Attirampakkam) over an area many square miles in extent [cf. V.D.K. Krishnaswamy (1947); B. and R. Allchin (1968), pp. 59 f.]. They also belong to the Lower Palaeolithic period and seem to be contemporaneous with the pre-Soan and Soan industries. Similar stone industries have also been found south

*Pebble tools are crude choppers made by removing a few flakes to form a cutting edge at one end of a pebble or lump of rock.

†A 'core' is a large stone from which parts are chipped off to give it an edge. 'Flakes' are the flat pieces which are chipped from a large stone.

**'Cleavers' are tools with one straight edge, shaped like an axe-head, probably for chopping meat and skinning. They are characteristic of the Acheulian period.

of Madras in the beds of the rivers Cauvery and Vaigai; near Bombay (at Khandivli); north of the Narbada; in the upper reaches of the Sone, a tributary of the Ganges; at a site near Allahabad; and in Orissa (Mayurbhanj) [cf. Dharani Sen and N.K. Bose (1948)]. But its centre is Madras and, therefore, it is known as 'Madras Industry'. The tools are pear-shaped or oval, flaked on both faces in such a way as to produce a continuous zig zag cutting-edge.

Who the peoples were who manufactured these tools is unknown as no skeletal remains of them are preserved. As the *Australopithecine* and *Homo habilis* forms at Olduvai (east Africa) apparently fashioned and used similar chopping pebble tools, the makers of the Indian Early Stone Age tools are sometimes believed to have belonged to similar hominid species [cf. H.D. Sankalia (1962), p. 278]. But the size of the tools speaks against this assumption, the small *Homo habilis* and *Australopithecine* creatures could never have held the rather large stone tools of the Indian Early Stone Age in their grip. It is, therefore, more likely that they belonged to the *Anthropus* group which was larger in size.

Zeuner [(1958), p. 292] maintains that the hand-axe is an excellent tool for digging up roots, grubs and other vegetable food from the ground, though it can be used for many other purposes as well—for instance, for making notches in trees to facilitate climbing. Hence, the hand-axe makers were probably vegetable and grub gatherers. Zeuner associates, on the other hand, the makers of the larger flakes and hollow scrapers of the northern regions of India with forests and believes that they were hunters. For, such flakes would be very suitable for cutting and dressing carcasses.

MacBurney [(1960), pp. 28, 31] has studied the distribution of hand-axes and flakes in western Europe and found that the hand-axe makers preferred the low, maritime and warm regions, whereas the flake fabricators liked the upland which was comparatively cooler. This would be true also for India.

The distribution of the hand-axe tools suggests that their makers lived on river banks in the open or on the edge of the forest avoiding the thickly forested interior, up to an altitude of about 2,000 feet. Higher, bare or heavily grown altitudes were probably avoided, because vegetables as well as game animals which they preferred and even the raw materials for making the tools they liked were scarce in such regions. They also preferred places near running water. On the other hand, they avoided the lower reaches of the rivers near the delta or near their mouth because of their swampy condition.

For these reasons alone we may explain the absence of Palaeolithic hand-axes in Assam and Kerala. The first was heavily forested, the second a coastal region. The same applies to Sind, Saurashtra and Rajasthan. These parts of India were probably, until the Middle Pleistocene times, covered by the sea.

In the south-east, the great number of sites and their richness in implements suggest that the Palaeolithic population was much denser in this region than in the west or north. On the other hand, the wide distribution of the tools might be due to the fact that the hand-axe makers did not carry the tools with them but made them, as and when required, on the spot. With their two main implements—the hand-axe, which they must have held in the bare hand as the pebble-butt indicates, and the cleaver—they dug up roots of plants, and cut trees as well as animal carcasses.

However, these speculations are no doubt based on observations culled from the remaining primitive peoples of the world. What is wanted is more positive data. The search for stone tools and especially for fossils in rivers and caves must be continued and even intensified.

The most striking feature of the Early Stone Age industries is their immense duration. For well over a million years the stone tools hardly changed at all. Even if the Early Stone Age had been considerably shorter in India, it lasted several hundred thousand years until the end of the last glaciation.

The Races of the Middle Stone Age

In the final phases of the Palaeolithic Age the type of tools changes in the lower Soan terraces and the upper Adamgarh layers. The tools are now all flake tools which vary considerably in shape. Since they are found on the same sites as the Early Stone Age implements, it is assumed by some prehistorians that the later tools have developed from those of an earlier date. But this need not be so; they could have been manufactured by a different race, the more so because Middle Stone Age tools are found in many other sites too, even in places where no Early Stone Age tools were discovered. It is possible that at Adamgarh and in the Soan sites fabricators of the Middle Stone Age chronologically followed the earlier settlers. They might have been immigrants from western Asia or Europe.

The implements of this age are generally smaller and of greater variety. They are flaked off pre-prepared cores and show bulbs of percussion where they have not been removed. Oval pebbles battered at one end are also quite numerous. Cores from which flakes have been split off sometimes show traces of use as hand-axes. But such hand-axes are much smaller in size than those of the Early Stone Age. There is a large variety of scrapers, borers and leaf-shaped pointed flakes, some with an incipient tang.

Middle Stone Age sites are fairly frequent in Central India, especially along the Narbada river. They are also found at Khandivli (near Bombay where K.R.U. Todd discovered them in 1938), in the Soan region (found by De Terra and Paterson) forming the so-called 'Late-Soan period', at Adamgarh (in the upper layers), at Nevasa in Maharashtra, in the gravels of the Luni river in western Rajasthan, and in the extreme north, in the Sanghao Cave in the tribal territory adjoining the former North-West Frontier Province (now in Pakistan) [cf. B. and R. Allchin (1968), p. 71]. Middle Stone Age tools are also found in eastern Maharashtra on the Wainganga and in Andhra (Gundla-Brahmesvaram).

The raw material for these tools is generally jasper, chert or chalcedony, while those of the Early Stone Age are mainly of quartzite or of volcanic stone. Though in India they have a character of their own, these stone tools still resemble the Mousterian type of culture. The people who manufactured them had obviously little use for implements like large hand-axes and cleavers. They preferred not only different tools but also ones of smaller size. All this suggests a basic change in the people who manufactured them, probably they were a different race. However, this is merely a conjecture, as no fossils of the makers of this tool type have so far been found. Until bone remains of the men of this industry are discovered, nothing definite can be stated about the race to which they belonged.

The frequent occurrence of spear-heads among these finds suggests that these tool-makers were a race of hunters [cf. H.D. Sankalia (1962), p. 123]. They might have migrated into India from almost anywhere. They might have come even from Africa, as the same type of tools can be found in the regions north and south of the Sahara. The makers of Mousterian tools might have been Neanderthalers. But as they were very ancient human types, it is not likely that they have survived in any of the living races of India.

THE RACES OF THE LATE STONE AGE

Immediately after the glacial period we find in Europe, north and east Africa and in Palestine various regional industries with the tendency to reduce the stone blades manufactured in the earlier period to often absurdly small dimensions. It can be presumed that such stone blades were merely the cutting edges of composite tools made largely of wood or bone. Such stone industries occur very widely also in India, especially in south and central India, also in Sind, and all over Pakistan, the Punjab and Baluchistan, though few scientific studies of these industries have been made in these areas. No microliths have so far been found in the Ganges plains and in the mountains north of them.

The microliths are mainly made of quartzite, jasper, agate and chalcedony; they consist of a variety of blades—parallel-sided, plain or retouched, pen-knife-type, etc.; points—crescentic, bi-marginally re-touched, leaf-shaped, shouldered or tanged, and simple points on flakes; burins; scrapers; and miscellaneous cores [R.V. Joshi, in B. and R. Allchin (1968), p. 85].

The Allchins believe that the Middle Stone Age developed gradually and organically into the Late Stone Age. It certainly does so at some sites, notably at Adamgarh. But there are many sites that begin with microliths on bedrock. Thus, peoples of various racial stock may have used the same technique, either developing it locally, or adopting it from other Mesolithic peoples, or bringing it along from outside India. This is also suggested by the wide distribution of the microliths. It is scarcely likely that at the Late Stone Age all the microlith stone fabricators in the whole of India belonged to one race.

The people of the Late Stone Age seem to have lived mainly by hunting and gathering. It must have been in this Mesolithic period that the bow and arrow were invented, or only microliths could be used as arrow-heads. While the situation of the earlier camp sites suggests that the people of the Early and Middle Stone Ages usually stayed in the open country, many Mesolithic sites are found in caves and in rock shelters. The rock shelters are sometimes decorated with paintings in various colours (usually purple, red and light orange-brown). Many of them depict wild animals or hunting scenes. This also suggests that their main occupation was hunting.

Bone remains of these Mesolithic peoples were found only at one site: at Langhnaj in Gujarat where thirteen skeletons could be excavated. They combine mainly Mediterranean and Veddoid racial features. They were fairly tall, of slight build, dolichocephalic, and with a slight prognathism.

According to Zeuner the Langhnaj people were hunters and fishermen because the animal remains found on the site belonged almost exclusively to wild species and the microliths found there were mainly barbs, points or arrow-heads. Some stray articles—like a copper knife, a large ring stone used as a macehead or weight for a digging-stick, a hammer stone—suggest that the Langhnaj people were already in contact with peoples of a superior form of culture.

It is quite possible that some living peoples of India derive their origin from these Mesolithic hunters. It is however remarkable that with the exception of the Veddas in Sri Lanka hardly any living tribals in the Indian subcontinent stay in caves and rock shelters. Even the most primitive tribes prefer to live in open country in huts or simply behind wind screens, even on trees, but scarcely ever in caves or rock shelters.

The Races of the Indian Neolithic

With the invention of agriculture mankind entered into a revolutionary new phase of its culture which affected all aspects of their life. This revolutionary change is also reflected in the tools which the new cultivators fashioned for their new tasks and needs. We call this type of stone culture the Neolithic or New Stone Age. It appears that man first became a cultivator in the Middle

East. Recent excavations made at Jarmo in Iraq, Jericho in Palestine, and Catal Huyuk in Turkey, show that cultivation started in these areas between the ninth and seventh millennia B.C. From the Middle East cultivation expanded to Iran and central Asia. It reached the Indian subcontinent comparatively late, only in about 3500 B.C. It is, however, possible that earlier cultivation centres might be discovered in northern India after a more intensified search for them.

The start of cultivation on the subcontinent, appears to have been made in Baluchistan (Pakistan). Kili Ghul Mohammed, near Quetta, Rana Ghundai in the Loralai valley, Anjira and Siah-damb in the Surab valley, and Mundigak in south-east Afghanistan are the sites which have been excavated and yielded typical Neolithic stoneware and pottery but no metal tools. The stone tools are of great variety, but blades prevail. They must have been used for the harvesting of crops. Arrow-heads suggest that the population still hunted, bone awls were used for stitching, grinding stones for grinding grain, and ringed stones as weights for the digging-stick.

The people also fashioned pottery of various sizes and shapes, often painted, and terracotta figurines of mother-goddesses obviously, and of humped bulls.

The fabricators of these stone and earthenwares appear to have been semi-nomadic; they built themselves mud houses and domesticated sheep, goats and cattle.

In a later phase of this culture, as excavations at Amri, Kot Diji and Kalibangan reveal, the buildings become larger and more elaborate, the pottery finer and more varied, and stone querns and pestles and balls (grain-crushers, or sling stones?) make their appearance. This development takes place towards the end of the fourth millennium and the beginning of the third. Geographically, chronologically and culturally this phase appears as the preparation for the Harappa or Indus Valley Civilisation. There is thus no urgent need for the assumption that the population of the Indus Valley Civilisation was of outside origin and brought its culture along when it entered India.

To the northern Neolithic belong also a small number of sites in Kashmir. The one at Burzahom near Srinagar has been systematically excavated in 1959. It provides some evidence of a culture sequence and shows affinities with Neolithic hunting cultures of western north China. But its ceramic industry is different and shows a local origin. These people buried domesticated dogs with their masters. This culture was obviously contemporaneous with the pre-Harappan and Harappan cultures in the Indus Valley and in the Punjab, though it had no contact with them.

The large number of polished stone axes in the Karnatak region in the valley of the Krishna river and its tributaries proves the presence of a wide-spread Neolithic culture in south India. Three phases can be distinguished which show a clear continuity of the culture sequence. The type of blades manufactured seems to suggest cultural links with central India and the Deccan. The people producing these implements must have been cattle-breeders though they also cultivated gram and millet. The human skeletal remains found in increasing numbers in the graves of this period show 'Caucasian' or 'Mediterranean' features. While earlier prehistorians believed that the peoples of the southern Neolithic entered India from the east, the Allchins [cf. B. and R. Allchin (1968), p. 170], favour their arrival from the north-west.

The hilly regions of Assam contain many Neolithic sites, with deposits of implements of various types and uses. Among the stone implements were large numbers of small ground axes—some with a rounded form and some with an angular outline. Both types are absent in the northern and southern sites; they are, however, found extensively distributed and in long use in China and south-east Asia. The pottery in the Assam sites also points towards China and south-east Asia. No metal was found at the sites.

Stone-axes in the Garo and Naga hills show a peculiar rounded-shouldered quasi-tanged form which might be either an earlier stage of the forms coming from the east (south China, Burma and Yunnan), or it was related to similar stone-axe forms of the northern and southern indigenous groups.

In eastern central India stone-axes have been found which, in their earlier forms, seem to come from the southern and central Neolithic sites, but the later forms obviously derive their origin from the east and are similar to those found in Assam.

The Races of the Indus Valley Civilisation

As explained earlier, the Indus Valley Civilisation is most probably a genuine gradual growth on Indian soil, not an importation by immigrant foreigners establishing a colony in India. The area in which the Indus Valley Civilisation flourished is very large—slightly less than half a million square miles—though it is restricted to northern India, with its strongest concentration in the Indus valley system. The uplands of Baluchistan were outside the influence of this civilisation, and in the south its boundary was the Thar Desert of Rajasthan. However, along the west coast the settlements of this culture extended further west almost to the Iranian border and south to the mouths of the Narbada and Tapti rivers.

The sudden, almost explosive rise of this civilisation and its spontaneous growth may have several causes. One of them was the favourable ecological situation of the Indus valley. The monsoon rains resulted in a regular recurrent flooding of the Indus plains. When the waters receded, fertile soil remained behind in which crops could be grown without previous ploughing. The main crops were wheat and barley, but also leguminous plants, field peas, sesame, mustard and dates were cultivated. The domestic animals raised were sheep, goat, fowl and also cattle. Pig and buffalo were probably not yet domesticated, but hunted as game animals.

The great fertility of the soil caused the population to increase rapidly and this strong concentration of people in the fertile plains was certainly an important factor in the amazing growth of this civilisation.* It was of course indispensable that the leaders of the population should have been sufficiently gifted to create such a civilisation. Other contemporary peoples of northern India obviously lacked this aptitude or were simply not interested in adopting it.

The Indus Valley people belonged to the Chalcolithic stage of

*Based on the quantity of grain milled in Harappa and Mohenjodaro, so far the two main known settlements of the Indus Valley Civilisation, J.M. Datta (pp. 8-10) estimates the population of Harappa as about 37,000 and that of Mohenjodaro as about 33,000. As many other settlements of the Harappan people existed in northern India, the population of this culture must have been quite considerable for that time.

culture. They used all kinds of stone, copper and bronze implements (no iron) and produced a great variety of pottery, as also articles for decoration. They also planted cotton, presumably for the production of cloth. They had some trade connections with the Persian Gulf and with Mesopotamia where Indian seals and other articles have been discovered.

This population built at least two large towns, Mohenjodaro and Harappa, with well-planned roads, an elaborate system of drainage, a public bath, and a large granary. They built their houses and city walls of bricks. But they seem to have built no temples though they must have had a religion as attested by the many engravings of a religious nature on their seals. For, they had a script which they engraved on square steatite seals together with pictures of animals and men of an obviously divine character. As the script has not yet been deciphered, in spite of many claims to that effect, it is not known what language the Indus Valley people spoke.

On the whole their culture bears a strongly utilitarian and competently practical character; the articles produced at the various sites—over seventy sites dispersed over a wide area are known so far—are so uniform and of a stereotyped make that their manufacturers must have been either very unimaginative people or otherwise restrained by higher authority form deviating from the accepted form.

Though initially the population of the Indus Valley Civilisation may have been of a uniform race, it did not remain so, for the skeletons found in the cemeteries of the sites show a mixed racial constitution. The Indus Valley people practised in early times a complete burial, but at a later period they changed over to fractional burial, in which merely the skull and some bones were deposited in painted jars. Graves were discovered in great numbers at Harappa, and the anthropometric analysis of 260 skeletons was published in 1962 by P. Gupta, P.C. Dutta and A. Basu [pp. 13–188]. The analysis confirms the earlier evaluation by B.S. Guha [(1937), p. 133] that the population of the Indus Valley Civilisation consisted mainly of two types. The older one represented a tall type of rugged and sturdy build, dolichocephalic, with pronounced brow-ridges, receding forehead, and a broad nose with a depressed root. And if we can trust their sculpture this type had a dark skin, wavy or curly hair, strong beard, broad flattish nose and protruding lips. The later type was shorter, of slighter build, also dolichocephalic, but with sharp, well-cut features, a fine, narrow nose, a longish face and smooth eyebrow ridges. According to Guha, it had close affinities with the Mediterranean race of Europe and West Asia. He also maintained that this race was probably responsible for the higher stages of the Indus Valley Civilisation.

But the Harappan cemeteries contained some other types too. At one cemetery some round-headed crania were found, at another skeletons of rather tall stature, with large and round heads, but also medium statured individuals, with a small or medium skull and a low face were discovered. These round-headed types were chronologically younger than the dolichocephals.

The population of the Indus Valley Civilisation was consequently not uniform, but consisted of several races, some of which arrived on the scene at a time when the development of this civilisation was already under way. Were the late-comers the ones who produced the apex of this culture, while the earlier races on the spot merely laid its foundations? Could it be that the late-comers came as conquerors and exercised a strict control over the earlier population? This would explain the stereotyped and dull uniformity of the cultural elements in spite of the wide dispersion of the sites.

The chronology of the Indus Valley Civilisation has experienced a considerable revision in recent years. According to J. Marshall's initial estimate, based on culture contacts with Mesopotamia, the civilisation lasted from 3250 to 2750 B.C. But new finds and Carbon–14 dating have forced the archaeologists to reduce the age of the civilisation considerably. Experts assume now that this civilisation flourished between 2300 and 1750 B.C. It thus lasted just about 500 years.

The reasons for its decline and final disappearance cannot yet be definitely stated. One cause might have been a disastrous alteration of the course of the Indus river resulting in destructive flooding of settlements and silting of fields. Another fatal cause was perhaps the general desiccation of the whole area. Even adverse tectonic movements have been made responsible for the decay of this civilisation which was certainly the more vulnerable as it depended so much on a very particular form of cultivation for its sustenance. Since the chronology has been revised and the end of the civilisation fixed at about 1750 B.C., the old hypothesis has been revived that the Aryan invaders—the early forerunners of the Rigvedic Aryans—might have destroyed the centres of Harappan Civilisation and killed or dispersed its population. The discovery of unburied skeletons on the steps of a building in Mohenjodaro seem to support such an assumption. However, if the hypothesis of some experts about a hierarchical order of the population in the Indus Valley cities is correct, the decline and final disappearance of this civilisation might also have been due to an inner decay of the ruling class, either physically through in-breeding, culturally and socially through a mixture with and an assimilation in the lower and less talented classes, or simply due to a degeneration of their superior talents which initially enabled them to gain their domination. But this assumption rests on slender evidence, as so little is known about the social order of this civilisation. It is even doubtful whether the decipherment of the script will give more substantial enlightenment about this particular aspect of Harappan culture.

Post-Harappan Development

In the last two decades much research was carried out to throw light on the post-Harappan period of northern India. More information must still be collected before the history of this development becomes clear, but certain features of the cultural expansion from the Indus Valley to the east and south have already become recognisable.

In the Kathiawar peninsula, at Lothal, the Harappan civilisation seems to have ended around 1860 B.C. The subsequent settlers of the site produced new pottery forms and styles of painting. This seems to suggest the emergence of a new provincial culture which, in a more primitive stage and underlying the prevailing Harappan culture, had all the time persisted in the area. Free from the control of the Harappan people, this suppressed early local culture now began to flourish, no doubt inspired by the Harappan culture. The same progress can be found at other sites, at Rangpur, Somnath, Rajdi and perhaps Desalpur in Cutch (Gujarat). After the withdrawal of Harappan influence a decline can be noted, but it is followed by a revival, with different forms and patterns of pottery. For stone tools, instead of the imported material, local jasper and agate are used as raw material and the copper tools increase in number and variety. Rice, millet and small grain cultivation is in evidence. This change signifies probably that a different population had taken over after the withdrawal of the Harappans.

A similar development seems to have taken place at the estuary of the Narbada river, and further in the north-east of Kathiawar, in the area of the Aravalli range. In the latter sites, especially at Ahar, a culture, not derived from Harappa, developed. It was developed either by earlier settlers locally or was imported by new immigrants. At Ahar no stone tools were in use; they had been replaced by copper implements. Copper was locally available as raw material. The settlers occupied houses built of stone and mud of a uniform pattern. Their pottery differs from that of the Saurashtrian sites. The large number of saddle querns and rubbing stones suggest that they were grain eaters, but they also hunted deer. Similar remains were found at Gilund, a large settlement. But here stone implements suggesting a blade industry were in evidence.

East of the Aravalli hills, in Malwa, two sites have been excavated, Nagda in the north and Navda-toli in the south, on the Narbada. While the finds in Nagda correspond closely with the early periods in Rangpur in Saurashtra, Navda-toli reveals a somewhat more independent development. In the earlier phases the population built square and round huts of wattle and daub, used stone blades and copper tools, kept cattle, sheep, goats and pigs, and cultivated grains like wheat, lentils and oilseeds. Their pottery included several varieties. The Kayatha site, east of Ujjain, contemporary to the phase of Harappa, seems to have had closer affinities to Harappan culture.

These post-Harappan cultures expanded further in three broad directions: one section advanced southwards into the Deccan where it contacted and even mixed with earlier Neolithic cultures. From the Deccan it moved eastwards to Andhra and Bengal. A second section moved immediately eastwards along the Narbada valley to the hills of central India, while a third section moved from north Rajasthan and the Punjab eastwards into the upper Gangetic valley and from there into the central Ganges region.

Whether the cultures of the post-Harappan time expanded by diffusion or were carried eastwards and southwards by the peoples who invented them, it is not yet possible to say. Carbon-14 dating has established that these cultures developed from about 1800 to 1000 B.C. After that a new era begins—that of the iron age.

Physical anthropologists [B.S. Guha (1937), p. 134] state that during this period, or earlier, a brachycephalic race of the Alpino-Dinaric type with a short to medium stature, a round and broad face, and a long prominent nose immigrated into northern India. B.S. Guha believes that this race had its origin in south-west Siberia during prehistoric times from where it spread to eastern Europe and southern Arabia. It probably proceeded to Afghanistan and penetrated into India. It descended from the Pamirs through Afghanistan, Baluchistan and Sind, and spread along the west coast into Gujarat and Kanara; one branch crossed over to Bengal, and in a more southern route over the Deccan to Tamilnadu. But it left out the Malabar coast.

Since the expansion of this race coincides in time and geography with the growth and spreading-out of the Indus Valley Civilisation and the post-Harappan industries, it is probable that this race was at least partly responsible for this cultural development in northern and central India. At Harappa and other sites skeletal finds have been made which bear the characteristic features of this race.

The Megalith-Builders of South India

Another important, much discussed, but as yet unsolved problem is the identity of the megalith-builders in south India. All over central south India, south of the river Krishna, thousands of large megalithic tombs are found. They are of various types, but the so-called 'port-hole cists'—box-shaped dolmens, frequently with a round hole in the front stone slab, the so-called 'soul-hole'—are predominant. Some of these cists are on the surface, but most of them are dug more or less deeply into the ground.

Megaliths can be found in many regions of India, in Assam as well as in north-eastern central India. But these megaliths are different in shape and function and are based on conceptions obviously at variance with those associated with the culture of the megalithic tombs in south India.

Since the megalith-builders knew the use of iron—in most tombs iron implements were found—the tombs must be comparatively recent, after 1000 B.C. and possibly not much earlier than 500 B.C.

Who the people were who built these megaliths is still under discussion. M. Wheeler believed that they were immigrants because their culture differs sharply from that of the preceding era. They used iron, but no bronze or brass. They had a peculiar form of pottery, the so-called 'Red and Black Ware'.

C. von Fürer-Haimendorf [(1955), pp. 162–6], R. von Heine-Gelden [(1932), pp. 558–617] and others connected the megalith-builders with the early Dravidians, that is, a people that brought the Dravidian language to India. They believed that they could trace these people back to Baluchistan where the Brahuis even today speak a language with Dravidian elements, and where W.A. Fairservis [(1961), pp. 22–9] had found at Edith Shahr near Bela, a large site of megaliths with port-hole cists of the south Indian type. R. von Heine-Geldern believed that the early Dravidians could be traced back to Iran and the Caucasus.

It appears, however, that the defenders of this hypothesis have unduly ignored the great variety of the megalithic tombs. The Allchins [(1968), p. 229 f.] believe that the different types of megaliths prove that several streams of influence combined in them. First, some grave types appear as developments of the indigenous Neolithic-Chalcolithic burial customs of the Deccan. Next, some other burial sites resemble in shape and form those of central Asia, Iran or the Caucasus, and might have been introduced by Indo-European immigrants. Third, stone cist graves, with or without port-holes, are found on the coast of south Arabia and in the Levant. India could have received such influences through maritime contacts with the Middle East. Fourth, a peculiar type, as for instance that of stone alignment, could have developed locally.

One should not omit mentioning that it is as yet impossible to date the various grave sites exactly. This also makes it illusory to connect certain forms of burial with particular peoples and races. Much more research will have to be done before the problem of the megalith-builders can be solved. Till then it must remain an open question.

The origin of the Dravidian languages, too, is an unsolved problem. It cannot yet be stated definitely whether the original speakers of the Dravidian language were immigrants or whether this language family is completely indigenous. Most experts, prehistorians as well as linguists, seem to incline towards an indigenous origin of the Dravidian language group. Experts point out the remarkable continuity of cultural development for over a thousand years in south Indian Neolithic sites prior to the appearance of iron. It is alleged that Neolithic peoples could very well have developed the Dravidian language during this time. These reasons are brought up against the assumption that the first Dravida-speaking people were comparatively recent immigrants to India.

The assumption that the megalith-builders of south India did not belong to a uniform (Dravidian) race is borne out by the anthropometric analysis of the skeletons found in the megalithic tombs. The skeletons found at Brahmagiri, for instance, belong to various races. The same is true of the Adittanalur (Tamilnadu) bone remains. Some of the skulls have elements in common with the Mediterranean race, others display Veddid or Australoid racial characteristics.

The Aryan Immigration

The racial immigration which took place in the last phase of prehistoric times and caused the most profound change in shaping the culture and history of India was that of the Aryans, somewhere in the second millennium B.C.

The Aryans, notable for the breeding of the horse and training it for the war-chariot, are believed to have come into existence as a nation in southern Russia. Archaeologists and linguists seem to agree on locating the probable area of Aryan origin as lying somewhere between the Danube and the Oxus, among the earliest cultivators of the south Russian steppes and the lands lying eastwards to the Caspian Sea. From this region they migrated via the Caucasus to Mesopotamia. Their presence in north Mesopotamia is recorded in documents; they appear from 1500 B.C. onwards as the rulers in the Mitanni kingdom from where they gradually extended their dominion as far as Syria and Palestine. Since by 1500 B.C. their conquest of the Mitanni kingdom was completed they must have appeared in Mesopotamia for the first time a few centuries earlier.

When exactly the first Aryans appeared at the border of India is still unknown. Prehistoric evidence for the early phase of Aryan immigration is very scanty. Excavations at Hastinapur in Uttar Pradesh, associated with the Mahabharata war, would suggest as a probable date 1200 B.C. In recent extensive and systematic excavations of the site various phases of habitation have been revealed. The earliest phase, lasting till 1100 B.C., represents an occupation of the site by a people with a crude ochre-coloured pottery. The settlements were flimsy and sporadic, with no metal implements, and no terracotta human or animal figurines. No structural remains are in evidence.

In the subsequent phase (1100 to 800 B.C.) a distinctive ceramic, called the 'Painted Gray Ware', commonly associated with the Aryans, made its appearance. Burned brick-bats were found, but without regular house plans, a few mud or mud-brick walls and some crude terracotta animal figurines. No iron could be found in this layer. A number of bones of sheep, cattle and buffaloes indicate that the people inhabiting the site had domesticated these animals at this time. Horns of antelope and bone-needles were indications that they also hunted wild game.

In the third phase of occupation at Hastinapur iron objects and even copper and silver coins were in evidence. The pottery of these residents was the so-called 'Northern Black Polished Ware'.

Further Aryan advance can be traced to some extent through finds of pottery now associated with them. It seems that the Aryans expanded mainly along the Ganges valley. Like Hastinapur, other settlements also in this area, known from Vedic literature as centres of Aryan dynasties, such as Ahicchetra and Kaushambi, can be traced back to almost the beginning of the first millennium B.C. Such a quick and strong colonising movement would have been impossible unless population groups from pre-Aryan times had also taken part in it. Were the conquered peoples those of the Indus Valley Civilisation? Or did they speak a Dravidian language? We do not know. But traces of Dravidian elements in Sanskrit would suggest the latter possibility.

Burrow [(1959), p. 386] claims that the Dravidian elements entered Sanskrit in northern India, not in Iran. The Dravidian elements are post-Vedic.

But we have so far no skeletal remains from ancient India which can be attributed to the early Aryans, except the remains of monks whose monastery at Taxila was sacked in the fifth century by the white Huns. The same racial type appears as the dominant element in the various Pathan tribes of the North-West Frontier, in the Kafir tribes, the Dards and Dums of Kashmir and the higher classes of the Punjab, of Rajasthan and upper India.

There is some linguistic evidence to show that the Aryan invasion took place in successive phases and not in one thrust [cf. T. Burrow (1959), pp. 27–32]. Still, their numbers must have been low; according to Heine-Geldern they were less than a 100,000, perhaps not more than fifty thousand.

The early Aryan settlers in India grew grain and pastured sheep and goats, but they were primarily cattle breeders, with a warrior aristocracy that possessed the horse and roamed in search of battle and plunder. The early Aryans had not reached the standard of a city civilisation and only knew the use of copper and bronze, not of iron. But they had domesticated the horse and possessed in the two-horse, two-wheeled chariot—from which the warrior, accompanied by a charioteer, would wield his bow or spear—a weapon of swift effect against the enemies.

BIBLIOGRAPHY

Agrawal, D.P.: *The Copper Bronze Age in India.* Delhi, 1971.

Allchin, B. and R.: *The Birth of Indian Civilization.* Penguin, 1968.

Banerjee, N.R.: *The Iron Age in India.* Delhi, 1965.

Burrow, T.: *The Sanskrit Language.* London, 1959, 2nd ed.

Chatterjee, N.K. and P. Gupta: *Report on the Adittanalur Skulls.* Delhi, 1963.

Clerk, J.D.: *The History of South Africa.* Penguin, 1959.

Datta, J.M.: 'Demographic Notes on the Remains from Harappa' in *Human Skeletal Remains from Harappa.* Calcutta, 1962, pp. 1–12.

Fairservis, W.A.: *Baluchistan Find.* Natural History, LXX, 1961, 6, pp. 22–9.

von Fürer-Haimendorf, C.: *New Aspects of the Dravidian Problem.* Actesdu IVe Congrès International des Sciences Anthropologiques et Ethnoslogiques. Vol. II, Wien, 1955, pp. 162–6.

Gordon, D.H.: *The Historic Background of Indian Culture.* Bombay, 1958.

Guha, B.S.: *An Outline of the Racial Ethnology of India.* Calcutta, 1937.

Gupta, P., P.C. Dutta and A. Basu: 'Human Remains from Harappa' in *Human Skeletal Remains from Harappa.* Calcutta, 1962, pp. 13–188.

von Heine-Geldern, R.: *Urheimat and Fruheste Wanderung der Austronesier.* Anthropos, vol. 27, 1932, pp. 558–619.

———Das Dravida Problem. *Anzeiger, Ost. Akademic der Wissenschaften.* Wien, 1964, So. 9, S 187–201.

Hutton, J.H.: *Caste in India.* Oxford University Press, 1951.

Khatri, A.P.: *Rock Paintings at Adamgarh (Central India) and Their Age.* Anthropos, vol. 59, 1964.

Krishnaswamy, V.D.K.: *Prehistory in India.* Ancient India No. 3, Delhi, 1947.

MacBurney, C.B.M.: *The Stone Age of Northern Africa.* Pelican, 1960.

Malik, S.C.: 'Levels in Indian Prehistory' in *Current Anthropology,* June 1964, p. 205.

Sankalia, H.D.: *Prehistory and Protohistory in India and Pakistan.* Bombay, 1962.

Sankalia, H.D., B. Subbarao and S.B. Deo: *The Excavations at Maheswar and Navda-toli.* Baroda, 1958.

Sen, Dharani and N.K. Bose: *Excavations at Mayurbhanj.* Calcutta, 1948.

Subbarao, B.: *The Personality of India.* Baroda, 1958.

De Terra, H. and T.T. Paterson: *Studies in the Ice Age of India and Associated Human Cultures.* Washington, 1939.

Zeuner, F.F.: *Dating the Past.* London, 1958.

CHAPTER II

The Aboriginal Races of India

FROM WHAT has been said in Chapter I it is clear that the aboriginal tribes in India are in most cases survivals from the later prehistoric population groups. Some tribes may even have degenerated from a higher standard of culture due to adverse circumstances. The Kurumbas of Tamilnadu are said to be the result of one such retrograde development.

The aborigines of the Indian peninsula do not form a uniform race, as has been made clear already in Chapter I. Entering India from various directions and from various regions of Asia, they also belong to different races. It has not yet been possible to arrange the aboriginal tribes of India into definite racial groups. Attempts were made by H. Risley, B.S. Guha and E. von Eickstedt, but so far they have not been satisfactory and convincing. More prehistoric and anthropological research is necessary before the racial and cultural history of India's aboriginal population can be cleared up.

Definition and Number

The question what Indian population groups belong to the 'aboriginals' has been solved more or less definitely by the Constitution of India, article 342. In order to provide special safeguards and more effective protection to these population groups the term 'tribe' had to be defined and a list of the 'scheduled tribes' had to be made. The latest list of such tribes can be found in the 'Scheduled Castes and Scheduled Tribes Lists Modification Order, 1956'. According to the Order, 414 main tribes besides a number of sub-tribes are listed as 'scheduled tribes'. The list can certainly be accepted as substantially accurate, though it leaves out a few tribes here and there, and includes other social groups whose tribal origin could be disputed. The list also contains tribes that do not need the assistance and protection of the Government though the tribes have been 'scheduled' just for this reason.

The Constitution of India nowhere states explicitly how a 'tribe' can be recognised and how it can be distinguished from a 'caste'. It did well not to try to give such a definition. In fact, there exists no satisfactory definition of the term 'tribe' anywhere. An East Asian Consultation, held at Sagada (Philippines), defined a tribal community as forming a 'group of people generally constituting a homogeneous unit, speaking a common language, claiming a common ancestry, living in a particular geographic area, generally lacking in scientific knowledge and modern technology and having a social structure based on kinship'.

According to the Oxford Dictionary, a tribe 'is a group of people in a primitive or barbarous stage of development acknowledging the authority of a chief and usually regarding themselves as having a common ancestor'. This is good enough as far as it goes; but it does not go far enough. Lucy Mair defines a tribe as 'an independent political division of a population with a common culture'. G.W.B. Huntingford maintains that a tribe 'is a group united by a common name in which the members take a pride, by a common language, by a common territory, and by a feeling that all who do not share this name are outsiders, "enemies" in fact'.

T.B. Naik [(1968), pp. 84–97] has proposed the following seven criteria by which a tribe can be recognised: (1) A tribe has the least functional interdependence within the community; (2) it is economically backward; (3) it is geographically isolated from other peoples; (4) it speaks a common dialect which may however be subject to regional variations; (5) a tribe is politically a unit under a common tribal authority; (6) a tribe's members are averse to change; and (7) a tribe has its own traditional laws which often differ from those of the majority communities. To be a 'tribe', a community must have all these attributes. It might be undergoing acculturation; but with a high degree of acculturation it would cease to be a tribe.

However, if these criteria are applied to the tribes accepted

as 'scheduled tribes' by the Indian Government, many would be disqualified. As far as Indian tribes go, the essentials seem to be only a comparatively simple and primitive economy, combined with a certain degree of residential instability, a simple, though not always, classless social organisation, and especially that feeling of being a different and separate social unit—apart from the majority communities of India. The social and political solidarity expressed either by a common name, a common distinct language or dialect, endogamy, similar customs and traditions of a social and religious nature appear less important. The Indian Government extends the privileges granted to the 'scheduled tribes' to those social groups which are not fully integrated into the Indian nation for reasons of economic handicaps, different ecological conditions, a different racial origin, and a different mental and religious world outlook and culture.

The term 'tribe' can perhaps be better understood in contrast with the term 'scheduled caste'. It appears to be easier to define a 'scheduled caste'. For a caste to be 'scheduled', it has to be economically and culturally backward, exploited by the peoples of superior culture and treated as socially inferior. But it has also to be sufficiently numerous to make special protective measures worthwhile. 'Scheduled castes' share many aspects of culture with the Hindus or, in some cases, with the Muslims of India, but they are backward economically, exploited and socially degraded and for these reasons often kept apart ('untouchables'!). Thus they require special protection if they are to be brought up to the level of the rest of the population. On the other hand, the 'scheduled tribes', though often backward and exploited, are rarely socially degraded.

To make the difference between the two social groups clear, the term 'self-sufficiency', proposed by U.R. Ehrenfels [in L.P. Vidyarthi (1968), p. 88], may be relevant in this connection: the tribals are, or want to be, self-sufficient in their cultural life. This desire for self-sufficiency may be one of the main reasons why they stay outside the mainstream of national life, why they hold on to their own traditions and values although they are only too often painfully confronted with the fact that these traditions and values are inadequate in modern life. Thus, while the majority communities in India marched on and progressed, at least in material culture, the tribals remained backward and were thus exposed to exploitation.

Members of the 'scheduled castes', on the other hand, though they also may be a people set apart, backwards and subject to severe exploitation, do not have that desire for 'self-sufficiency'. If they form a society apart and are backwards, it is because they have been socially rejected by the majority communities and, due to their social degradation and economic exploitation, do not have the physical and moral strength to rise up to the level of full-fledged members of the Indian nation. A 'tribal' is so because he belongs to a society with a particular frame of mind, while the 'Harijan', belonging to a 'scheduled caste', is, though in a peculiar cultural position, of one mind with the majority communities and has no desire to be different from them.

The Census of India 1961 enumerates 29,883,470 Indian citizens as belonging to the 'scheduled tribes'. They form 6.81 per cent of the total population of India.

The 'scheduled tribes' go under various names. They are called either 'Aboriginal Tribes', 'Primitive Tribes', or 'Adivasis', (i.e., the original inhabitants of India). Instead of 'scheduled tribes', a term which has too juridical a connotation, we shall here use the term 'Aboriginal Tribes', placing the emphasis on the word 'tribe' and less on the assumption that they are the 'original' inhabitants of India.

The Present-day Races of India

The available evidence about the racial composition and history of the living races in India is as scanty as the prehistoric evidence. Much research must still be done before a competent and reliable racial history of India can be written. Very little is known regarding the nature and routes of migrations into India and inside India even after the arrival of the Aryans. Therefore, all attempts at a reconstruction of the racial history of India have to be based on a lot of conjectures. Our knowledge is particularly vague and hazy about the origin and subsequent history of the numerous aboriginal tribes in India as well as of the low castes. On the other hand, research into the racial composition of the Indian population should not be too difficult and should prove very rewarding, for though the various communities and populations in India carried on a lively exchange of ideas and goods and thus influenced each other culturally, the strict enforcement of the laws of caste and tribe endogamy prevented much racial miscegenation. It could not be prevented absolutely, but it never became great in depth and extent. The various communities lived side by side, and interchanged ideas and goods, but not their blood.

Though anthropological evidence shows that in each cultural region distinct racial strata do exist which can be correlated to some extent to social strata, one racial element is not always and everywhere socially supreme; the social position of different race groups often changes from region to region.

In the following we adopt the classification which B.S. Guha gave in the Census of India, 1931. Whenever his classification appears to be deficient we shall make the necessary corrections for which we shall offer our reasons.

THE NEGRITOS

Guha thinks that the Negritos were the earliest racial element in India. He believes that the Kadar, Irulas and Panyans of south India have a Negrito strain, though even he admits that they are not pure Negritos. The German anthropologist E. von Eickstedt agrees with Guha and states that there is definitely a Negrito component in the Malid sub-group of the south Indian Veddids. But D.N. Majumdar and S.S. Sarkar deny the existence of any Negrito strains in south India. The small stature of these tribes, their dark skin colour, their occasionally frizzly hair with short spirals—admittedly Negrito elements—are found also in other races. But what is decisive is, they say, that these tribes are not brachycephalic as the Andamanese and their blood-groups show a different proportion. The Indian tribes have a small B incidence whereas it is high among the Negritos.

Guha has to admit that as yet in India no skeletal remains of a Negrito race have been excavated from any prehistoric sites. If the Negritos had ever entered India, as he claims, if they lived here and again disappeared, nothing is known about their original homeland, the time of their arrival and the reason for their disappearance, and whether they died out, were exterminated or assimilated by other races.

E. von Eickstedt calls these Negritos of Guha, Proto-Negritos. Hutton believes that the existence of Negritos in Assam is fairly probable. Their former existence in this area reveals itself by the occasional occurrence of a strikingly 'Papuan' profile, a low stature, curly or even kinky hair and a dark complexion. He also asserts the survival of many items of material culture showing Melanesian affinities. The Konyak Nagas, for instance, have a tradition of having driven out an earlier race of 'monkey people'. Others must have been exterminated. Hutton states that shortly after he left the Naga hills a village where people of low stature and curly hair predominated was exterminated by hostile neighbours. Curly hair is intensely disliked by the Nagas.

S.S. Sarkar has found traces of Negrito strains among the very primitive Maler, and similar features can perhaps be found among the many small vagrant tribes of India, who live the life of foodgatherers in spite of very adverse conditions and are generally of small stature and dark complexion. Their often infantile appearance is remarkable and is particularly noticeable in their women. Curly hair is often found in these tribes. The nose is broad, with a deeply sunken root. Unfortunately, these tribes have not been studied anthropometrically.

THE PROTO-AUSTRALOIDS

The second-oldest racial group, according to Guha [(1937), p. 130 f.], is that of the Proto-Australoids. A somatic study of the aboriginal population of India shows little marked differences in the shape of the head, form of the nose, projection of the face, skin colour, form and structure of hair. But in central and south India there are many tribes which have well-developed supra-orbital ridges along with a sunken nasal root. Guha compares these tribes with the Veddas of Sri Lanka and the aborigines of Australia, and finds that the three groups are essentially alike, though the Australians are taller and have more marked brow ridges. It would therefore appear that the Indian tribals retained the more basic characteristics of this race; while the Veddas and the Australians developed some peculiar features in a more marked manner. Guha [(1944), p. 11] consequently thought that the term 'Proto-Australoid' was most suitable for Indian tribals of this type and race.

It seems that the majority of the central and south Indian tribes belong to this racial type, though they may speak different languages. The same can be said of the tribes in western central India and of the partially Hinduised groups in the Gangetic valley. There are of course variations from tribe to tribe and from region to region, but they are comparatively slight, while more marked differences can be explained by racial mixtures with tribes of another racial type or with the later settlers in India.

E. von Eickstedt [(1935), vol. I, p. 38], however, does not agree with this classification of Guha's. He groups Guha's Proto-Australoids differently: he distinguishes a Veddid race which he sub-divides into a southern Indian Malid race (from *mala*, meaning mountain) and a central Indian Gondid race. Then he distinguishes a Melanid race of Europo-Negroid character and origin. Its only difference from the Europid race of this type is that it has a very dark skin colour. He discovers this race in the Carnatic type of the highly civilised South-Dravidas (in Tamilnadu) and in the Mundas, Hos and Santals of Chota Nagpur (in the Kolid type of the primitive Austro-Asiatics). It is, however, difficult to understand how the Austro-Asiatics (Mundas) could be grouped with the Tamil Melanids. I believe that Guha's theory is sounder, grouping, as he does, all the aboriginal tribes in south and central India as Proto-Australoids. But Guha is probably wrong in including among the Proto-Australoids the Mundas, Hos and Santals who are Austro-Asiatics. By somatic constitution and language they seem to belong to a different race. Their language at least would suggest an origin from the East.

It appears that both Guha and Eickstedt do not take sufficiently into account the linguistic differences of the tribals in north-eastern central India. Linguistically, the tribes in this area are divided into three groups: one group speaking a Mundarian language, another a Dravidian tongue, and the third—the largest—speaking Aryan dialects. While among the Aryan-speaking group of tribes there are many which have adopted their present form of speech fairly recently, some of the most primitive tribes, which at the same time claim to be the oldest settlers in the region, also speak an Aryan language. Certain cultural evidence would suggest that they adopted their Aryan speech in very ancient times.

This fact suggests strongly that they adopted their present language at a time when the Mundari and Dravida-speaking tribes had not yet arrived in north-eastern central India. If the Mundari-speaking tribes arrived in this region after the adoption of Aryan speech by the earlier settlers of the region, this immigration of the Mundas cannot have taken place earlier than about 800 B.C., because it was only around that time that the Aryans advanced into Bihar and central India. However, some time was necessary for the early primitive tribes in the region to adopt the Aryan language. S.S. Sarkar [(1954), Chapter 5] claims that there is also anthropological support for the assumption that the Munda tribes are comparatively recent immigrants in north-eastern central India. And he contradicts Guha's earlier assumption that the main Mundari-speaking tribes (Mundas, Hos, Santals) do not differ racially from the other two linguistic groups. He proves by anthropometric evidence that the Mundas do not show that close racial affinity with the Dravida-speaking tribes of the south which Guha claims.

The assumption of a comparatively late arrival of the Munda tribes in Bihar and Madhya Pradesh is contradicted by the theory of R. von Heine-Geldern [(1932), pp. 561 and 609], which holds that the Mundas are a Mongoloid people who entered India from the north-east and brought a Neolithic culture with them. Heine-Geldern connects them with the so-called 'shouldered axe' and claims that this axe appeared in north-eastern central India in the first half of the second millennium B.C. However, A.H. Dani has recently proved that the shouldered axes—he calls them 'tanged stone axes'—found in this region are copies of earlier bronze types and therefore must be set at a much later date [D.H. Gordon (1958), p. 124]. Their association with the Munda tribes is very doubtful. Moreover, neither the Mundas nor the other neighbouring tribes have any tradition that they ever used these stone implements. Indeed, wherever they find them, they rebury them quickly because they believe that these stones attract lightning—a belief found among many other tribes as well.

But even if the Munda tribes can be associated with the stone imitations of bronze axes, it would only prove their late arrival in their present habitats. On the other hand, if the Munda tribes did not use tanged stone-axes at all when they entered India, this fact, too, would prove their comparatively late arrival in India. For no doubt as Austro-Asiatics they did possess such stone axes around 2000 B.C. If they had already exchanged them against iron axes at the time of their entering India, then their arrival must have taken place considerably later than the time assumed by Heine-Geldern.

However, the problem of dating the arrival of the Mundari-speaking tribes in India can only be solved after we know by which route they had entered India. Even this is uncertain. The controversy about the origin of the Munda language has not yet subsided. W. Schmidt [(1906), pp. 13–17] had long ago classified the Munda languages as belonging to the Mon-Khmer languages of Indo-China. He named this language group the Austro-Asiatic language group. But W. von Hevesy, a well-known Hungarian linguist contradicted Schmidt and tried to connect the Munda languages with the Finno-Ugrian language group. This theory, however, was never accepted by the linguists.

J.H. Hutton [(1951), p. 12], too, has a theory of the origin of the Munda language. He associates the Austric speech with the Kolarian group of tribes which, according to him, entered India by two routes, one 'round the west end of the Himalayas' and the other, the Mon-Khmer speaking group, from the east of the Himalayas. His assumption of a partly western origin of the Munda tribes was probably prompted by the general belief that the Bhils, a large tribe in the western central India, are related to the Mundas, Hos and other cognate tribes. But there is no linguistic or racial evidence that the Bhils are closely related to the Munda group [cf. C.S. Thompson (1895), p. vi].

In spite of these and other dissenting opinions [cf. A. Burgmann (1954), pp. 637ff.], most linguists hold that the Munda languages are related to the Austro-Asiatic language group and that the Mundas consequently must have entered India from the East. A strong reason in favour of this theory is doubtless also the fact that, with the exception of the Korkus perhaps, all Mundari-speaking tribes are located in eastern and north-eastern central India. These are the Korwas, Cheros, Turis, Asurs, Kols, Mundas, Kharias, Birhors, Bhumij, Kharwars, Mahlis, Hos and Santals. The Korkus, who also speak a Munda language, are now widely separated from the main Munda group and live in central Madhya Pradesh, while the Juangs, Gadabas and Bondos have their habitats in the south-eastern region of central India. A link between the Mundas on the one side and the Mon and Khmer peoples on the other is formed by the Khasis of Assam and the Nicobar islanders, who also speak Austro-Asiatic languages.

The third linguistic group which can be found in the north-eastern region of central India speaks a Dravidian tongue. Some tribes of this group hold the tradition that in former times they had been living in south India. In fact, Gondi, Kurukhi, Malto and Kolami are grammatically more closely related to Kanarese than to their immediate southern Telugu-speaking neighbours [cf. A. Aiyappan (1955), p. 43].

The Dravida-speaking tribes arrived in their present habitats in north-eastern central India after the Munda tribes had occupied their present territory. This can be assumed from the fact that one tribe of the Munda group—the Korku tribe of Madhya Pradesh, over 200,000 individuals strong—was split off from the main stock through this immigration that passed like a wedge through the Munda group. This tribe is today separated from the other Munda tribes by over a thousand miles.

Cultural evidence is not lacking in support of the theory that the Dravida-speaking tribes had originally lived in south India. This is maintained by A. Aiyappan [(1955), p. 43] and D.H. Gordon [(1958), p. 172]. The latter states: The most northerly Dravidian types of speech such as Gondi, Khondi and Kolami are those of people whose traditions indicate ancestral connections with the south.

The Dravida-speaking tribes of Bihar, Madhya Pradesh and Orissa are the Maler, Oraons or Kurukh, Mannewars, Kaikaris, Gonds, Marias, Murias, Bhatras, Parjas, Kolams and Khonds or Kondhs. They number several millions. Most probably they were expelled from their southern habitats by a superior agricultural people.

Whoever the people may have been who pushed them out—whether they were the original settlers who had developed a superior form of agriculture in their homelands, or immigrant new-comers who had brought their advanced forms of agriculture along from outside India, whether they were Dravida-speaking or not—it is certain that they were the megalith-builders of south

India. These people were a well settled agricultural race who used even tank-irrigation to increase their yield. The great number of megaliths in this area suggests that their numbers had increased considerably. They were obviously in need of arable land as they took great care that their megalithic monuments did not encroach on land suitable for cultivation. They must have looked with greedy eyes at the fertile fields which the shifting cultivators had wrested from the jungle and, being more numerous and powerful, they soon succeeded in dispossessing the tribal shifting cultivators of their land and finally pushing them out altogether. Unable to resist this superior race and unwilling to submit to its domination, at least a part of the indigenous tribes yielded and moved northwards. They finally settled in the hills and jungles of eastern and north-eastern central India. But their path of migration is fairly clear, for they had left traces of their migration along the way. All the way from the south, in Andhra Pradesh, eastern Maharashtra, south-eastern Madhya Pradesh, Orissa and north-eastern Madhya Pradesh, aboriginal tribes speaking Dravidian dialects remained back and settled down. Linguists have established a close connection of Ollari, Poya and Parji, spoken in southern Madhya Pradesh and Andhra, with Kolami and Naiki, spoken in northern Madhya Pradesh. All these five dialects have close affinities with Telugu. This would suggest that the Ollari and Poya speaking Gadabas, the Parjas, Kolams and Naikas came from the Telugu-speaking areas in Andhra Pradesh. North of these tribes is the area of the Gonds who, too, at least partly, speak a Dravidian dialect, the Gondi.

These languages, however, differ from the Dravidian Kurukhi and Malto, languages spoken by the Oraons and Maler in southern Bihar and West Bengal. Linguists believe that these languages are more akin to Kanarese. Their speakers consequently must have come to their present habitats by a different route and from a different region of south India, probably much earlier.

It is obvious that not all the tribes moved out of south India. Many must have remained, retreating perhaps still further into the inaccessible forests and mountain ranges of south India, or being enslaved and assimilated by the superior cultivators. They may at present form the low-caste population of south India or the many landless tribal labourers living on the fringe of the forests or in the forest areas.

Racially, the Dravida-speaking tribes who had migrated towards central India and further north may belong to the so-called Proto-Australoids or Veddids, as Guha and Eickstedt call them. In fact, there is a close physical resemblance between them and the tribes that remained back in south India. They also seem to be related to those tribes in central India who speak ancient Aryan dialects and claim to be the oldest settlers of the north-eastern regions of central India.

The date of this northward migration is uncertain. But it cannot have taken place much before 500 B.C. At that time the Munda tribes had already settled in the same area. However, there was ample land for the newcomers from the south. Both races, the Mundas from the east and the Proto-Australoids from the south, lived more or less peacefully side by side, not mingling much because of the difference in language and culture. Nevertheless, the long duration of neighbourly residence did result in some exchange of cultural traits.

THE MONGOLOID TYPE

In the sub-Himalayan regions, in Assam and in the lands adjoining the eastern frontiers and Burma, Mongoloid races have settled. In the plateaus south-east of the Karakorum ranges adjoining Tibet there are the Chiangpas who are of pure Tibetan origin. The north-eastern Ladakhis and Baltis also show distinct Mongoloid features (high cheekbones, epicanthic fold), but also the racial strains of the Oriental race. From the Chiangpa to the Bhutan hills north of Assam, the Mongoloid strain appears as the dominant element among the Lahoulis, the Limbus, the Lepchas and the Rongpas. The chief characteristics of these tribes are: medium to tall stature, a brachycephalic head and broad face, high cheekbones, a long flat nose, the epicanthic fold, little hair on the face and body, and a light-brown skin colour. In Nepal the same type can be found in the east and north, but the basic type there is non-Mongoloid. The Gurung, Murmi and Gurkha tribes only represent the Mongoloid element.

The racial history of Assam appears as follows: The first inhabitants, according to Hutton, might have been Negritos, or at least a Negrito-like race. It was followed by the Khasis and the Syntengs who belong to the Mon-Khmer linguistic group.

Then came the invasion of the Bodo group, comprising the Garos, Kacharis, Tipperahs, Lalungs, Rabhas, Mech—'head hunters' like the Nagas, from the western mountains. The Nagas followed. They too were originally natives of north-east Tibet, but seem to have reached Assam by the south, driven back by the Kuki-Lushai-Chin population who followed them. This movement is not yet over; its course can still be observed.

To explain this curious circuit it must be assumed that there was first a migration of the Nagas from north to south, which was followed by the better evidenced and still continuing migration from south to north.

These tribes represent a different racial type with a sub-medium stature, mesocephalic head-shape, tending towards dolichocephaly, a flat (euryprosopic) face, a mesorrhine nose, but their cheekbones are high; they have the epicanthic fold and the scanty hair of the Mongoloid races. Their skin colour is of a brownish-yellow. They appear to belong to that great race which was originally settled in south-west China, and whose main body moved through Burma and Malaya to the Indonesian Islands. However, it left a side-stream in the Assam hills as represented by the Miri, Bodo and Naga tribes. It underlies also the population, excepting the higher strata, of the Assam Valley in general.

In the beginning of the Christian era small groups of Bengalis began to move into and settle in the plains of Assam. There is also a theory current that 'pre-Vedic' Aryans had crossed the north of India and Assam and sent out a swarm to western China and to the Indo-Chinese peninsula.

Lastly, at the beginning of the twelfth century, a tribe called Thai (or Shan), the Ahoms, invaded Assam from Burma, and became the rulers of the whole country. They gave their name to the State, 'Ahom' meaning Assam.

There are a number of tribes and peoples who do not enter into the above account and whose anthropological position is only vaguely defined. Among them are the Assamese of the plains, who form a mixed population of Shans and Bengalis. The anthropological study of a number of mountain tribes is still too fragmentary to allow any reconstruction. Perhaps a brachy-cephalic Mongoloid type can be distinguished: the Chakmas of Tripura, and the Mog tribes of the Arakan-Yoma hills belong to it. They are a short and rather dark race, and came probably from Burma.

AN ORIENTAL RACE

B.S. Guha [(1937), p. 137] and the German anthropologist E. Fischer, distinguish in north-east India also an Oriental type which, according to them, is represented by the Badakshis in Badakshan (north Afghanistan). It is dominant in north Afghanistan and from there spread from Dir to Kyber, and from Chitral to west Nepal. It is now found all along the sub-Himalayan regions, as for instance, among the Ladakhis and Baltis. The Muslims of upper India, at least in their higher classes, also represent this type. The race has at rosy-white skin colour, but black eyes and hair, contrary to the older Aryan type. The nose is markedly long and aquiline.

VARIOUS LATER IMMIGRATIONS

The Aryans and Orientals were followed in the subsequent centuries by various invasions on a smaller scale. Between 500 B.C. and the beginning of the Christian era, north India was invaded first by the Persians and Greeks, and then by the Sakas or Scythians and by the Kushans, who were a nomadic tribe from central Asia.

In the fifth century, another horde of nomads from central Asia, the Huns, found their way into India. They are considered, by some, the forefathers of the Rajputs and Gujars, though others believe that these two peoples came along with the Huns and then settled permanently in north India.

In the eighth century the Muslim invasions began with an Arab invasion of Sind, followed by various aggressive incursions of Muslim leaders with their warlike hordes bent on loot and conquest; these invasions went on until in the sixteenth century the Moghuls established themselves permanently and founded their empire.

Similar, but smaller, invasions took place on the west coast of India, in Malabar. We may only mention the Arabs, Jews, Syrians and, in the sixteenth century, the Portuguese, and still later the Dutch. The descendants of these colonists have survived in small groups, with their peculiar cultures and religions, though racially they became more or less diluted by intermarriages with the indigenous population. This applies also to the Bene Israels who were probably Jewish refugees, who arrived at the Konkan coast in an earlier immigration. But it is not true for the Parsees, Iranian Zoroastrians, who have not mixed with the local population. Much greater, however, is the number of the so-called Anglo-Indians (111,637 in 1951). They are generally the progeny of British settlers and Indian women of various castes. Descendants of purely white immigrants from England and other European countries, but born and domiciled in India, may also call themselves Anglo-Indians. There was also an infiltration into the community from lower-class 'Indian Christians' and the descendants of alliances between Portuguese (Luso-Indians) and Dutch colonists with Indian women.

LANGUAGE

The previous pages clearly show that the aboriginal tribes of India belong to various racial groups. These diverse races naturally had their own languages. A large portion of the Indian tribal population, however, has given up the original language and today speaks the dialects of the neighbouring peoples possessing a superior culture and also a more developed speech form. But these tribes may have retained in their newly adopted languages certain syntactic and phonetic peculiarities of their old idioms, even a number of words. A more exact analysis of the tribal dialects would probably bring this out.

Only two large tribal goups have retained their original languages, the Munda and the Sino-Tibetan tribes.

The Munda languages belong to the Austro-Asiatic sub-section of the Austric language family. This linguistic family is spread from central India, through Assam and Burma as far as Malaya and Indonesia. It extends even into the eastern, northern and southern extremities of the Pacific, to the Hawaii Islands in the north, to Easter Island in the east and to New Zealand in the south. Austric languages are also found in Madagascar not far from the east African coast.

The Austric languages are divided into the (1) Austronesian and (2) Austro-Asiatic language groups. The latter group includes the Munda languages in central and eastern India,

Nicobarese, the Mon-Khmer languages of Assam (Khasi), Burma (Mon or Talaing, Paloung and Wa), Indo-China (Khmer or Cambodian, some lesser known dialects like Steng and Bahnar, possibly Cham of Vietnam and the Sakai dialects of Malaya).

In India the Munda or Kol tribes in central and eastern India speak Austric languages, as also the Khasis in Assam and the Nicobarese islanders. It is of course possible that some earlier tribes in the neighbourhood of the Munda settlers allowed themselves to be assimilated by them, at least partly accepting the Munda language and Munda culture. The Nahals of central India seem to be an example of this. They still have remnants of a language which according to F.B.J. Kuiper is unrelated to any other existing language group of India. But today Nahali has adopted so many Korku words (Korku is the westernmost Munda language) that Nahali is considered a Munda dialect by many Indian linguists. The original features of the Nahali language are so obscured by Korku and Marathi accretions that their very existence has been largely ignored. A similar tribe might be the nomadic Birhor of Chota Nagpur who also speak Mundari, but all traces of an eventual original language have long been lost.

The Munda tribes themselves have so far preserved their original languages because they have, at least in their core, always formed a fairly compact racial and cultural group so that the superior cultures around them had never such an overpowering influence on the Munda tribes that they could destroy their tribal, racial and cultural identity. Still, a number of marginal Munda tribes may have abandoned their Austric idiom and adopted either an Aryan or Dravidian form of speech. Only a penetrating study—which has yet to be done—of the physical features and cultural peculiarities of these tribes could establish proof of such a change.

The origin and early history of the Munda languages is largely unknown. But it is generally assumed that the Munda tribes entered India from the east. This hypothesis was not shaken by W. de Hevesy who, some decades ago, attempted to prove that the Munda languages belonged to the Finno-Ugrian language group. The linguistic experts found his propositions inconclusive.

It is not improbable that in the past the Munda languages were spread over a larger area of India than at present. Their expansion was stalled by the inroads of Aryan, Dravidian and Tibetan languages. Thus, some tribes in Kulu and Lahoul are believed to speak languages which were originally Mundari, though at present the vocabulary is Tibetan. These languages are Kanawari, Malana (or Kanashi) in Kulu, Bunan, Manchat and Tinan in Lahoul.

At present the Munda languages are divided into the following sub-groups:

(1) Northern Munda (or Kherwari): It consists of Mundari, Santali and a large number of dialects, the more important of which are Asuri, Birhor and Ho. The Kherwari dialects are the best known of all the Munda language group. They are spoken mainly in Bihar.

(2) North-western Munda, or the Munda dialects: Spoken in Madhya Pradesh, namely, Koraku, Korowa, Mowasi and Korku. Korowa and Koraku (spoken in Surguja District) are allied to Korku, spoken in Betul, Nimar and the adjoining districts, but they have special affinities with the Kherwari group. Mowasi is a dialect of Korku and is mainly spoken in the Chhindwara District.

(3) Central Munda: It consists of Juang (spoken in Keonjhar and Dhenkanal Districts of Orissa) and Kharia (in the southern parts of Ranchi District in Bihar and its neighbourhood).

(4) Southern Munda: It consists of five distinct languages, namely, Didey, Bonda, Gutob, Parengi and Sora. All these languages are spoken in Koraput, the southernmost District of Orissa.

The second largest group of aboriginal tribes that speaks its own original languages is composed of tribes living mainly in the northern and north-eastern border regions of India and in Assam. These tribes speak Sino-Tibetan languages. The Sino-Tibetan language group is sub-divided into two main groups: (1) the Tibeto-Burman and (2) the Thai-Chinese groups. The language from which all Sino-Tibetan languages are derived can be proved to have existed originally in west China; the inhabitants of China, Thailand, Burma and Tibet trace their idioms back to this language. The modern languages developed, in the course of time, highly sophisticated literatures written in scripts of their own invention.

But the Sino-Tibetan languages spoken by the Indian tribes

in the Himalayan highlands and in Assam did not develop to that high standard; they remained comparatively primitive until modern times. As is natural, in the often isolated hilly regions, these languages developed numerous local differences and modifications. Some of these dialects are spoken by a few hundred individuals only.

The Tibeto-Burman languages spoken in India are divided into several sections: the Himalayan group, spoken by the peoples on the sub-Himalayan slopes west of Bhutan, is sub-divided into two sections: the so-called 'Pronominalised Dialects' (showing perhaps Austric influence) and the 'Pure or non-Pronominalised Dialects'. The Pronominalised Dialects are divided into a western group (Kanauri and Lahuli, among others) and an eastern group (Kiranti, Limbu and Dhimal, in eastern Nepal). The non-Pronominalised dialects are spoken mostly in Nepal, like the Murmi, Magar, and the Newari, among others. (Recent studies have revealed that the language of the Lepchas does not belong to this group, but is a Naga dialect.)

Another language group of this type is found in north Assam. It includes the idioms spoken by the Akas, Abor-Miris, Daflas and Mishmis.

More important is the Assam-Burmese group which is divided into two sub-sections: the Bodo-Naga group and the Burmese-Kuki-Chin-Kachin-Lolo group. The Bodo language was, in former times, used by the tribes residing in the Brahmaputra valley of Assam, north and east Bengal. But due to the expansion of Aryan languages such as Bengali, Assamese and Maithili, the Bodo language has been split up into isolated islands like Koch, Rabha and Mech in north Bengal and the Assam plains, Kachari in the Kachar hills, Garo in the Garo hills and Tipra in Tripura State. Similar to Bodo are the Naga dialects, spoken by the Angami, Sema, Rengma, Ao, Lhota Nagas and other clans, as also by the Lepchas. These dialects have developed such distinct peculiarities that they are often mutually unintelligible.

Of the Burmese-Kuki-Chin-Kachin-Lolo group only the Kuki and Chin idioms are spoken in India. The most advanced language of this group is Meithei or Manipuri, the state language of Manipur State. Lushai too is a Kuki language.

In addition to these languages, there are a number of intermediate dialects, such as that of the Mikir, related both to the

Naga group and the Kuki-Chin group, while the Empeo, Khoirao and Kabui dialects are related to the Naga and Bodo groups.

The Tibetan (Bod, Po or Pho, or Bhuta) dialects are comparatively recent arrivals in India. They are spoken in Bhutan, Sikkim, Baltistan and Ladakh.

Mention should also be made of the Ahom and Khamti languages which belong to the Dai or Thai group of the Thai-Chinese branch of the Sino-Tibetan linguistic family. Ahom is now extinct in India, as the Ahoms themselves have abandoned their original language in favour of Assamese. But Ahom survives in numerous manuscripts written during the time of Ahom rule in Assam. Khamti, another Thai dialect, is spoken in the extreme east of Assam by recent immigrants from Burma.

While thus a considerable part of the Indian aboriginal population speak Austric or Sino-Tibetan languages, only a few other tribal groups possess a language of their own. There is one spoken in an almost inaccessible area beneath the peaks of the Karakorum and Hindukush, in Hunza and Nagyr in Gilgit: it is the Burushaski or Khajuna language. This language cannot yet be affiliated with any known language group. It is obviously an enclave dating from pre-Aryan and even pre-Austric or Sino-Tibetan times.

Another isolated and exclusive language is spoken by the aborigines of the Andaman Islands. It is an idiom of equally unknown affinities. The Andamanese language is divided into several dialects which however are closely related to each other.

By far the largest part of the tribal population of India today speaks languages which are not indigenous to them; they are either Indo-Aryan or Dravidian type. The Indo-Aryan languages are all derived from Sanskrit, the language which the Aryans spoke at the time of their arrival in India. While the later civilisation of Hindu India certainly resulted from a fusion between the Aryan and pre-Aryan cultures, such a fusion did not take place between their respective languages. Though a small minority, the Aryans succeeded in imposing their own language almost fully on a large part of the earlier population of India. Wherever Aryans settled down they imposed their rule and language on the indigenous population and practically obliterated the languages of the latter. Around 600 B.C. Sanskrit ('polished', i.e., according to the rules of grammar) was spoken by most of the peoples residing in the northern Indian plains, from the Punjab eastwards along the Gangetic valley as far as the eastern borders of Bihar. But this did not mean that the indigenous languages did not exert any influence on Sanskrit. In fact, by the middle of the first millennium B.C. various local versions of Sanskrit appeared which were called Prakrit—the 'unrefined' population dialects which in course of time evolved further and further away from the codified Sanskrit. The earliest stage of Prakrit is represented by Pali, which arose in the last centuries B.C. as the language of a school of Buddhism. It is still in use as the religious language of the Buddhists in Ceylon, Burma and Thailand.

Gradually the differences in the various Prakrits increased as these dialects spread further over northern India into Sindh, Rajasthan, Gujarat and northern Deccan, and also to Bengal and the sub-Himalayan regions. Later these Prakrits, which also go under the name of Middle Indo-Aryan dialects, continued to develop and expand until between A.D. 600 and 1000 the modern Indo-Aryan languages began to take shape.

The present-day Indo-Aryan languages are divided into various sections: (1) The North-Western group, including Hindi or Lahnda, or western Punjabi dialects, and Sindhi with Kachhi; (2) the Southern group, including Marathi and Konkani; (3) the Eastern group, including Oriya, Bengali, Assamese, the Bihari dialects, Maithili, Magahi, Bhojpuri with Sadani and Halbi; (4) the East-Central group, including Kosali or eastern Hindi in three dialects (Awadhi, Bagheli and Chhattisgarhi); (5) the Central group, including Hindi proper (with Khariboli, Bangaru and Brij-bhasha, Kanauji and Bundeli), Punjabi (including Dogri), the Rajasthani-Gujarati group including Gujarati, the Rajasthani dialects like Malvi, Marwari, Jaipuri and Mewari, and the Bhil dialects, besides Saurashtri and Gujari; and (6) the Northern, Pahari or Himalayan group, including Gurkhali, Garhawali and Kumaoni, Chameali, Kului, Mandeali, Kiunthali, Sirmauri, and others. A seventh section also exists which includes extra-Indian groups like Sinhalese in Ceylon, with Maldivian, and the Romani or Gypsy dialects of western Asia and Europe.

In the areas where these Indo-Aryan languages are spoken the aboriginal tribes either speak the local dialects or form dialects of their own, with usually slight but characteristic differences in pronunciation and syntax. Linguists might perhaps be able, through an analysis of these peculiarities, to reconstruct or at least to conjecture approximately the type of languages these tribes were originally speaking. Practically all the tribes living in the areas where Indo-Aryan languages are spoken have lost their own idioms.

In Kashmir, in the extreme north-western mountain region of Pakistan and in Afghanistan, the so-called Dardic languages are spoken. Most scholars now believe that the Dardic languages constitute a distinct language group within the Aryan branch of Indo-European, the other two groups being Indo-Aryan and Iranian. While some of the Dardic languages, like Kashmiri and Shina, have developed into literary languages, a number of Dardic dialects are spoken by small and rather primitive tribes. Such dialects are, for instance, the Kho-war or Chitrali, Bashgali and Pashai.

Two important languages of the Iranian group, Pashto and Balochi, also belong to the subcontinent (now Pakistan). Each of the two has two distinct dialects.

While the tribals of northern India speak either Austric, Sino-Tibetan or Indo-Aryan languages, all tribal groups of southern India have replaced their original idioms by the regional Dravidian languages. Dravidian is the second important language family in India. It forms a solid block in south India, including four great literary languages (Tamil, Malayalam, Kannada and Telugu) and a number of less important languages such as Tulu, Kodagu or Coorgi, Badaga, Toda, Kota and Kolami (in Andhra).

But in central and eastern India several rather primitive Dravidian dialects are spoken by aboriginal tribes: Gondi (in Madhya Pradesh, Andhra and Tamilnadu), Kandh or Kui, Praji and Ollari (in Orissa), Kurukhi or Oraon (in Bihar and Orissa), and Malto in the Rajmahal hills (Bihar). Further, in Baluchistan, the Brahuis speak a language which has a strong admixture of Dravidian elements. It is perhaps an indication of the route by which the Dravidians entered India.

It is yet very uncertain how these primitive tribes came to speak Dravidian languages so far distant from the Dravidian area. In Chapter I an attempt was made to give the various explanations by which prehistorians and linguists try to account for the origin and spread of the Dravidian language group. While some of them favour the theory that the Dravidian languages came into existence in the south of India, these languages must have spread to the north and east by migration. Others believe that the Dravidian languages had spread all over India in pre-Aryan times, and it was the Aryan advance which restricted the area of the Dravidian languages but which left pockets of Dravidian speech in the more inaccessible jungle regions. While the Dravida-speaking peoples of the north were either pushed southward by the advancing Aryans, or assimilated Aryan culture and language, some tribes retained their Dravidian idioms and thus form remnants of them in the east and north of India.

The tribes residing in the southern areas where the Dravidian languages are spoken by the non-tribal population have all lost their original dialects. They now speak Dravidian languages, often with certain peculiarities in pronunciation and grammar. As these tribal languages have not yet been studied by linguists, it is impossible to say whether they contain some pre-Dravidian elements.

In conclusion it may be stated that the tribal languages wherever they still exist are on a steady decline and are perhaps condemned to final extinction. Attempts at their revival have so far not met with much success. This decline of the tribal languages has set in a long time ago; the wide adoption of the Indo-Aryan and Dravidian languages by a large part of the tribal population of India is proof of this assumption.

There are various reasons for this development: One reason obviously is that the tribals were detribalised and assimilated by superior Dravidian or Aryan immigrants who either forcibly occupied their habitats or subjugated them gradually. It is also possible that the tribals themselves sought contact with the newcomers who so obviously possessed a superior culture. As the tribals had no words for the new goods and values which they encountered they naturally adopted the names which the newcomers used. Gradually, they completely adopted the new languages, especially if they became economically dependant on the immigrants. The tribal languages are generally deficient in abstract terms and lack the richness of expression found in civilised languages.

The most effective reason for the tribals adopting the superior languages in modern times is school eduation. Education is generally imparted through the medium of the regional language; even elementary education is rarely given to tribal children in their own language. The inevitable result is that the children become more fluent in the regional language than in their own and increasingly neglect the latter. It happens not seldom that educated tribals feel ashamed of their tribal language and refuse to speak it.

The usual process of changing from the tribal language to the regional one begins with the men of the community. They are more exposed to contact with the outside world, and for this reason find it necessary and profitable to learn the regional language. The women of the community may continue to speak the tribal language for a longer time. But slowly they also acquire some fluency in the use of the regional language, especially in the villages with a mixed population. Once the women begin to speak the regional language, the fate of the tribal language is sealed. This decline of the tribal languages may be regrettable, but it is the natural result of cultural change and cultural progress. Against the overwhelming superiority of the present-day Indo-Aryan and Dravidian languages the tribal languages cannot compete. They are doomed to extinction.

Economy

FOODGATHERERS

Many of the aboriginal tribes in India were without doubt in ancient times simply foodgatherers and primitive hunters. When their hunting and collecting grounds were gradually appropriated by cultivating immigrants coming from distant lands in great numbers and in the possession of a superior culture, the food-gathering tribes had to yield to them. Some of the tribes allowed themselves to be subjugated and assimilated by the newcomers, others escaped into areas still comparatively free of settlers, and again others retained their nomadic and collecting way of life in defiance of the new situation. They refused to abandon their collective economy and their traditional freedom of wandering about in their old hunting grounds; the new settlers who had usurped their land began to accuse them of vagrancy, thieving and cheating. And the Government, being all along on the side of the cultivating classes who pay revenue, began to treat the foodgatherers as unwanted vagrants and thieves. The British administration branded them as 'Criminal Tribes and Castes' and placed them under police supervision. Attempts at 'reform' were made by Government and private welfare agencies, and the foodgatherers were urged to live in permanent settlements and to take up farming.

But the nomadic mode of life is based on a peculiar mental attitude or a specific world outlook; it is sometimes deliberately chosen by some individuals belonging to a different type of culture or retained by whole communities in which it is traditional. The wandering urge and the love for complete freedom which are deeply ingrained in these people may often be incomprehensible to people belonging to a different form and standard of culture. This lack of understanding and sympathy has often resulted in very harsh and unjust treatment of the nomadic collecting communities. Though after independence the former 'criminal tribes and castes' were classified as 'denotified', their treatment has changed little. Most of these tribes are still placed in the same category as 'criminal castes'.

Still, an exception was made for some foodgathering tribes. They were never included among the criminal or denotified tribes, but among the aboriginal or scheduled tribes. The reason was because they lived in predominantly 'tribal areas', where their foodgathering activity created less disturbance in the life of the settled population. Such tribes are, for instance, the Birhor, Korwars and Hill Kharias in Chota Nagpur, the Kadar, Yanadis and Chenchus in south India, and the Katkaris or Kathodis in Maharashtra and Gujarat.

The foodgathering tribes living in the plains among a cultivating rural population are economically in the worst position. There is really no place for them in the rural areas. The land has all been distributed among the farmers; its produce is closely guarded and there is nothing left for the primitive children of nature to live on.

But in modern times all the nomadic foodgatherers of India are on the decline and dwindling in numbers. The fast growing population of India cannot afford to leave sufficient space for a foodgathering economy which requires a large uncultivated area to live on. Not only is the cultivable land getting scarce, but also the forests are being increasingly cleared, and in the remaining forests their produce is placed under an increasingly stricter control by the Forest Department. New diseases against which the primitives have no resistance and know no medicines also take their steady toll. The smaller their numbers become, the greater is the danger of inbreeding and the bad effects this entails. Thus it is only a question of time before the foodgathering tribes disappear from the Indian subcontinent. It is a wonder that they have survived so long.

PRIMITIVE CULTIVATORS

In 1961, 89.2 per cent of the tribals were engaged in cultivation. Agriculture is, therefore, going to be the predominant pattern of tribal economy for a long time to come. However, the form of agriculture which is practised by most of the tribes is primitive and low in yield. Originally, most tribes were shifting cultivators, burning the forest and sowing their seeds in the fertile ashes. Many tribes in south India, in central India, in Chota Nagpur and Bengal, on the slopes of the Himalayas, and in Assam practised, until fairly recent times, this slash-and-burn cultivation for which no plough animals were required. The only implements required for this type of cultivation were the axe and the digging stick.

This type of cultivation made a greater variety of field products possible and was not restricted to the cultivation of grain alone. Garden fruits ripening at different times were also grown. This made for more balanced nutrition.

But in most regions of India plough cultivation was forced on the tribes by the Government which found shifting cultivation wasteful and damaging to the forests.

However, 'shifting cultivation' is not merely one form of cultivation which can easily be replaced by another, i.e., plough cultivation. 'Shifting cultivation' was an integrated part of the economy in the tribal culture, and as it grew out of a particular mental outlook it also affected all other spheres of their cultural life. The tribes which preferred shifting cultivation deliberately chose hilly and forested country for their habitats, and left the plains and broad river valleys to the plough cultivators. Moreover, the shifting cultivators always lived close to the jungle, and found ample time and leisure to get away from the dull routine of heavy farm work. They felt free to roam in the jungle for a hunt or the collection of forest produce. They required no cattle as plough animals and were thus less tied down to their homesteads and stables.

Their whole mental constitution and spiritual outlook differed from that of plough cultivators. Thus the change-over to plough cultivation forced upon them by an unsympathetic and undiscerning Government resulted in a serious disturbance of the very basis of their traditional culture. No wonder, they now feel insecure, confused and disoriented. It is not a sign of low intelligence nor a lack of adaptability nor extreme conservatism that makes the tribals inept and inefficient in a form of cultivation which has been forced upon them more or less abruptly. For, the abandonment of shifting cultivation entails a change of their whole cultural life in all its various aspects. This has been largely overlooked while making policies designed for the uplift of the tribals and their integration in the national life of India.

TYPES OF LAND TENURE

In Central India

Among shifting cultivators land is generally owned by the village community. Land for cultivation is redistributed either every year, or after a period of three to five years among the members of a clan or village community.

In India during the rule of the Maurya and Gupta dynasties feudalism developed and the rights of land became divided among the chiefs of state, the village communities and the individual cultivators. The cultivator had the usufructuary right on payment of a share of the produce, the community the ownership, and the rulers or their deputies had the right to collect tributes from the village communities. Ultimately, the State claimed ownership of the hand and it collected its share of the produce through tributary chiefs or feudatory princes.

On the eve of the Muslim invasion the monarchy had gone into a decline and the feudatory princes had largely become independent. They usurped proprietory rights over all the land and largely disowned the village communities. It was this land system which the Muslim rulers inherited and further developed. They introduced the *zamindari* and *jagirdari* systems by which a new class of landlords emerged, while the cultivators were reduced to the status of tenants.

As long as land was freely available, the new tenant cultivators were scarcely aware of this change and where the new ownership was enforced they could always retreat into the virgin forest, clear some land and prepare new fields. But feudalism spread even into the heart of the tribal communities when prominent clan, village, and district headmen of the Mundas, Gonds and Korkus, the Bhils and other tribes turned themselves into chiefs or *rajas*, adopted the royal style, usurped all the land of the community over which they ruled and gave parts of the lands to Brahmin priests and court officials. Their tribal subjects thus were reduced to mere tenants in their own country.

In the second half of the last century the British Tenancy Acts took away all the communally-owned land which still remained with the tribals and gave, sold or auctioned it off to landlords. The result was that even those tribals who had till then retained their lands, were reduced to tenants. They were now at the mercy of landlords who often, in order to get a better return, gave their land to more efficient Hindu farmers for cultivation. Oppressive exploitation and increasing scarcity of arable land were the consequences. This resulted in severe tribal unrest and occasionally in armed revolts. The Hos, Santals, Mundas, Maler and Kols repeatedly revolted against their oppressors, but only with disastrous consequences to themselves, as the British administration protected the system which they had either introduced themselves or found in existence when they occupied the country.

In Western India

In western India, before independence, a great number of large and small princely states were in existence. In these states the *jagirdari* system of land tenure was in force. The *jagirdar* exercised control over his tenants; in fact, he behaved as if he were the owner of the land. He fixed the rent for the land, much in excess over the amount he paid to the Government. He also usurped the right of turning out tenants and taking others who promised to pay more rent. Lands were let out to the highest bidder resulting in rack-renting. In addition, the tenants had to do forced labour and to render other services also. Moreover, they had no security of tenure. No wonder that tribal discontent in western India was high and sometimes exploded into bloody revolts. The Bhils, Naikdas and Kolis often revolted when exploitation became unbearable. The *jagirdari* system was only abrogated in 1952, with an amendment in 1954.

In Assam

The tribal land belonged either to the village or clan community. Field plots were distributed to the families by the clan or village elders. Plots under cultivation were either inherited from generation to generation, or redistributed at certain time-intervals. But everywhere there was that slow but inexorable advance of the land-hungry Assamese or Bengali peasant population which greedily appropriated every available field-plot. The tribals were no match for the peasants of the plains in efficiency of farming or in holding on to the land.

In South India

The majority of the tribals in south India were either foodgatherers or shifting cultivators. During the 'settlement transactions' most of the tribal land was appropriated by cultivators and by large estates, tea gardens, coffee and rubber plantations which were started at that time. As long as land was plentiful, the tribals were allowed to live on their old hunting and collecting grounds as before. But gradually labourers and farmers from the plains were introduced or invaded the hills and jungles and settled down to farm. The jungle tribes were deprived of their hunting grounds and had to hire themselves out as field and plantation labourers; at the most they were assigned a small plot of land for cultivation.

LAND ACQUISITION FOR INDUSTRIAL ENTERPRISES

In modern times vast areas of land have been acquired by the Indian Government for the building of steel factories, giant industrial estates and for the building of dams and hydro-electric works. As these new enterprises were established mainly in tribal areas, the tribals lost their land in most cases. Up to 1961, a total of 14,113 tribal families were thus deprived of 62,228 acres of land; they were rehabilitated on an area of only 8,314 acres.

The Dhebar Commission found that in Gujarat, for instance, due to the changes and defective execution of the land revenue laws, 20 per cent of the tribals had in recent times lost their land. In Madhya Pradesh, between 1959 and 1960, no less than 1,135 tribal families were displaced. Of these 1,135 families only eighty were rehabilitated. The others were given indemnification in cash, after an often very arbitrary and unfavourable evaluation of the property they lost. The tribals often squandered the cash which they received instead of buying new land.

HANDICRAFTS

Members of the aboriginal tribes are often skilled artisans and able to manufacture all their agricultural implements for themselves. Some of the tribes are professional blacksmiths, mat and basket makers, weavers, carpenters and carvers of wood and stone. While their skills are sufficient for the traditional needs in their own village, they would require a more adequate training for employment in industrial concerns or in the manufacture of articles of modern design.

ANIMAL BREEDING

Very few aboriginal tribes specialise in the herding and breeding of animals, such as the semi-aboriginal Ahirs, Gujars, Dhangars, etc., and in the south the Kavundar, Idayar, Todas and Lamanas. For some tribes, like the Bhois, Dhimars, Mogers, Paravar, Bagatas, Valar and Aryar, fishing is the traditional profession. Their methods of breeding cattle and sheep, and fishing, are still most primitive and often inefficient and unproductive. The domestic animals of the tribal cultivators are generally of the poorest quality and badly neglected. Sound and productive husbandry is often impossible due to religious and social prohibitions.

ACCULTURATION

The Indian Government is making strenuous efforts to acculturate the aboriginal tribes and to improve their primitive economy.

For, the tribals can be called backward and primitive mainly for economic reasons.

It is still largely unknown what exactly hinders the cultural progress of certain tribal communities. Is it congenital low intelligence? But this can be true in only a few instances, for a large part of the tribal children who were given the opportunity of an education showed largely the same intellectual abilities as children of other communities. Perhaps a more relevant factor may be the adverse environmental and geographical conditions which impair their cultural advance, the isolation which follows from living in remote and inaccessible hills, and the lack of stimulating contacts with people of a superior culture. But many tribals do live in proximity to people of a superior culture, and still remain backward and aloof. The reason for such behaviour might be less an extreme innate conservatism of which they are often accused, but more the bad experience they have had with members of the superior culture. Often they have been hurt and oppressed and mercilessly exploited and unjustly treated by these outsiders. Representatives of the same class come and make all kinds of new proposals, assuring them that these changes will benefit them and bring them relief in all their troubles. No wonder the tribals distrust them and oppose their schemes, the more so as the schemes often prove impractical and rarely pass beyond the experimental stage. The tribals cannot take any risks of experimentation, as they are already living in very precarious economic conditions.

The schemes proposed by the various welfare and development agencies not only often disturb the tribals' economic equilibrium, but also entail changes in their social life for which the tribals are mentally unprepared. For, they set a high value on personal freedom and they will reject any proposal, however advantageous economically, that ties them down to a life of dull routine. Deeply attached to the free and exciting life as hunters and food collectors in the jungle, or at least to the clearing of the forest and the sowing in virgin soil, they will reject any occupation that leaves no room for an occasional breakaway from the drudgery of daily life. And when in the right mood, they want a day off for singing and dancing and for the celebration of feasts and important events, such as weddings and funeral feasts.

It is consequently mainly the mentality of the tribals and their world outlook which would have to be changed before they are ready to welcome any form of merger into the national life of India.

Social Structure

The social organisation of the tribes in India is very diverse and often quite complicated. This is quite natural as they come from so many different races and cultures which are at various stages of development. They have also been much influenced by the surrounding superior cultures whose social structure they may have adopted though often quite incompletely.

Among the nomadic foodgathering tribes the social structure is based mainly on the natural family. Usually several such families, united by ties of kinship, form a local group. They live together, hunt and collect together and share out among themselves what they have gathered. They have obligations towards each other, and support each other in want, sickness and old age. Social life, however, is not entirely restricted to the local group wherever it exists. The local groups meet occasionally to celebrate feasts, for the arrangement of marriages and other important matters.

Generally they observe local group exogamy, that is, members of a local group have to select their marriage partners from outside groups. The marriage bond is loose, divorce frequent, and the women and girls not infrequently earn additional income by prostituting themselves. This is however not the custom among the tribes living in the forest, but more among the tribes living in the plains among the rural population. The local group is generally headed by the oldest male member who is, however, not rarely replaced by a clever and enterprising younger man. The headman has not much authority, but he acts as spokesman with the police and other Government officials, decides when to strike camp and where to go, and tries to settle disputes and quarrels arising between the members of the group or with outsiders.

While some tribes of north-eastern central India have adopted, or retained, the—often totemistic—clan system, with clan exogamy and clan taboos, the nomadic tribes in southern India, in particular those in Kerala, have adopted the matrilineal system partly or fully. In some tribes this has resulted in a breakdown of the family system and led to practical promiscuity. Divorce is frequent and premarital and extra-marital sex relations are at least tolerated. These tribes, too, live in small local groups, with a permanent or temporary headman, whose authority depends more on his personal character and ability than on his office. The male members of a local group with their families are free to separate and join other groups if they so desire and are accepted by another group. But often they are united by ties of kinship or affinity and prefer to stay together more or less permanently.

The social structure of the tribes which practise a primitive form of cultivation is more developed. The nuclear family of the foodgatherers expands frequently into a joint family, the sons remaining after marriage with their father and helping him in the fieldwork while the women look after the house and the children, and also help in the fieldwork. Since members of one group now settle in more compact villages and stay permanently together, the local group develops into a village community. Descendants of one ancestral village regard each other as relatives. They practise village exogamy, that is, members whose ancestors were residents of the same village cannot marry each other. The common bond which unites persons hailing from the same ancestral village often has a religious significance. The final funeral ceremonies for a deceased must be performed in the ancestral village and even memorial pillars of stone and wood may be erected in these places. This is for instance the custom among the Mundas and Gonds of central India.

In the past, new villages were often founded by an enterprising man with the help of a few of his kinsmen and their families. That is why village exogamy had to be observed. Later, other families may also have joined the village community. These outsiders were accepted into the village community and were gradually granted equal rights. The village community, consisting of members of one tribe, arranges, witnesses and supervises wedding and funeral feasts. It settles marriage disputes and declares a divorce. It discusses property disputes, settles quarrels and chastises those who offend against the tribal law. It excommunicates, punishes or fines the culprits. It deals with outside communities.

Many tribal cultivating communities possess a so-called clan-system. The clan is centred on a personal ancestor, not a place or village as in the village or territorial system. Sometimes a tribe, like the Gonds and Baigas of central India, may have both systems side by side, which of course complicates matters considerably. In the beginning, a clan community may have been identical with a village community, that is, members of one clan only formed a whole village community. In the course of time this order was often disturbed and members of several clans settled in a village. Commonly the bonds of the village community appear stronger than clan ties and authority rests in the village community and less so in the clan fellowship.

But in communities with a matrilineal social structure the clan solidarity may prove stronger. This seems to be the case in Assam among the Khasis and Garos. A village is usually occupied by a single clan, with matrilineal descent, and a female clan head, who is generally the head of the oldest and highest family in the village. The management of the clan need not always be exercised by a woman; often it is her brother who acts in her name. Thus, the male element reasserts itself. The kinship ties may be so strong that neither husband nor wife are prepared to separate from their kinship group. Consequently, a man does not live with his wife, but visits her only at times fixed by convention. This is called a 'visit-marriage'. In the past this custom was found among some Naga tribes (in Manipur) and also among the Khasis.

The clans of many tribes are totemistic in character. Totemism in its various forms can be found in wide areas of the Indian peninsula. It is absent only in the north of India and in its southernmost corner. It is not at all restricted to tribal communities. It is strongest in central India from where it probably spread out into Bihar, Orissa, Maharashtra, Andhra and Kanara (in Mysore).

It is still disputed who the original carriers of totemism in India are. It has been suggested that the Proto-Australoid tribes had totemism first and later handed it in modified forms on to the agrarian peoples of the Deccan, Andhra and Kanara. In their migrations they carried it along as far as Chota Nagpur. But the Munda race too seems to have been totemistic from the beginning. In Chota Nagpur and eastern central India the

Proto-Australoids and the Mundas met and mingled to some extent; this might well be the reason why totemism is so strong in this area.

The totem of the Proto-Australoids is either an animal, a plant (tree) or any other object, animate or inanimate. In Chota Nagpur animal totems predominate (the Mundas, for instance, have 150 animal totems, eighty-seven plant totems, or those of minerals, metals, etc.; the Asuras have ten animal totems and three plant totems; the Bhumias have thirteen animal totems out of fifteen totems; the Santals with seventeen totems have four animal, nine plant and four object totems; the Oraons with sixty-eight totems have forty-three animal and nineteen plant totems). Totemism with predominant animal totems is also found in Bengal and northern Tamilnadu. But no caste or tribes has animal totems exclusively.

Plant totems predominate in Maharashtra. Of 137 *devaks*, sixty-two are plants, twenty-eight animals and twenty-four inanimate object totems. The Bhois seem to have exclusively plant totems. The Maravar in Travancore, too, seem to have only plant totems (six in number). This predominance of plant totems seems to have spread northwards to the Bhils, and north-eastwards, where the Dahaits of Jabalpur and even the Korkus of the Melghat have predominantly plant totems.

In the east and north-east of India other objects (of various kinds, like ocean, gun, corals, cakes, garden, island, magic, darkness, white and red colours, etc.) prevail as totems.

But the list of totems is not at all complete, and information is sketchy.

Totemism is found in patrilineal as well as in matrilineal societies. Totem membership is inherited in the paternal line in Chota Nagpur, in the Deccan and in the south-east of India. Totem membership is inherited matrilineally in Assam among the Garos and Khasis, perhaps also among the Lalungs and Kacharis. In south-west India, in south Kanara, the Tulu-speaking castes, like the Billavas, Devadigas and Madivalas, inherit totem membership and property in the female line, while the Kanarese-speaking castes of North Kanara inherit both totem membership and property patrilineally. These are the Halvakki Vakkals, the Gam Vakkals, Mukris, Gabits, and many others. But there are also other castes, like the Bants, Moger, Hallpaiks and Kelasis, who inherit totem membership in the female line, but property in the male line. So in south Kanara do the Patvegaras, Holeyas, Bili Maggas, Nalkes and Nador. Thus it seems that totemism is secondary in matrilineal castes and the result is a mixture of cultures.

The strong emphasis on exogamy of the totem clans is typical. Among the primitive tribes at least it is usually strictly enforced.

However, among certain tribes, the strict enforcement of clan exogamy is disturbed by the existence of territorial exogamy which seems to be an older form of social organisation in India. It is the usual social structure in north India where totemism is absent. Members of such a group bear the name of their ancestral village or territory, and may not intermarry. This system is also found among the more primitive tribes of central India, especially those who are probably pre-Munda and pre-Dravidian, and consequently the oldest settlers in this region.

Where aboriginal tribes have adopted Hinduism, they often give up their clan exogamy and adopt the Hindu system of relationship exogamy in various grades and degrees, orthodox Hindus forbidding marriage within seven, others only within three degrees of relationship. Clan exogamy may also be relaxed when the population of a tribe has been reduced so much that no marriage would otherwise be possible. For, tribes and castes are endogamous. The Pahiras and Parjas are examples of this. Frequently, a tribe or caste consists of several sub-divisions, each with a certain number of exogamous totem clans, but this type of division seems to be more recent than the existence of undivided tribes and castes.

Sexual totemism is absent in India. Individual totemism has been discovered in one tribe only—the Asuras. It is very likely, however, that individual totemism was more widespread in former times in tribal India. A number of folktales collected in central India seem to contain elements which are found in individual totemism. It may also have been in existence among the Lakhers of Assam.

The ceremonial character of totemism is well developed in India. Taboo regulations are general and perhaps of most ancient origin. Mourning for the totem is found as a characteristically local development in central India and more in the east of India. The veneration of the totem is either a general 'reverence', 'respect', or even 'worship'. Some tribes, like the Bhils, must bow down when they meet their totem while the women veil their faces.

Among many tribes the totem is worshipped at weddings. This is done all over the Deccan, where the *devak* is worshipped. As a matter of fact, it seems that this custom has its origin in Maratha totemism from where it spread to central India. But it is found also among the Buruds of Hyderabad, and the Chadars, Basors and Dehaits of central India who venerate a figure or painted picture of the totem.

The representation of the totem in sculpture or painting (drawing) is found mainly in places where the totem is venerated at weddings. It may be represented in clay, dough, in the form of a dagger or post, or painted on the wall. Tattooing of the totem on the body is found among primitive tribes only, for instance, the Bhils, Bhainas, Dhanwars, Gonds, Kawars and others. The Khadals, Khangars and Gonds also sacrifice to the totem at marriages. In south India such a ceremony is found only among the snake clan of the Kanarese Toreyas (of Coimbatore and Salem). The Oraons and Birhors in Bihar have totem deities whose figures they venerate on certain occasions. It is noteworthy that these totem deities are often, at the same time, village deities. Some eight clans in central India mourn when they hear of the death of their totem or when they see its dead body. The mourning is carried out in the same manner as if a near relative had died. Most of these clans break their earthen pots in mourning. The same custom is found among the Kacharis in Assam.

Rules of avoidance regarding the totem are very common. Animal totems may not be killed, wounded or eaten, plant totems may not be touched, cut or used for food. A breach of the taboo rules is believed to cause sickness or misfortune. Taboo rules are prevalent not only in south India (Mysore, Madras, Trichinopoly, etc.), but also in the north-west of India among the Bhils, in the north-east, Chota Nagpur and Orissa where such rules are observed by almost all tribes and castes as far as Assam (among the Khasis, for instance). It is remarkable that such taboo rules are often prevalent in the aboriginal portion of a caste or tribe, while the Hinduised part of the tribe does not any longer observe the same rules. This shows the destructive role of Hinduism with regard to totemism; it is a parallel to the disappearance of clan exogamy in the same tribes and castes.

The inner relation between the totem and the respective clans is conceived as a kind of kinship. The Asurs of Chota Nagpur believe that the totem animal is a kinsman. Breach of clan exogamy is consequently considered as incest. This is so not only among the Asurs, but also among the Santals, Birhors, Oraons, Korkus, and among the Bants in south Kanara. The Garos believe that the totem is their ancestor; the Halepaiks in south Kanara also think so. The Kanwars believe in descent from their animal and plant totems, not however from inanimate object totems. But many tribes and castes strictly reject the idea of genetic descent and have some other explanations of their dependence on the totem, like the Mundas, Gonds, Janappans, Kharias, Korkus, Birhors, Majhivars and others.

The various forms which totemism in India has assumed make it apparent that totemism in India is not a peculiar growth, but stood once in historical connection with similar forms existing in other parts of the world [J.V. Ferreira (1965)].

Political Organisation

The political organisation of the aboriginal tribes in India, now much disturbed and partly superseded by the modern Indian Government, comprises a wide range of forms.

Among the nomadic foodgatherers and hunters, and also many of the vagrant tribes and castes, the disciplinary and juridical matters of the groups are managed by the heads of the family groups. They have usually no chiefs.

The governing body of the primitive cultivators is usually the council of elders of the village community. It is called *panch* or *panchayat*. There are no chiefs but headmen; these headmen do not have much power over their subjects. Matters concerning the welfare of the tribal group and especially racial and ritual purity are controlled mainly by a democratic tribal or caste council whose members consist either of all adult males or several elders of the village community. In rare cases a tribal council consisting of the headmen of a number of village councils may meet and decide matters of great importance.

The tribes in north-eastern central India, however, of much

greater numerical strength and more conscious of their importance, have a more elaborate political organisation. They have not only village councils and more influential headmen with other village officials in support, but often well established headmen over a number of villages, a sort of confederacy of village communities. There is an annual meeting, often initiated by a ceremonial hunt and other ceremonies. In the past these headmen often assumed princely powers and became *rajas*, often with disastrous consequences to their tribal subjects.

In the eastern regions of India, Assam and the adjoining regions, democratic tribal councils exist side by side with the institution of chiefs, either elected or inheriting their position. There is also a more pronounced hierarchy within certain tribes, with ruling families, commoners, and even slaves. Some of the tribes have open-air assemblies which settle judicial cases, decide over the tribal policy and execute administration. The individual members are bound to attend these assemblies (*darbar*). Without the sanction of these assemblies the chiefs cannot dispose over land or forest, cannot impose taxes nor promulgate new laws.

In many tribal communities of central India, Assam and even south India, the so-called dormitory system is in existence, though it is now going rapidly out of use. While in some areas, especially in the south, youth dormitories have scarcely any other function but the prevention of incest, in Bastar and in Assam the dormitory system has educational, economic and social functions. The young men and women can be asked to help in communal agricultural activities, but their dormitories can also be used for entertainment, singing, dancing, council meetings and the performance of religious ceremonies.

The traditional political organisation of the tribal communities in India, permitted to function until recent times by an ineffective or indulgent Government during the pre-British and even throughout the British times, is now since independence threatened by the increasing pressure of the administrative control of the Indian Government. Though M.K. Gandhi and the Congress Party viewed the traditional *panchayat* system of the tribals and of the rural population in general with benevolent approval and tried to incorporate it into the administration of India, this was not very successful. The *panchayat* system sponsored and protected by the Indian Government often acts as a parallel governing body, working side by side and often against the traditional *panchayat* system still in force. This has resulted in the decay and often complete breakdown of the traditional as well as the newly introduced Government *panchayat* systems.

In recent times the Indian tribals have in some areas started active movements for a certain degree of political autonomy and self-rule or even for complete independence. Such movements are not found in south India where the tribals are more scattered and are often completely demoralised and without any influence. In Chota Nagpur, where the tribals are especially strong and vigorous, live in great concentration and are numerically very strong, where they also have a tradition of self-rule in the past and even boast of rulers and princes of their own, the Jharkhand Movement was born and found a powerful leader in an educated Munda, Jaipal Singh. Even after his downfall and death, the Jharkhand Movement did not die out though it faces strong opposition from the non-tribal classes of the area as well as from the Congress Party. The carriers of the Jharkhand Movement aspire at an autonomous state within the Indian Union in which the tribals would rule themselves.

In Nagaland, it was especially the Mizos (Lushais) who demanded autonomy and even complete independence. Various attempts have been made to achieve political independence, sometimes even with the assistance of neighbouring countries who have an interest in the existence of small buffer states between themselves and India. The leaders of these independence movements are partly Christians since the Christians in these areas form the most educated groups and consequently more fervently desire self-rule and political independence.

EFFECTS OF THE CASTE SYSTEM ON THE TRIBES

The Indian caste system is so powerful and all-pervading that few tribes can entirely escape its consequences. Though the tribes may keep as far as possible to themselves, they must maintain some relations with the outside world. In dealings with the Hindus the tribals also fall under the influence of the caste system, for the Hindus judge and class them according to their own standards. They accord them that rank in their society which, in their opinion, the tribes deserve as judged by the tribals' habits regarding food and behaviour. Thus tribes that eat beef and the flesh of other 'unclean animals' or carry on a profession which is ritually unclean are regarded as impure and their touch is polluting. Many nomadic tribes of north and south India fall under this category, as they are not discriminate in their food habits and undertake ritually impure professions such as domestic service, mat and broom making, playing musical instruments, public singing and dancing, etc.

However, the Hindus are quite prepared to judge the tribals more leniently and not to apply the same strict standards on them as on members of their own society, especially if these tribes are wealthy and powerful. Though they may practise habits which the Hindus abhor, such as drinking liquor, permitting divorce and remarriage of widows, eating meat (as long as it is not beef and the flesh of the domestic pig), these tribes may still retain a relatively high level of social status in the eyes of the Hindus, provided they remain tribals and keep at some distance. But as soon as the tribes aspire at a full incorporation into Hindu society, they must conform to the whole set of rules and regulations demanded by Hinduism or accept a lower rank in the caste system.

The majority of the tribes have always aspired at the Kshatriya rank and in particular claimed incorporation in the Rajput community. Most often they made this claim on the real or fictional assumption of being the descendants of Rajput ancestors. And, in fact, many Rajput adventurers, and also many fugitives from Mughal rule seem to have intermarried with the upper strata of tribal society. There are too many reports of such alliances to be merely relegated into the sphere of fairy-tales. Such stories may sometimes even claim a historical documentation. Thus it is well-known that Rani Durgavati, mother of the last Gond king of Mandla, was a Rajput princess of Mahoba. It is also certain that Rajputs married into the chief families of Korku and Bhil tribes and became the ancestors of mixed tribals who claim a higher rank than other members of the tribe because of the Rajput blood in their veins however attenuated it might have become after many generations.

These tribes may prefer admittance into the Rajput community also for the reason that the latter have the reputation of being more liberal in the observance of the Hindu caste rules. They eat meat, even the flesh of the wild pig which they hunt, drink liquor and, at least in the lower ranks, permit divorce and widow-marriage. The tribes find their society more congenial than that of vegetarians and puritans.

In order to maintain a respectable caste status, some tribes refuse to accept food from any low caste member though originally such discrimination is foreign to them. Thus the Khandesh Bhils do not eat food cooked by Mahars, Mangs and Chamars. Gonds do not eat food cooked by Baigas, Chamars, Balahis, Pardhans, etc. Certain tribes refuse to accept food from any outsider, even were he a Brahmin. They are not yet able to make a correct distinction between pure and impure castes and do not want to take any risk. Thus they disdain from accepting food even from a Brahmin.

On the other hand, the employment of Brahmins for religious services is regarded as a sign of good caste standing. Often a tribal community introduces certain religious ceremonies for this very purpose of being able to employ a Brahmin priest, while for their traditional tribal ceremonies they invite their own priests, or priests of another tribe—the Baigas, for instance.

The caste system has affected the tribes not only in so far as their relations with the Hindus are concerned. A certain caste discrimination also exists within the tribal society. First of all, there is the distinction between a Hinduised section and a tribal section. Such a distinction exists in many tribes, as for instance among the Baigas (Binjhwars and ordinary Baigas), Korkus (Raj-Korkus or Muwasis and Patharias), Gonds (Raj-Gonds and Dhur-Gonds), Bhilalas (Bara Bhilalas and Barelas), etc. In each case the Hinduised section considers itself superior and refuses to interdine and intermarry with the tribal one. This separation is maintained though both sections are well aware of their common origin and often still retain their tribal names. At the most the Hinduised section takes wives from the tribal section, but refuses to give its daughters in marriage.

The tribe may be further influenced by the Hindu caste system in the treatment of other tribes. They may regard tribes that eat beef and other unclean food as polluting as if they themselves were Hindus of good caste. They may also regard tribes as inferior who serve them and accept cooked food from them. Thus the Gonds treat Ojhas, Pardhans and even Baigas as inferior because these tribes act as their exorcisers, minstrels and priests. The Korkus and Bhils treat the Nahals as inferior, because the latter serve them as their field labourers and accept cooked food from them. It is stated that in the past all these tribes interdined and even intermarried frequently and without any unpleasant consequences. This caste discrimination was introduced when the leading tribes came into contact with the Hindu castes and gradually adopted their caste principles.

This short survey shows that in spite of all deliberate aloofness which the tribes intend to keep from the outside world, Hindu ideals and principles are being gradually adopted. However, from the point of modern developments, this adoption may be considered as retrogressive because among the more progressive and modern Hindus the tendency is to abandon the full rigours of the traditional caste system. While on their part the caste system is liberalised, it is being introduced in its full strictness in the tribal areas by the more conservative Hindu classes.

RELIGION

The original religion of the tribal population in India is commonly characterised as 'animistic'. Animism is the doctrine that inanimate objects as well as living beings are endowed with indwelling spirits of various kinds. Indeed, belief in such spirits and their veneration and worship is common to all Indian tribes. Mountains, rocks, rivers, trees, etc., are believed to be inhabited by deities and spirits. The whole world is populated by a host of spirits, good and evil. These spirits can be invoked, propitiated and even forced to help or harm human beings by various magical means and practices. Naturally, not all spirits are equally favoured by the tribes. Some tribes prefer the worship of the spirits of the forest, of rivers and mountains, others concentrate on the spirits of the earth, or of the heavenly bodies, sun, moon and stars. Even spirits of disease are believed to exist, and they must be propitiated.

But there is also the belief in a high-god. The term 'high-god' was coined by Andrew Lang in his book *The Making of Religion* (London, 1898). For Lang the high-god is a personal god, separate from and altogether superior to all other deities and spirits, the master, and often maker, of the universe and of men, the creator and guardian of the moral code, master over life and death, himself benevolent, immutable.

The concept of a high-god is very likely indigenous in the tribal religions of India. When they came into contact with the Hindus, they began to identify him either with the 'absolute being' of Hindu religion, or with its main incarnation or personification. As the Hindus call this being Parmatma, Parmeshwar, Param Shiva, or Bhagwan, the tribes often use the same names for their high-god. But in north-eastern central India he is often identified with the 'spirit of the sun' (which is the exact translation of the word Sing Bonga, the high-god of the Mundas, or of Beru Deo, the high-god of the Gonds). In eastern central India he is also called Dharmesh, or Dharmraj, due probably to Buddhist influence. The name Bhagwan is very common. The rural Hindu castes understand Bhagwan as something like a high-god. The tribals have obviously adopted the name Bhagwan from them.

In most tribal religions of India, the high-god is today regarded as an otiose deity, that is, he is invoked but rarely worshipped. He has become a distant deity who leaves the world and men at the mercy of the minor deities, the spirits and demons. Generally the tribals do not fashion an image of the high-god, though some tribes in south India, and the Gonds and Baigas in central India erect a formless stone slab under a tree for this purpose. They also occasionally address prayers to the high-god and even perform sacrifices in his honour, usually right in the beginning of an elaborate sacrificial ceremony.

But other deities seem to be more important for the emotional and ceremonial side of tribal religion. Prayer and sacrifice are particularly addressed to them. The Earth-mother is first in importance for primitive cultivators. She receives mainly bloody sacrifices of goats, fowl, buffaloes, and sometimes even human sacrifices. The Earth-mother, now often bearing an Aryan name, such, as Prithvi-mata, Dharti-mata, but also simply Kali, Durga, or Parvati, is often at the same time the village goddess (Gram Devi). Much worshipped are also the goddesses of disease, such as the so-called 'Seven Sisters', chief among them being Marai Mata, Sitala Mata, etc. They are venerated especially during epidemics like cholera, small-pox, chicken-pox, plague, etc.

Various Hindu deities, like Vishnu (especially in his incarnation as Krishna), Shiva (Mahadeo, Shankar), Hanuman, Ravan, and the epic heroes, such as the Pandava brothers, play an important part in the religious life of the primitive tribes. But no doubt, the rural Hindu castes have also adopted tribal gods and given them a place in their pantheon. One of these is certainly the 'Bamboo-mother' (Bans-mata or Banhi-mata); the 'Tiger-god' (Bagh Deo), Dulha Deo (the bridegroom killed on the way to his wedding), the 'God of Animals', etc., belong also to this category. There is a special god for each particular need. Sometimes the god has retained his tribal name, but often this has been replaced by a corresponding Hindu name.

In fact, all tribal religions have to some extent absorbed elements of higher religions, especially of Hinduism, and some of the main Hindu gods—Shiva, and Vishnu (in his incarnation as Krishna)—are incorporated in the tribal religions or identified with former tribal gods. The Pandava brothers of the Mahabharata, and especially Bhima among them, are favourite figures in the tribal myths and folktales of central India. Ayyappan is widely venerated by the tribes of south India. Perhaps he is a tribal god who has been adopted by the Hindus.

The foodgathering and hunting tribes are perhaps the least influenced by Hinduism, while almost all cultivating tribes have imbibed a generous portion of Hindu religious beliefs. In fact, the degree of Hinduisation often decides the social status of the tribes in Hindu society. Many tribes are divided into 'superior' and 'inferior' sections according to the higher or lesser degree of absorption of Hindu religious beliefs and practices.

Many primitive tribes have special rites of veneration for their ancestors, on the occasion of a death, on certain feasts. All primitive tribes hold the belief in the survival of the soul after death. Often they believe in a plurality of souls: the shadow, life-spirit, the ego. The belief in the transmigration and reincarnation of souls is fairly widespread, but need not always be the result of Hindu influence. Many tribes believe that the future life is determined by the good or bad deeds a person has committed in his earthly life. But more important are certain religious rites and sacrifices without which even a highly virtuous life is of no avail. Many tribes, especially in central India, erect memorial pillars for their dead, of wood or stone, sometimes artistically carved. Only with the erection of such a pillar is the soul of a deceased finally laid to rest and enters the realm of the ancestors. An elaborate ritual surrounds the erection of these pillars.

Ignorant of the true laws of nature and the cosmic order, the tribals have developed a largely magical world outlook. They believe that the whole world and every individual life are mainly governed and directed by superhuman powers, personal and impersonal. They are convinced that they can effectively influence these superhuman powers by means of magic and sorcery.

In particular the cure of disease is in the hands of magicians who by their divination or while in a trance indicate the nature of the disease, its natural or supernatural cause, and means and rites by which a cure can be achieved. The tribals are well aware of the fact that some diseases have natural causes and can be cured by natural remedies of which they know quite a lot. But they are convinced that many cases of sickness or accidents are caused either by supernatural agencies or by persons who wish the patient evil.

In the opinion of the tribals a person may expose himself to the nefarious influence of evil spirits either by accidentally stumbling on them, or by the machinations of black magic. A person may get possessed by an evil spirit that will make him sick and cause his death unless the spirit is exorcised. A person may also fall sick and die when he has committed an offence against the tribal law or offended a certain deity or spirit by neglecting to fulfil a vow, etc. It is not necessary that the offence be committed intentionally. The actual commission of a reprehensible deed or the omission of a prescribed action deserves punishment. It is the task of the diviner or magician to find out the real cause of a disease or misfortune.

The diviner employs various natural methods of finding out the will and desire of a deity or spirit. Such methods are, for instance, the repeated counting of a handful of grains, the repeated measuring of grass stalks by passing the fingers alongside, the swinging of a lamp hanging on a string held in the hand, the irregular flicker of a light in a saucer, etc.

A shaman believes that he can induce a spirit or deity to possess him and to speak through him, while he himself is in a trance and unconscious. In contrast to the Siberian shaman, the Indian (tribal or low-caste) shaman usually does not maintain that his soul leaves the body and seeks contact with superhuman beings in places beyond the earth; his body is simply possessed by a superhuman deity or spirit who then speaks through him, while he is usually unconscious. Shamanism can also be practised by women.

While the diviners and shamans use their alleged powers for the benefit and cure of suffering or unlucky tsibesmen, the black magicians and the witches use their powers for evil purposes. The tribals firmly believe in the efficacy of black magic and witchcraft. Occasionally serious crimes are committed either in the pursuance of magic practices, or in defence against them, and revenge for them. Persons suspected of witchcraft are in danger of death. In the opinion of the tribals the evil eye, the uttering of a curse and bad omens may also cause misfortune and sickness.

The tribals firmly believe in good and bad omens; ordinary events happening during the day may have a prophetic significance. Dreams can also be omens. Their interpretation is the task of the diviner. The clients regulate their activities accordingly.

Among the rural Indian population the belief is widespread that the tribals are great experts in the invention and practice of the magical arts. But, in fact, magic is practised no less frequently and confidently in the low caste communities. It is not impossible that the practice of magic and witchcraft has spread from the low-caste Hindus to the tribes, and not vice versa.

Ever since the arrival of the Aryans in India and the development of the Hindu religion, tribal communities must have been assimilated and incorporated in the Hindu creed. When the Muslims arrived in India, many individual tribals and whole communities must have embraced Islam. This religion gained many followers among the tribals of northern India and East Bengal. But a much larger section of the tribals has become Hindu. No doubt the overwhelming influence of the Hindu religion made itself felt wherever the tribes came into contact with Hindus, and many tribes grew gradually and imperceptibly into this religion, without any sudden and spectacular formal conversion. Wherever the tribals lived for some time in intimate contact with the Hindus, the tendency towards a slow and gradual assimilation into the Hindu fold was strong. Government officials, landlords, merchants, fellow villagers, Hindu monks and preachers, all did their part in infusing Hindu beliefs and practices into the tribal religions and cultures.

Of course, there were also formal mass conversions of tribals to Hinduism. Thus in the 18th century the Manipuris, Kcches and Kacharis were declared by the Brahmins true Hindus of Kshatriya status, and provided with a fictitious genealogy. And to this day a Naga or Kuki, on conversion, is at liberty to describe himself accordingly, and to assume the sacred thread of the twice-born. Brahmins similarly bestowed in recent years the sacred thread on large numbers of Rajgonds in Mandla District. In Gujarat Vaishnavite Brahmins came as missionaries and converted thousands to Hinduism. Thus the Brahmin Vaishnava monk Swami Narayan converted many thousands of tribals and low castes to Vaishnavism at the beginning of the 19th century. The Brahmin Viswanath (who died in 1945) converted 75,000 Bhils and Dhankas to the Hindu religion. Other Hindu monks, mainly Vaishnavas, worked as missionaries among the Oraons, Santals and the Bhumijs.

However, the conversion of the tribes to the Hindu religion was rarely a complete one. Most Hinduised tribes have retained a large portion of their traditional religious beliefs and practices. As this process of Hinduisation was slow and without undue strain, the tensions usually arising out of a change of culture did not make themselves felt. Only in recent times—with the rapid increase of the Indian population, the development of industries in the tribal areas, the increase of communications and the ever stricter and more oppressive control of the Government administration—did serious tensions arise, rendering the pressure for change too overwhelming for the tribals to accept Hinduisation without resentment.

An alternative to Hinduism was offered by the Christian missionaries and a considerable number of tribals adopted the Christian religion instead. Fairly large numbers of tribals, altogether about a million, have been converted to Christianity in Chota Nagpur and Assam. These are the regions where the tribals live in greatest concentration, where they are more aware than elsewhere of their tribal identity, and where encounters with the Hindus have not been altogether happy, but resulted in serious tensions. Feeling that in this struggle their traditional tribal religion and world outlook would prove inadequate, the tribals turned to the teachings of Christ for a solution of their spiritual problems.

Such conversions are often regarded with resentment by the majority community, for many Hindus are inclined to identify national culture with Hindu culture. Though India is a secular state according to the Indian Constitution, this does not mean that all Indian citizens share the convictions of the eminent men who composed the Constitution and those who made it the law.

Christian missions were started in the tribal areas relatively late, only in the middle of the last century. Neither the Syrian Christians who came to India in the early centuries of the Christian era nor the Portuguese who arrived in 1499 were interested in the conversion of the aborigines. The first Christian mission among the tribals was started in 1841 by Protestant missionaries in Assam. Even this first attempt was half-hearted and soon abandoned. But after a few years it was restarted and then proved successful.

Art

In comparison to other primitive tribes in Africa, America and in the Pacific, even Australia, the Indian tribes appear to be less talented in the fine arts. V. Elwin, who wrote a book on *The Tribal Art of Middle India* (pp. 1-8), believes that this is so for several reasons: one reason is that certain materials were prohibited for the tribals due to the Hindu prejudice with regard to certain occupations using 'unclean' materials. Thus, work in iron and bronze, in clay (pottery), even weaving and basketry work were carried out by 'impure' and often 'untouchable' occupational castes. The tribals who wanted to attain and keep the status of a respectable caste were thus not allowed to use these materials and could not acquire the necessary skills for the production of works of art. Moreover, the members of the higher Hindu castes have, in modern times, convinced the tribals of the inferiority of the latter's art products, and consequently most tribals have given up the production of articles of their own creation and replaced them by the products of the traditional artisan castes whose work is indeed superior in the quality of the material (gold, silver, etc.) and in the perfection of the technical execution of the objects, but vastly inferior in originality of conception. The real superiority of tribal art has only been recognised in modern times since originality of conception and the apposite expression of an idea are more highly valued than the quality of the material and technical perfection. An intriguing fact is that survivals of tribal art are often found in the jewellery of the rural population which is a translation into metal of the ornaments of grass or seeds and fruits worn by the aboriginal tribes.

It must be admitted that in present times only poor remnants of the former flourishing tribal arts are still in existence in various regions of India, mainly in central India and in Assam. In the south of India the tribes are generally not known for any artistic talents, nor those in the northern regions, except perhaps the Kafirs who used to carve wooden vessels and tripods, and wooden memorial figures of their dead. Other tribes in the north may be skilled artisans, but they cannot be called true artists.

In central India and in Assam certain tribes still produce articles of true art, though much less so now than in past times. These art creations are all produced for practical purposes, not primarily for art's sake. Such articles are produced either for decoration of one's person, or of a person's attire, of the house and of implements of work, or for special festive occasions (at marriage and funeral feasts, for instance) and dances, and for religious and magical purposes.

In the decoration of the body, tattooing is a widely practised art though in present times it is often carried out by semi-aboriginal professioal tattooers, usually women. They have their traditional patterns, which often differ for each tribe. Thus, Gond and Baiga women are often tattooed all over the body, but for each tribe the patterns are different. Painting of the body is rarely done, except for certain dances.

For decorative purposes, the tribals use various materials, perishable ones like flowers, leaves and feathers, but also more durable seeds, beads and shells, or ornaments of bamboo, wood and metal. Thus the Khonds and Gonds wear hairpins of horn, bone, wood or metal; also head bands for the hair and various other ornaments; likewise ornaments for the ear, nose, neck, and for the arms and legs.

The dress, especially of tribal women, formerly often consisting of leaves or bark cloth, is now usually of cotton cloth. The colour combination of the cloth is often traditional and differs with every tribe. Though weaving is now usually done by professional weavers and the tribals buy their weaving apparel in the weekly markets, the weavers pay due attention to the wishes of the tribes and produce the cloth in the desired colour and quality. For further decoration of their dress the tribes of central India often use cowrie shells.

A special decoration for the hair is the comb, itself often specially carved and decorated. It is of horn, bone or bamboo. Gond and Baiga lovers often exchange their combs, and a boy or girl wearing a new and artistically decorated comb thus gives an indication that he or she is in love.

A special artistic head-dress is worn by the Bison-horn Maria Gonds of Bastar. Their turbans are decorated with bison-horns and peacock feathers. These turbans are worn at their dances.

Gonds, Khonds and other tribes of central India often possess tobacco cases which are decorated with elaborate carvings, usually of geometrical patterns.

Several tribes of central India have artistically carved wedding poles, while the crowns worn on the face by groom and bride are plaited of palm leaves.

The Santals carry the bride and groom in litters which are often decorated with figures of men and animals in relief.

Several tribes, such as the Khonds, Gonds, Saoras and Oraons, carve and draw the figures of various tribal deities and demons for their feasts. The same tribes, as also the Korkus and Bhils, make funeral pillars and memorial posts of wood and stone, often with figures in full or in relief. A rich ceremonial surrounds the erection of these pillars.

Decorations of a more secular nature are usually found on doors and house walls. The youth dormitories especially are often decorated with carvings and paintings. The figures of men and animals are often highly stylised, often in silhouette or in simple geometrical outlines. A common method of symbolisation is the production of a part for the whole: thus for a woman the breasts or the vulva are depicted, for a bird its wings, for a fish its bones, and so on. Totemic emblems are found especially among the Oraons of Chota Nagpur.

For the dance, the tribals wear not only special dresses and decorations, but also use masks of various designs, hobby-horses and specially decorated drums and other musical instruments. Thus a dance provides a special stimulation for the production of artistic objects.

Most tribals display their artistic talents in basketry work. They plait baskets of various shapes and designs, well adapted to the purposes for which they are intended. The material used differs according to the size, nature and purpose of the baskets: it is of leaves, reeds or bamboo, often dyed in various colours in pleasing combinations.

Though the productive arts of the Indian tribals are now decaying and may disappear soon, the same tribals are still rich in other spheres of human art: they are good story-tellers, accomplished singers, musicians and dancers. They know many myths, legends, folktales, ballads and riddles which contain their musings, beliefs and traditions about all happenings in the world, about the origin of the world, of man and human institutions, about the universe and the earth, fertility, human life and death, the soul, about deities, spirits and demons, about religion and magic.

The myths and legends are recited on certain festive occasions, especially at the time of the first sowing, and at a sacrifice. Folktales and riddles are told whenever there is a gathering of people, on the winter evenings when they sit around a warming fire, or in the nights when they must keep awake watching their fields.

Songs are sung alone or in company, when grazing the cattle, doing fieldwork, on long journeys or in the evenings and especially at dances. Songs differ according to the seasons. They run the whole range of human emotions; they sing not only of the eternal beauty of nature, but of all human relations, of love and hatred, praise and mockery, reverence and bitter sarcasm. Many songs deal with religion, the praise of God and the gods, they may be prayers and invocations. Songs accompany wedding and funeral ceremonies. Occasionally they describe in ballad form important events in the history of the tribe, or the life of heroes. Women sing when rocking the cradle to lull their babies into sleep, or when they are grinding the grain early in the morning; sometimes in gatherings of women and of course during the dance.

The melodies of the tribals are usually very simple and have no wide range of tunes in complicated keys. They please, and often intoxicate, singers and audience more through incessant repetition than through the variety of melodies.

The tribals have various instruments to produce their simple music. Often they manufacture their musical instruments themselves, out of primitive materials ready at hand. Their main instrument is the drum. They usually have a great variety of drums. Rhythm is the most important basis for their singing and dancing. Accomplished drummers are much sought after and often invited for meetings and dances. Second in importance is the flute which is played in certain seasons, often by boys herding cattle and goats. Many tribals make a variety of wind instruments out of the dried shells of gourds. String instruments are fabricated of bamboo or wood with strings of gut or other materials. These instruments are usually used in accompaniment to songs. But the main instrument is the drum.

The tribals have a great number of dances which are danced only in certain seasons. A special feature of tribal singing and dancing is that of their social character. Tribals hardly ever sing and dance *singly*. They sing and dance for their own pleasure in jolly company and good fellowship, not for the entertainment of an audience. Men have their own dances, as have also the women, but certain dances are in mixed company, a row of men facing a row of women, with the musicians standing and playing between the two rows which advance and retreat. The most famous dance in eastern central India is the Karma dance with a branch of the sacred tree kept in an upright position in the centre of the dancers. But the tribals have also mimic dances in which they imitate certain animals, the peacock, or the tiger, for instance. For some dances they put on masks, or ride hobby-horses, or dress up as Hindu mendicant monks, as Government officials, policemen or Europeans with a tropical helmet on the head.

Most of the dances, danced communally, follow a simple pattern. They please and intoxicate the tribal people mainly through the incessant repetition of certain simple rhythms and tunes in harmony with corresponding dance steps and body movements. The tribal dancers can carry on for hours and often throughout the night, fortified with strong alcoholic drinks which they take at intervals.

Mixed dancing, and the generous consumption of alcoholic drinks during the dance, are viewed with strong disapproval by puritanical Hindus and Hinduised tribal leaders. For this reason communal dancing among the tribals is gradually being abandoned. With the decay of tribal dancing, the other arts, too, suffer. No one bothers any more to prepare the elaborate dancing costumes or to fabricate the musical instruments used in the dance; the songs inspired by the rhythm of the drum and the melody of the instruments remain uncomposed, and tribal life becomes dull and drab, lacking the excitement of the senses caused by this artistic combination of sound, rhythm and movement.

A Pseudo-Romantic Image of Aboriginal Life

To passing tourists, the life of the aborigines may appear beautiful and romantic: the country with its gurgling hill streams, its dense jungles abounding with game, the smiling fields basking in bright sunshine, the villages perched on steep declines, the well-swept village lanes and courtyards in front of the houses, the house walls painted with artistic designs and quaint figures, the gardens at the back with fruit trees and vegetables, the chatter of the women walking early in the morning in single file to the village well, the carefree and exciting life of hunting and collecting of jungle produce; the strange ceremonies of birth, marriage and death, the picturesque rites on feast days and occasions of sacrifice, the tireless shuffling of dancing feet on full-moon nights to the rhythm of the drums, accompanied by the singing of simple but appealing melodies, interrupted occasionally by hoarse yells in the ecstasy of the dance; the narration of folktales and myths, at night in the fields, to watchmen sitting around a warming fire, the impressive tribal art kept alive by the habit of adorning doors and walls with drawings and by the remodelling of dancing costumes—all these things make the life of the aborigines appear happy and exciting.

There is, however, a reverse to this bright picture: the poor condition of the soil on the steep hills, the danger of erosion through ever-recurring torrential monsoon rains, the primitive and indifferent methods of cultivation, the back-breaking work during the agricultural season, the lack of working animals and adequate agricultural implements, the ravaging of fields by birds and wild animals, the danger from snakes and beasts of prey, the severe restriction on hunting and collecting of jungle produce, the abject poverty and penury of aboriginal life, the near-starvation in many houses during times of unemployment or failure of crops, the exploitation through usurers and Government servants, the heavy drinking, the clash of temper and lure of passion at dances, the loose morals and easy divorce, the suppression of individual enterprise and prevention of progress through over-conservative caste-elders, the draconian fines for breaches of often meaningless caste laws, the frequency of death in child-birth and in infancy, the ravages of diseases like tuberculosis, epidemics like small-pox and cholera, venereal diseases, the superstitions and the abject fear of witchcraft and black magic, of the spirits of evil, disease and death, the absence of the higher forms of religion, the ignorance of higher values and privation of spiritual pleasures and the lack of education. Add to all this a general feeling of insecurity and loss of mental balance, the hurt pride and impotent anger when the aboriginal has to face the contempt, ridicule or oppression of the superior classes, and you obtain a more impartial picture of the true situation which today confronts the aborigines of India.

Nor is the daily life of the aboriginal all dancing and enjoyment. S. Barkataki [(1969), p. 4] describes the daily life of a hillman in Assam in the following words: 'One can hardly imagine the difficulty with which a Mizo or a Zemi Naga has to eke a livelihood out of his little patch of land. From before daybreak the womenfolk of a village march in processions, carrying a number of bamboo tubes in a cane or bamboo basket, hundreds of feet down to a spring or a stream to collect water for the day's use. The return journey uphill with the load of water on their backs is strenuous. Immediately after their return they have to get busy preparing food for the family before they accompany their husbands to help them in their work in the *jhum* (cultivation). About half-an-hour is spent at mid-day in eating the pack-lunch (consisting of rice, salt and chillies) they carry with them to the *jhum* and then work goes on again till sun-down—hoeing, sowing, weeding, whatever work at a particular stage it might be. In the evenings the menfolk snatch a few moments of leisure and relaxation which they devote to *zu* (rice-beer or spirit) drinking and singing, while the women have to carry on with their household chores—cooking and attending to the pigs, the fowl and their own little ones. On special occasion, there is dancing both by men and women in addition to *zu*-drinking and music. This is, or at least was, till very recently the normal routine of the average tribal's life in the hills.'

Still worse is the lot of the mere foodgatherers who are always on the verge of starvation, who are often hunted and despised by the outsiders, who are helplessly exposed to the ravages of the elements and of diseases, much afraid of super-human spirits and deities. They too have a claim to the elementary human rights, a right to a share in a decent life, in knowledge and in spiritual values.

These realities of tribal life are the best justification for the sincere attempts by the Indian Government to uplift the aborigines of India.

BIBLIOGRAPHY

Aiyappan, A.: 'The Tribes of South and South-east India' in *The Adivasis.* The Government of India, Delhi, 1955.

Avery, J.: *The Tibeto-Burman Group of Languages.* Transactions of the American Philosophical Association, 1855, vol. XVI.

Baines, A.: *Ethnography.* Strassbourg, 1912.

Barkataki, S.: *Tribes of Assam.* New Delhi, 1969.

Bose, N.K.: *Tribal Life in India.* New Delhi, 1971.

Burgmann, A.: *P.W. Schmidt als Linguist. Anthropos,* vol. 49, 1954, pp. 627–58.

Burrow, T.: *The Sanskrit Language.* London, 1955.

Caldwell, R.: *A Comparative Grammar of the Dravidian Languages of South India.* London, 1913.

Census of India. 1931 and 1961.

Chatterji, S.K.: *Languages and Literatures of Modern India.* Calcutta, 1963.

von Eickstedt, E.: *The Position of Mysore in India's Racial History* in L.K. Anantakrishna Iyer: *The Mysore Tribes and Castes.* Mysore, 1935, vol. I, pp. 33–80.

Elwin, V.: *The Tribal Art of Middle India.* Oxford University Press, 1951.

Ferreira, J.V.: *Totemism in India.* Oxford University Press, Bombay, 1965.

Fuchs, S.: *Rebellious Prophets.* Bombay, 1965.

Ghurye, G.S.: *The Scheduled Tribes of India.* Bombay, 1959.

Grierson, G.A.: *Linguistic Survey of India.* 20 vols., Calcutta, 1903–28.

Guha, B.S.: *An Outline of the Racial Ethnology of India.* Calcutta, 1937.
———*Racial Elements in the Population.* London, 1944.
Hevesy, W. von: *Finnisch-Ugrishes aus Indien.* Wien, 1932.
Hoffmann, J. and A. van Emelen: *Encyclopaedia Mundarica.* 13 vols., Patna, 1914ff.
Hutton, J.H.: *Caste in India.* London, 1951.
Indian Government Publications: *The Adivasis.* Delhi, 1955.
Karve, I.: *Kinship Organisation in India.* Poona, 1953.
Kuiper, F.B.J.: *Nahali, A Comparative Study.* Amsterdam, 1962.
Naik, T.B.: 'What is a Tribe? Conflicting Definitions' in L.P. Vidyarthi (ed): *Applied Anthropology.* Allahabad, 1968.
Patel, M.I.: *Agro-Economic Survey of Tribal Mandla.* Delhi, 1969.
Risley, H.: *The People of India.* Calcutta, 1915.
Sarkar, Amal: *Handbook of Languages and Dialects of India.* Calcutta, 1964.
Sarkar, S.S.: *The Aboriginal Races of India.* Calcutta, 1954.
Schmidt, W.: *Die Mon-Khmer Volker, ein Bindeglied zwischen Volkern Zentralasiens und Austronesiens.* Braunschweig, 1906.
Thomas, M.M. and R.W. Taylor: *Tribal Awakening.* Bangalore, 1965.
Thompson, C.S.: *Rudiments of the Bhili Language.* Ahmedabad, 1895.
Vidyarthi, L.P.: *Applied Anthropology.* Allahabad, 1968.

CHAPTER III

The Aboriginal Tribes of Northern India

THE TRIBES IN NORTH-WEST INDIA

THE AREA in the extreme north-west of India, in British times called the North-West Frontier Territory, now a part of Pakistan, once belonged to Afghanistan. This area is inhabited by three population groups, the Baluchis, the Brahuis and the Pathans. The political frontier, however, does not also constitute an ethnic boundary; the same peoples are found in Afghanistan who are living in Pakistan and India. A line drawn from Dera Ghazi Khan through the Sulaiman range due west to Quetta roughly separates the Pathans in the north from the Baluchis in the south. But the latter have expanded both towards the north of this limit in the Indus valley and towards the south where they have established large colonies in upper and middle Sind.

BALUCHIS

The Baluchis hold the tradition that their original home was Aleppo in Syria from which place they were expelled on sectarian grounds. But it is more probable that they are of Iranian stock and lived originally on the shores of the Caspian Sea. They moved southwards and migrated through Baghdad and Kirman first to Makran where they stayed for many generations. Then they proceeded to Khalat and occupied the south Sulaiman hills which they wrested from the Pathans.

The Baluchis are divided into two large sections, the northern or Sulaiman Baluchis and the southern or Makrani Baluchis. They are separated from each other by the Brahuis.

A large portion of the tribe was expelled from Baluchistan in a tribal dispute and settled in Sind. Members of these expelled clans joined with related tribes of the plain to give assistance to the Emperor Humayun when he tried to regain his dominion after his expulsion from India. After his successful return the grateful Emperor rewarded them with grants of land along the Indus from where they have now spread well up the Chinab and Sutlej valleys. The result of this migration is that there are now more Baluchis in Sind and the Punjab than in their native country, where they are outnumbered by the Brahuis.

The Baluchis are divided into tribes, each headed by a chief whose office is hereditary in a particular family. But they freely admit outsiders from other tribes into their ranks; these are given wives and assigned a share in the tribal lands, once they have proved their worth in a fight.

The predominant section is that of the Rinds, from which most of the rest claim to be descended. The Rinds, originally of Arab stock but racially now fully assimilated with the Baluchis, colonised a part of upper Sind, but they have not spread much elsewhere outside Baluchistan.

The Lasaris stand next in rank, but they have suffered severely through intertribal feuds and were at one time almost annihilated. They have never really recovered from this massacre and are now found in dispersed groups only in middle Sind.

The tribes best represented on the frontier and along the rivers are the Marries, with their hereditary foes the Bughties of the hills, and the Mazaris, Gurchanis, Legharis, Lunds, Bozdars and, of course, the Rinds themselves. The tribes have, higher up the rivers, mixed freely even with the Pathans and the Jats.

In south-west Punjab, indeed, every camel driver is called Baluchi. In spite of this racial intermixture, the Baluchis, as also the Pathans, have developed a specific mental attitude. They are very independent and individualistic, and show little regard for the observance of the artificial restrictions of caste as also for the rules and restrictions of religion. Even Islam could not tame them. It should be remembered that many centuries ago the people of these tracts already possessed the reputation for great religious indifference and 'neglect of rites'. The Vedic singers on the Saraswati called them 'godless' and assigned them to the status of Mlecchas.

The wealth of the Baluchis consists of camels, cattle, sheep and goats. The tending of the herds forces them to a continuous change of pastures. But the Baluchis enjoy this kind of life, they are nomads by instinct and inclination. However, they are being gradually forced to settle permanently in one place as cultivators. Still, it is usual that only the chief has a permanent place while the others erect mud or stone walls for a house over which they place detachable roofs. When they shift to new pastures, they take along the roof while the walls are left for the accommodation of the next-comers.

A supplementary occupation to the rearing and tending of the herds is embroidery and carpet making. However, they also supplement their income through robbery and cattle lifting; they bear the title Rahzan (highwayman) as a title of honour.

The Baluchis practise female as well as male circumcision.

BRAHUIS

Among the populations of Baluchistan and upper Sind the Brahuis are of special importance because their language contains undoubted traces of Dravidian character. It is now considerably influenced by Sindhi and Baluchi, but the original Dravidian structure is still unmistakable. It is not known whether Dravidian is the original language of the Brahuis or whether they inherited it from another people with whom they lived in long and close symbiosis. They themselves have a tradition that they are of Arab descent and that their original home was Aleppo. But this tradition is also held by other tribes in the vicinity and does not prove that the Brahuis did not occupy their present habitats for many centuries.

The Brahuis have certain physical features which distinguish them to some extent from the other tribes: they are shorter and darker in complexion. But these differences tend to disappear more and more since they have begun to intermarry with Baluchis and Jats and admit adult members of these tribes into their community.

The Brahuis enjoy a good social status among the peoples of Baluchistan. Their main occupation is the rearing and pasturing of camels. They love their wide grasslands and rarely leave them; they are not like their Pathan neighbours who often leave their homeland and accept more lucrative jobs elsewhere.

The Brahuis are remarkable for the custom of moulding their children's heads. The reason for this custom seems to be that they greatly admire the short Iranian head; thus they bind their children's foreheads and give them soft pillows of millet, till the backs of their heads are permanently flattened.

PATHANS

If the theory identifying the Pathans (or Pakhtuns) with the Paktyes of Herodotus is correct, as is now generally assumed, these tribes have been, since several thousands of years, residents of the inhospitable hills of Baluchistan and north-western India. If they are such old settlers in these regions, they must at one time have been converted to Hinduism and later to Buddhism. It is well-known that Buddhism survived and lingered on in these secluded villages and on the highway to India which passes near them. Already in the tenth century, however, the Pathans had accepted with equal zeal and devotion an exceedingly narrow and superstitious form of Islam to which they still adhere. Anything less like the mild and tolerant character of the Indian Buddhist than the present temperament and habits of the frontier men of present times can hardly be imagined.

But there is evidence to show that the Pathans are extremely varied in origin. It can safely be assumed that many of the tribes now living in these regions came at various periods with the different waves of migration that have carried the peoples of central Asia, Persia and the Middle East thousands of miles from their original homelands. These later immigrants may have assimilated or exterminated the original settlers, and developed in their fierce struggle for survival in a hard and cruel country the present violent and greedy temperament.

One such original tribe that has survived might be that of the Malchis, thin, ugly and of servile character. Their stony fields can support them only for three months of the year. For nine months they must find some employment or live by begging.

Not subject for centuries to any authority, the Pathans have become fiercely independent. They lead a free, wild, active life in their mountains. They are exceedingly proud, but at the same time extraordinarily superstitious. They are a faithless race; no promise, no oath is sacred to them. They fight with one another as fiercely as with outsiders. They are inveterate robbers, and human life has little value among them.

At the same time, the Pathans, like all highlanders in the tribal stage, have a certain charm in their manly independence and in the practice of a few virtues in which they excel. They have a moral code of their own with three main obligations, namely, the necessity of revenge (*badala*) by retaliation; the right of asylum, which compels them to shelter even an enemy who asks for protection; and open-handed hospitality (*melmastia*) to all who demand it. Of these three precepts the last is the greatest.

The Pathans have an exaggerated regard for honour and manliness. The least loss in person or property received at the hand of another must be requited in full; forbearance and forgiveness are regarded as cowardice. A man who fails to take up a feud where tribal custom demands it is branded for life. Children point at him with fingers: 'There goes a woman and no man!'

And there are many occasions for feuds and revenge. The least slight or injury may result in violent reaction, as the Pathans are very hot-tempered and touchy. Revenge is sweetest where the actual offender is punished; but honour is equally satisfied if the offender's brother or another near relative is made to suffer. Thus, many Pathans go daily in fear of their lives. No wonder they react violently and aggressively, as they live constantly under severe tension.

Those who settle in the plains of the Punjab, even though they might remain in continuous and close contact with their fellow tribesmen in the hills, soon lose their hardiness and fierce independence. And the more they prosper the less respect they show for the hard life they have left behind. They have now spread practically all over India. However, not all those who call themselves Pathan are always so by blood and descent. The title of Pathan is assumed by any member of the Hindu military caste who is converted to Islam. Such men find admittance into the Pathan ranks and are adopted by a clan or tribe in the same manner as some wealthy aboriginals are admitted into the Rajput caste.

The Pathans are divided into some dozens of tribes varying in numbers from thousands to hundreds of thousands. In appearance they vary considerably. Some are fair complexioned, with grey eyes and brown hair, many have a long head and aquiline nose, are tall of stature and strong in build. Other tribes are much shorter in height, with medium noses, broad faces and a darker complexion. The Pathans, though claiming descent from the Jews, belong really to the Turko-Iranian type, with generous racial intermixtures with earlier local populations. The northern Pathans are certainly related to the Dinaric race which was expelled from Russian Turkestan during the Mongol invasions and settled in the Hindukush.

The term Pathan is now commonly used to denote anyone speaking the Pakhtun language, or Pushtu, and thus includes the Afghans, a foreign race which, however, has impressed its name upon a whole country.

The Afghans, whose Semitic origin is still a matter of controversy among the experts, first settled in the tracts of Ghor and Hazara. From there they descended upon the Helmond valley then occupied by the Gandharis, a Pathan tribe, which had been expelled from the Peshawar valley by one of the Scythian invaders. The Gandharis were dominated and then converted by the Afghans who finally intermarried freely with them. These people, however, took the first opportunity of returning to their former habitat, where they now reside under the names of Yusufzais, Mohmands, and others.

The Afgnans, by this time known as Tarins, Siranis and Abdalis or Durranis, remained around Kandahar until the 18th century when they established their headquarters at Kabul.

The Ghilzais, probably of Turkish origin and related to the Khalaj tribes north of the Tien Shan mountains, arrived across the Bamian from Ghor, like their predecessors. They believe themselves to be descendants of Noah. After assisting Mahmud of Ghazni on his raids into India, the Ghilzais were given possession of the country between Jalalabad and Qal'at-i-Ghilzai, and have since spread east and west of that centre.

In the extreme north, not far from the Hindukush, lies Chitral. The Chitralis are a people of mixed race and doubtful origin; they may have come from Wakhan and the Pamirs and bear the blood of Mongolian invaders. There is also an Indo-Afghan strain in them; and like other Pathans they are Muslims. They are a bright, cheerful people, impervious to fatigue, fond of laughter and song, and devoted to polo and dancing.

Besides the Ghilzais and Chitralis, along the frontier, there are other tribes like the Mohmands, Shinwaris, Afridis (said to be former Parmar Rajputs or the 'Apaariti' of Herodotus?), Orakzigs, Bannuchis, Waziris, Dawaris, Marwats, Mahsuds (who live in the mountainous central tract of Waziristan, and whose fighting strength is traditionally put at 18,000. Actually their number is much more. They are more intelligent than the other Pathan tribes, fanatical, tough, independent, fearless—and to be feared.), Bhitannis, but also Turkish tribes like the Turkmen, the Kazaks and Chagatai Turks, and Mongol tribes such as the Hazaras, descendants of the Tatar regiments of Genghis Khan. All these constitute the Pathans of today.

The territories occupied by the ancient people of that name, however, have been much altered. The (Scythic) Kakars nearly obliterated the Dadis of Sewistan; the Kathaks and Afridis were dispossessed by the Turks to a great extent. But through intermarriage and the adoption by all of the Pushtu language, all have been welded into one nation, with the usual fictions about common descent in order to explain the fusion.

The modern Pathan inhabitants of upper India were first introduced by the Lodi and Sur dynasties, and consisted chiefly of Ghilzais who at that time were neither Afghans nor Pathans. They were soon followed, however, by large bands of other tribes who were generously endowed with estates by the Ghazni chiefs and also by Babar, whose original army grew like a snowball as he moved across the hills to the fertile plains.

The tribes most numerously represented in this distribution were the Yusufzais, the Orakzais, Lodis, Kakars, and Karlanris. The tribal organisation gets weaker, as is only to be expected, as the distance from the frontier increases, and is scarcely to be found in its original form east of the Jumna, where the Rohillas, well known in history, form probably the best-knit of the larger groups of this race. At the same time they are also the most prosperous of them.

In addition to the Pathan colonies and the converts claiming that title for themselves, the Powindahs form a floating population of 100,000 to 150,000. They are itinerant traders of Pathan nationality. They belong chiefly to the Ghilzai tribes though their connection with their kinsfolk is not very close owing to their nomadic life. Large caravans assemble in the autumn to the east of Ghazni, and march in armed bodies through the dangerous country of the Waziris and Kakars to the Indus at Dera Ghazi Khan. Here they deposit their arms, leave their families on the grazing grounds along the river, under the guardianship of a detachment of their fighting men, and wander off across upper India, often as far as Bihar, selling the goods and horses they have brought from Kandahar and central Asia. When these have been disposed of, the Powindahs act as pedlars on behalf of the merchants in the larger towns. In the spring they reassemble on the Indus, and wend their way once more back to Kandahar, dispersing from that centre by their various routes through Herat and Kabul to the north. A few of the bands engage in contract labour for the season.

Many Pathans migrate to India where they seek employment in the cities and towns. They stay on permanently, but pay periodical visits to their northern homes. They set up as itinerant hawkers of sundry goods or as moneylenders. Others find employment with moneylenders (*sowkars*) to recover debts or collect rent from backward tenants. A few take up simple contracts for earth-work, or obtain jobs as peons and guards in public offices. Others become petty shopkeepers, knife-grinders, private watchmen and servants. The moneylenders among them are invariably given to extortion and tyrannical practices, and never lose sight of a loan.

Some Pathans have taken to crime. In organised dacoity they are not averse to committing acts of violence. But they also steal and cheat, or act as receivers of stolen property.

The tribal organisation of the Pathans is based on kinship. A tribe (*khel*) is composed of a number of kindred groups of agnates; descent is in the male line. But the tribe admits a certain number of alien groups which are said 'to live within its shade'. These foreign allies are supposed to assist the protecting clan in any blood-feud in which it is involved. A tribal group is subject to constant loss by fission. The nomadic habits of the Pathans frequently force a group to break away from the main stock and to look out for new lands and pastures. This separation may be temporary or become permanent. Then a new clan comes into existence.

The Pathans are intensely democratic, and the clan leader

(*malik*) has no chance to rule as an autocrat; he only maintains his position through constant exertions. He is, however, head of the *jirga* or council, the decisions of which are ruthlessly enforced.

Within the family, however, the husband is a law unto himself. If he wishes, he can put his wife to death for adultery, and punish a daughter who has disgraced the family as severely. Pathan women are, in fact, little more than chattels. They are property to be bought and sold, much like camels. They are purchased by their husbands from their father or brothers, and if their husbands die, they become the property of the other brothers or other relatives. Usually, one of the brothers marries the widow; if, however, an outsider wishes to marry such a widow, he must pay for her.

Family solidarity is not much in evidence. Cousins may murder each other in order to keep a plot of land intact in their possession, instead of dividing it according to Muslim law between the heirs. This type of murder is called *khei*. It means the deliberate extinction of a family by those entitled to inherit from it, in order to obtain possession of its property.

KAFIRS AND OTHER TRIBES

On the edge of the Pathan country, towards Dardistan, a number of non-Pathan tribes can be found. They inhabit the valleys of the Kunar, Panjkora, Swar and Indus rivers. They speak dialects of their own which belong to the Pisacha, Burushaski or Dardic language groups. Ultimately, they all seem to trace their origin to Chitral, for which they feel much attachment. Until recent times, some of these groups, especially those of Dir-Kohistan and Kalam, paid a tribute to the Mehtar of Chitral.

These tribes were formerly called 'Kafirs' (unbelievers), not being Muslims. Towards the end of the last century, they were converted to Islam by force, and the name of their country was changed from Kafiristan to Nuristan—'Land of Light'!

The Kafirs are said to have been, till recent times at any rate, head-hunters, speaking an Indo-European language closely akin to Sanskrit. In view of their language and their physical appearance with fair hair and grey eyes, tall stature and long heads, it seems likely that the Kafirs represent the nearest approach to the original stock of the Indo-European invaders of India in the second millennium B.C. They are divided into various sections—the Safed Posh (white-robed), the Siah Posh (black-robed), the Kamos, Ashkuns, Maigelis and Jashis. The latter, however, have been expelled or absorbed by the several immigrations into the valley of Bashgal.

They use carved wooden vessels more suggestive of Scandinavia than India, and tripods described as Grecian in type. One account describes them as a warlike people in the past often raiding outsiders, but also other sections of their own people. As they observe the law of blood revenge they have an excuse for frequent raids on other villages. This is the reason why the Kafirs live in compact settlements, surrounded by a wall interspersed with watch towers.

Kafir society is based on social equality; but they keep slaves. They have, however, headmen (*jast*) with a council of elders (*urir*). All important matters of policy, foreign and domestic, are discussed noisily in tribal meetings. Disobedience to the decisions of the *jast* and council is punished by burning down the house of the culprit and destroying his property. Those who aspire to the dignity of a *jast*, must give twenty-one feasts within three years.

The Kafirs are organised in clans. They practise clan exogamy. A Kafir may not marry a girl of his father's or of his mother's clan. They practise polygamy. Women are practically household slaves. Theirs is a life of incessant toil. Divorce is easy. Extramarital sex relations occur frequently.

The Kafirs are good farmers. They grow millet, wheat, barley and maize on terraced fields, but no rice.

They bury their dead in wooden coffins, often several dead are laid into one coffin. In memory of the dead they erect wooden effigies of them; a great feast is held at the erection of a memorial figure, which is celebrated with much dancing one year after the death.

The Tribes of the Himalayan and Sub-Himalayan Regions

The plateaus south-east of the Karakorum ranges adjoining Tibet and also Ladakh, Lahaul and Spiti as well as the sub-Himalayan regions in general are inhabited by tribes of a definitely

Mongoloid racial type. But there are also tribes which belong to the so-called Oriental race, such as the Dards, Chaks, Galawans, and others. They have longer noses, a darker complexion and broad or shorter to longer skulls.

But in general, in the sub-Himalayan regions from Ladakh to Nepal, Sikkim and Bhutan the population is of a Mongoloid type. They have a medium or tall stature, round head and face, high cheekbones from which the face rapidly narrows downwards, and a small retreating chin.

On the inhospitable slopes of the rugged country in which they reside the tribes are generally cut off for six months of the year from contact with the outside world by heavy snow. The poverty of their country, which can support only a very scattered and sparse population, has prompted them to adopt the Tibetan form of family life, if they did not bring it along from Tibet. It is the system of fraternal polyandry, in which a number of brothers share a wife between them. In this manner they are able to keep the number of children down and the family property together. By religion most of them are Buddhists.

The upper valley of the Indus, near Gilgit, is inhabited by the Dards. They speak a dialect akin to Sanskrit and are supposed to be of Aryan stock. They are broad-shouldered, with brown or brownish hair, of fair complexion and middle height. They are remarkable for their aversion to the cow: they abstain from the use of milk and butter, and even refuse to burn cow-dung.

Related to the Dards are perhaps the Chaks, a tribe in Kashmir. A legend relates that Pando Chak, their ancestor, was the offspring of a Kashmiri woman and an amorous demon; his descendants were very tall. The Chaks are Shia Muslims. Today they are quiet and peaceful cultivators, but in the sixteenth century they waged war against the Mughals and once defeated Akbar's forces.

The Shins are a tribe or caste, widespread in the upper Indus region, from Kohistan into Gilgit and Baltistan. In some districts, they form the vast majority of the people, or even the entire population. The Shins are now Muslims, but it is believed that originally they were a higher Hindu caste, forced to emigrate from Kashmir into their present homeland. Reasons for their Hindu origin seem to be their concern with caste, their refusal to eat beef, their belief that the leather of cows is polluting, and the fact that the Shins are called *dangarike*, i.e., 'cow people', by their neighbours.

It is interesting that they look on cattle with abhorrence and avoid contact with them. Cattle are used for ploughing, but Shins have as little as possible to do with the animals. They believe that a goddess, or fairies and demons, are responsible for this prohibition. They would punish them with lameness or blindness, or withdraw their protection in the dangers of the mountains, if they even touched a cow, ate beef, drank milk, or burned cow-dung as fuel. Though Mohammedans, the Shins still believe in deities, fairies and demons.

Another tribe of probably similar origin are the Dums. But they claim descent from a Hindu king who became afraid of his numerous sons and scattered them all over Kashmir, giving them the job of village watchmen and police power. Even today the Dums follow this vocation. They wield considerable power and so are in a position to annoy and injure the villagers.

Another tribe of similar racial type is that of the Galawans, who are either descendants of the Dums or of the Chaks. They are of a dark complexion. Originally they earned their livelihood by grazing horses, but in the course of time they developed criminal tendencies. They moved about in large parties, all mounted and armed with long, heavy clubs. They raided threshing floors and frequently attacked wedding parties depriving the wedding guests of their jewellery and sometimes carrying off the bride. The Rajas of Kashmir finally made efforts to suppress this lawlessness and succeeded in killing nearly half of the Galawans. The rest were settled down and forced to become cultivators. But raiding is in their blood and sometimes the Galawans return to their old habits. They eat horse-meat.

A similar Kashmiri race is the Chaupan. The Chaupans are the shepherds of the villagers. In racial features they are not distinct from the peasants of the valleys, but they form a separate society, intermarrying only among themselves and occasionally with the Galawans. The mountain grazing lands are divided between the various Chaupan families, and intruders are quickly expelled. In winter and early spring the Chaupans live in the villages and sometimes cultivate land. The sheep are kept in stables. The Chaupans are supposed to know medicinal herbs which they collect while grazing their sheep.

The Chaupans are notorious for their dishonesty—a reputation which they share with the Galawans—and are said to occasionally sell a sheep entrusted to their care pretending that the animal died of sickness or was killed by wild animals. The Chaupan receives a fee for each sheep which he grazes; the fee is usually in kind—a certain measure of maize or rice. When an aminal dies he has to produce its head or skin, to prove that he has not sold it.

The tribal character of these peoples is often doubtful. As regards their origin they may belong to one of the peasant communities of the area in which they now reside. But then their occupation and half-nomadic life has marked them in a special manner and they lead a life which has little in common with that of the ordinary farmers.

There is less doubt that the tribes descending from Tibetan stock belong to the 'Scheduled Tribes'. They differ clearly in racial features and in their manner of life from the peasant communities. One of these tribes is that of the Baltis, obviously of the same race as the Ladakhis. They have Mongolian features, high cheekbones and slit-eyes, but the nose is not so depressed as is the case with the Bhotias of Ladakh. Also, the Baltis are slighter in build, though taller.

By temperament they are good-natured and patient. In spite of their hard life, they are merry and light-hearted, always ready to laugh. It has often been noticed that the Tibetans are a cheerful type of people in spite of their adverse environment.

The Baltis dress in coats and trousers of wool, wear skull caps and raw skin boots made comfortable by grass quilted inside. They shave their heads, leaving long elf-locks growing behind the temples into which they entwine flowers.

When the Baltis embraced Islam and became Shias, they gave up the practice of polyandry, with the result that their population has increased in excess of the area available for cultivation. In Ladakh, where polyandry prevails, the population has been kept in check. The constant sub-division of the land held by a Balti family leads to holdings too small for profitable cultivation, and the owners are forced to desert their land and to turn to other means of earning a livelihood. Many Baltis consequently emigrate to India in search of work or become porters carrying loads to Gilgit and Ladakh.

Cultivation depends on irrigation; and where water is plentiful, excellent crops can be raised. The actual work of cultivation, except ploughing, is done by women, as the men are away tending their herds on distant pastures or carrying loads to Ladakh and Gilgit, or repairing water-courses and field terraces.

Next come the Gaddis (51,356) in Himachal Pradesh. They claim to be immigrants from the north Indian plains, of low Rajput stock. They left Rajputana, fleeing before the Muslim invaders. At present they exclusively inhabit the range which divides Chamba from Kangra. A few Gaddis have wandered down to the valley at the base of the range, but the great majority live on the heights above, on an elevation between 4,000 and 7,000 feet at an altitude with little or no cultivation.

The Gaddis are semi-nomadic: they spend half the year in search of fodder for their herds, and the other half they spend in their villages cultivating their meagre crops. They are a sturdy race, often bow-legged (from carrying great weights), of wheatish or brown complexion. They are short and stocky in build and inured against cold and exposure.

The Gaddis are sheep and goat herders. They graze their herds with the help of dogs so fierce that they can repel bears and panthers. The Gaddis rear their animals for wool, food, sacrifice and sale. They spin the wool of their sheep and goats and weave them into cloth and blankets.

The Gaddis are Hindus by religion and worship Shiva as their main god. But they venerate other gods too and a host of spirits to whom they sacrifice their animals. They expect health and prosperity from Shiva, while they greatly fear the evil spirits who cause sickness, abortion in childbirth and epidemics among the animals. They must be propitiated with the sacrifice of goats and sheep. The Gaddis also believe in the power of magic.

The Gaddis practise fraternal polyandry and occasionally also polygyny. Their system of polyandry keeps the number of children low, saves the family property from uneconomical division and makes the family a closely knit unit. However, women are considered of inferior social status.

The Gaddis are a cheerful people. They like to sing and dance; every shepherd carries his flute to while away the time. The

Gaddis are not very clean as they never bathe nor wash their clothes. They brew a liquor, which they call *sur*, out of barley flour and a root growing locally. *Sur* is only slightly intoxicating.

The buffalo herding Gujars (16,805 in Himachal) are regarded as 'scheduled tribes' only in Himachal. But they are found also in Kashmir, Jammu, Uttar Pradesh and generally in north India. Thousands of them live in Bombay rearing buffaloes and selling milk and milk products. In Himachal Pradesh the Gujars are nomadic throughout the year. They live in the jungles, valleys and grasslands for only a while and move on when their cattle require fresh pastures. The forest meets their needs for wood in order to build temporary shelters and for fuel.

As their name suggests, they claim to come from Gujarat. But this etymology might be wrong. It was probably they who gave their name to Gujarat. They do not know when and why they left their alleged home country. At present they are at home practically all over northern India.

In Himachal they are Mohammedans. They do not seem to be very orthodox and regular in their religious duties. They are monogamous, patrilineal and patrilocal. But they have neither clans, nor do they observe the rules of endogamy or exogamy. This may be due to their conversion to Islam, as Islam permits cousin marriage.

They pay a rather high bride-price. Marriages are arranged by the parents. Child-marriage is quite common among the Gujars. Polygyny is not forbidden, but rare. The Gujars live in large joint families.

Their nomadism has kept them from modern influences. They are very conservative and averse to changing their traditional habits.

Another tribe in Himachal Pradesh are the Kanauras or Kinnaras (27,093), also called Kinners. They inhabit the frontier district of Kinnaur in the east of Himachal, near the Tibetan frontier. The Kinnaras are of mixed blood. Originally from northern India, they have intermarried often with Tibetans and Gurkhas and thus acquired definite Mongoloid features. They have a fair complexion.

They are divided into two classes, one higher than the other. The Kinnaras are a pastoral people, rearing sheep and goats for wool. But they also cultivate fields and keep gardens. The men do the ploughing once a year, the women do all the rest of the field work. They also sell the field and garden products in the market.

The Kinnaras practise polyandry and polygyny. Most of them are Buddhists but they also worship Hindu deities, such as Badrinath, Maheshwar and Bhagvati. They offer animals and liquor to the deities. They believe in various types of evil spirits which can make them sick and must therefore be propitiated.

In the valley of Pangi another aboriginal tribe can be found: the Pangwals (7,724). They are divided into two main sections, a high class and a low class. Each section is sub-divided into four castes. Intermarriage and inter-dining between the two sections are prohibited, but the four castes of each section may freely inter-dine and intermarry.

Marriages are usually arranged by the parents, though marriage by exchange, by service and by capture is also permitted. Widows may remarry.

Pangwal women may freely divorce their husbands and remarry. Inheritance is in the male line.

The Pangwals worship the Hindu gods. They also believe in evil spirits of various kinds and try to appease them by the sacrifice of goats and sheep. They are particular in the observance of ritual purity.

Another tribal community in Himachal, beyond the Kulu valley towards the high hills, is that of the Lahulis or Lahaulas (2,850). They, too, are divided into two sections, an upper class and a lower class. The upper class is sub-divided into four castes, the lower class into three. These castes are endogamous.

The Lahulis are polyandrous; but a Lahuli woman can have only two brothers as husbands. A third brother must get himself a new wife. Divorce is easy.

The Lahulis are mainly cultivators; but most of the field work is done by the womenfolk. The men enjoy the results of the women's hard labour.

The religion of the Lahulis is an impure Buddhism, grafted on an ancient serpent and mother-goddess cult. Not only in religion, but also racially the Lahulis are of mixed origin. Originally of north Indian stock, they have intermarried a good deal with the Tibetans.

Besides Pangwals and Lahulis, there are lesser tribes, such as the Jads, Khampas, Swanglas and Bhots (or Bhotias). The Jads and Khampas are originally inhabitants of Tibet. While the Jads are mainly cultivators, the Khampas are pure nomads. Both these tribes are polyandrous and patrilineal.

The Bhotias inhabit not only the hilly regions of Himachal, but also the Kumaon Himalayas. They are a semi-Mongoloid people of Tibetan origin. Numbering nearly 27,000 in both states, they inhabit the alpine valleys of the central Himalayas. They are well acclimatised to high altitudes.

Though they call themselves Hindus, they are free of caste prejudices and freely inter-dine with the Tibetans. They also drink liquor which they distil from barley. They use *jhaboos*, which are yak and cow hybrids, and goats and sheep as carrier animals for their trade in salt and borax. Their womenfolk weave blankets and brightly coloured carpets for sale.

The Bhotias have several endogamous sections. Geographically they are divided into the western and eastern Bhotias. The difference in dress between the two sections is conspicuous. Linguistically they are divided into those speaking an Aryan dialect and those speaking a Tibeto-Burman one. All Bhotias are further divided into two classes, the upper or Rajput class and the lower or Dumra class. The two classes do not intermarry.

The eastern Bhotias practise polyandry. Women are free to choose their husbands or to indulge simply in free love without marriage. Marriage is not compulsory. The Bhotias have a social institution called Rangbang. It is a kind of club, found in every village. All the unmarried boys and girls are admitted, also married women who have not yet become mothers. The meetings are held in a house or on a level spot in the open air. The participants pass the night singing, dancing, eating, drinking and smoking around a fire. The Rangbang is also a place for courting and match-making, and occasionally for love-making.

In religion the Bhotias profess to be Hindus, though they also worship their ancient traditional gods. Chief among them is Gabla, their high-god, whom they worship for health and prosperity. Then there is Kebang-Rang-chim, who is both male and female. The Bhotias are full of superstition and greatly afraid of evil spirits who in their opinion cause all the sickness in the world. Everywhere they erect prayer poles and stone pillars to fend off evil spirits and ghosts from their homesteads.

In secular matters the Bhotias are a practical and hard working people with a good sense for business. They are good bargainers. Men and women are always busy. Even in their idlest moments they spin yarn for weaving.

Further east we meet the tribes of Nepal. There is a great variety of races and cultures in the isolated regions of this mountainous kingdom. Most of the communities are endogamous, thus perpetuating these racial and cultural peculiarities.

The Mongoloid element, which forms the bulk of the population of tribal Nepal, is strongly expressed in their features and cultural convictions and habits. All this proves that most of these tribes came originally from the north of Tibet and even from further to the east, and their tribal languages confirm this. On the other hand, much of their culture, literature, script, art, music, songs, and many of their dances have come from India through Hindu immigrants, often of high caste. They were mostly refugees, fleeing from the Muslim invaders seeking a new home in the hospitable valleys of distant Nepal.

Though many tribes of Nepal are thus not only culturally but also racially influenced by the peoples of the Indian plains, the degree of influence varies much and a number of Gurkha subdivisions definitely belong to tribal culture. Especially in their religion the Gurkhas have still retained a good deal of tribal worship and ritual, and Lamas are often substituted for Brahmin priests, especially when there is a need for sorcery or witchcraft.

The Gurungs, for instance, are certainly of Tibetan descent though their precise origin may be unknown. Linguistically, they belong to the Tibeto-Burmese group.

The life of the Gurungs is agricultural and pastoral, cattle breeding being an important element of their economy. They live in the mountains close to the snow line. As these districts are very isolated, they have preserved their original customs to a large degree.

The whole tribe is divided into two distinct sections—the Char Jat and the Sora Jat. The Char Jat is divided into four exogamous clans, and each of these clans is sub-divided into a large number of lineages. The Sora Jat has lineages only. In the past the members of the Char Jat considered themselves superior in rank and refused to intermarry with the members of the Sora Jat. This class distinction is fast disappearing and inter-marriages are now on the increase.

Until a short time ago a cross-cousin marriage was much preferred, but at present it is less frequent. The Gurungs eat buffalo meat, but abstain from pork.

They practise cremation and burial depending on local customs or on omens at the time. In religion, they are Tibetan Buddhists, with Hindu admixtures. In former times they offered a bull in sacrifice at funerals. Under Hindu influence this custom has been abandoned. Their Lamas are expected to ward off hail, prevent storms, exorcise those possessed by evil spirits, and to perform many other feats of magic.

The Tamangs, also called Murmis, are much like the Gurungs, not only in physical appearance but also in language and religious ceremonial. They probably entered Nepal from Tibet and settled north of Katmandu. They are clearly of Tibetan stock modified, however, by Nepalese admixtures. They have two main divisions of unequal social rank; each division is divided into a number of kindred groups. The Tamangs have not been much Hinduised, and even eat beef. In Nepal they are farmers. But many have emigrated to Darjeeling where they work as coolies in the tea-gardens.

The Magars, another Gurkha tribe, are concentrated in central Nepal, south of the Gurung country, but they are found also in other parts of Nepal, particularly in the north-east, which is supposed to be their original home. They form nearly one-third of the whole population of Nepal. They are more Hinduised than the other tribes and even employ Brahmins for their religious ceremonies. Racially, the Magars show less Mongoloid features; the epicanthic fold is often absent and the nose is generally long and slender.

Before the arrival of the Rajputs the Magars consisted of twelve large joint families (*thams*), each of which was governed by a chief. Now they have seven clans which are exogamous. But these clans are not of equal rank. Those working as smiths, miners, stone workers, etc., are somewhat looked down upon. One clan, the Ghartis, is purely pastoral. Cross-cousin marriages were once the rule among the Magars, but they are at present less common.

Their tribal priests are Lamas who are trained in Tibetan

lamaism. The Magars are good farmers. Their staple crop is barley; except for the Pun clan, they abstain from buffalo meat and pork.

Speaking a similar language as the Puns are the Thakalis—a Nepalese tribe whose ancestors lived in the village of Thak, hence the name. They live together with the Puns in the steep valley of the upper Kali between Dana and Mukinath. It appears that they are genetically related to the Puns. The Thakali women run many of the inns (*bhattis*) which are found on the main routes of central Nepal. In physical appearance they are like the Tibetans, and their priests are Lamas. Their religion too is similar to that of the Puns. Their chief occupation is trade in borax and salt, which they transport on sheep bred by themselves.

Another tribe related to the Magars with whom they formerly intermarried are the Sunwars. They seem to have entered eastern Nepal coming from the west. But they have typically Mongoloid features. They are somewhat shorter than the average Nepalese. Though they are cultivators at present, they were formerly hunters as their traditions reveal. Another occupation was dress and basket making. They are said to have been split originally into three clans which are now sub-divided into exogamous kinship groups.

The Sunwars conform in their religion closely with the Magars, but employ Brahmins only for some religious ceremonies, when a new-born baby is named or at a wedding for casting the horoscope. Children are married at the age of about five years.

Remnants of a former hunting tribe, the Kusundas, are found in a small village Satobati, near Gorkha in central Nepal. They call themselves 'people of the forest', or 'Kings of the forest'. The Kusundas were originally divided into four exogamous patrilineal clans of equal rank. Of these, only two are left—the clans Shing and Shian. Traditionally, they lived from hunting, the collection of jungle produce and of alms in the villages. Since the jungle has largely disappeared, the Kusundas now have settled down and started farming. In the past, they hunted only birds and animals living in the trees. They are now partly Hinduised, as they have adopted particularly those Hindu rites which are connected with the life cycle.

The tribes of eastern Nepal are collectively known as Kirantis.

Included in this group are the Limbus, the Rais, the Khambus or Yakkus.

The Limbus have a tradition that they came originally from Banaras. But they as well as the Rais are rather more Mongoloid in appearance than the Gurungs and Magars. Any attempt to place their origin in the plains of northern India is probably due to the desire to show a Rajput origin. It is more likely that they are early settlers of the tracts they now occupy, and from their appearance it seems that they were originally from Tibet. They have the flat nose, the epicanthic fold and the yellow complexion of the Mongoloid race.

The Limbus speak a language of the eastern Tibeto-Burman sub-group. They have many local dialects. They are divided into ten sub-divisions, with a chief at the head of each. These ten sections are sub-divided into fifty or sixty exogamous kinship groups. They do not appear to have any clan system. They never had the custom of cross-cousin marriage. The Limbus bury their dead. They profess rather indifferently a kind of Shaivism when among the Hindus, but employ Lamas when among themselves in the hills. They believe in a supreme God who appears to them in various disguises. They have a myth about man's creation which is very similar to that of the Korkus, a Munda tribe in Madhya Pradesh: both tribes believe that it was a horse which several times prevented God from making man and giving him life [cf. M. Hermanns (1954), pp. 10-11]. The Limbus also worship female deities. They have their own priests and employ, like the other tribes in the neighbourhood, exorcists (*bijua*) against the evil spirits whom they greatly fear. The Limbus are also found in Sikkim where they are chief cattle merchants and butchers.

The Rais or Khambus, neighbours of the Limbus, live on the southern range of the Himalayan heights. Those among them who own land call themselves Jindars. Numerically they are the strongest tribe of Nepal. Racially they are definitely Mongoloid, with a prominent epicanthic fold. But they have longish faces which suggest some Indian admixtures.

By religion they are now Hindus who employ Brahmins as priests and for the casting of the horoscope. But for the performance of their ordinary religious and domestic ceremonies they have men of their own tribe. They believe in a supreme

God, creator of the world and of men. They also worship a goddess of fertility, in whose honour they perform dances.

Their marriage customs conform to those of the other eastern tribes. Marriage is between adults; pre-marital sex relations are tolerated, but a man must marry the girl he has made pregnant.

The Rais or Khambus now bury their dead; in the past they also cremated them, or simply threw the bodies into the nearest river.

The Newars, who live in the central regions of Nepal, in the District of Katmandu, are not a caste in the strict sense of the word, but the aggregate of the early inhabitants of Nepal, compartmentalised into functional groups which gradually developed into castes. The Newars are both Hindus and Buddhists. The Buddhists stay close to the Tibetan frontier while the Hindus among them settle more on the southern ranges and valleys. The two sections have no social relations with each other. The Newars in Indian territory, no more controlled by their caste authorities, have grown lax in the matter of intermarriage, and thus have lost their social status when they return to their native land.

Their language is of the Tibeto-Burman type. But racially they show a strong mixture of non-Mongoloid blood, probably of the Indians of the plains. The epicanthic fold is mostly absent, their nose is well formed, and their skin the colour of wheat.

The descendants of a liaison between a Newar father and a Gurung or Magar woman are called Nagar Kotis. Many of them have a fine physique.

The other tribes in Nepal are Tibetan in origin. The Sherpas, for instance, belong to this category. They reside in Nepal and Sikkim. The tribe is not very strong numerically, and although the Sherpas may be found throughout the uplands of eastern Nepal and in larger numbers in the Darjeeling District, their true home is in the Solu and Khumbu tracts, in the upper regions of the Dudh Kosi. Owing to the high altitude at which they live they can only grow barley, maize and potatoes, and the sale of seed potatoes is one of the main sources of income for them.

They are extremely strong and are able to carry heavy loads for long distances. Recently, the Sherpas made a name for themselves as high altitude porters with Himalayan expeditions.

Tenzing Norgay, the Everest climber, is a Sherpa.

There are at least two endogamous classes in the society of the Sherpas and possibly more, though they cannot yet be called castes. The vexed 'question of Sherpa polyandry and polygyny is largely structural and not so much a sexual problem, and children of polyandrous marriages tend to continue to marry polyandrously presumably for the reason that the property of one's father still requires to remain undivided to support the family at the same standard of living. All brothers have a right in property and daughters have a right to dowry. Rather surprisingly the Sherpas allow a woman to be married only to one or two husbands at once but not to more.

The Sherpas are closely affiliated to Tibet; they profess Buddhism in its lamaistic form. Their language is Tibetan in origin. Their Lamas are of the Red Hat sect and are allowed to marry. The Sherpas do not celebrate the usual Gurkha festivals of Dunuja and Lorsa. But a substantial substratum of religious concepts seems to persist among the Sherpas which is foreign to Buddhism and may represent the remnants of an older folk religion. They have retained, for instance, the cult of the mountain gods, the cult of the clan gods and of family deities, which are called *lu*, and are serpent spirits. Sherpa shamanism is another prominent feature. They also seem to have retained traces of a megalithic culture, and build stone platforms and stone walls in memory of decased kinsmen and for an increase of personal merit and prestige.

Another Tibetan tribe north of the Nepal valley is that of the Yolmos. They too are Buddhists of the Red Hat sect and their Lamas may, therefore, marry. Similar to the Yolmos are the Saisaphas, but they speak a slightly different Tibetan dialect.

The Chepangs are a nomadic forest tribe near the junction of the Kali with the Seti and Trisuli rivers; they build themselves temporary huts in the forest or live in caves and are continuously on the move. They are no Buddhists, but worship the spirits of nature. They are short in stature and have a dark complexion. Some anthropologists believe that they belong to the Munda race.

On the southern slopes of the Himalayas, in the malarial Terai, are the Tharus (nearly 38,000 in 1941). They are certainly aboriginals, but have completely abandoned their tribal culture and are now considered a backward Hindu caste. They themselves claim to be the offspring of Rajput women who fled from Chitorgarh (Rajasthan) and sought refuge in these regions. They married local men whom they still dominate. Agriculture is their main occupation, and they have developed a primitive system of irrigation by damming hill streams. They supplement their livelihood by rearing buffaloes and cattle, pigs, goats and fowls, and by hunting and fishing. They used to be employed as mahouts for the elephants which work in the forest areas. They imitate the Hindus in all their religious ceremonies and worship the Hindu gods. But they also worship Bansapti Mata, the dreaded mother-goddess of the forest. The Tharus are much feared by the people for their alleged knowledge of magic, but they themselves, on the other hand, are very fearful of the spirits lurking in the jungle.

It is not certain whether the Bhoksa (12,047 in 1961), residing south of the Kumaon hills in Nainital District, are an independent tribe or just a sub-division of the Tharus. Racially and culturally, the two tribes differ little.

The Bhoksas are economically not as efficient and hardworking cultivators as the Tharus. Though jealous of the Tharus' greater prosperity, they declare with resignation that the Tharu women are more accomplished magicians than Bhoksa women and that this accounts for their better crops. Being poor farmers, the Bhoksas are always heavily in debt with the money-lenders and in danger of losing their small land holdings, rarely exceeding eight acres, to Rai Sikhs and Punjabis.

They cultivate their fields by very primitive methods and grow paddy, millet, wheat, gram, barley and mustard. They have a kitchen garden in which they grow vegetables. They keep cattle and buffaloes, but no pigs, goats and sheep. Their animals are of poor quality.

The Bhoksas live in nuclear families, have patrilocal residence, practise monogamy and pay bride-price.

They live in small villages of from fifty to three hundred inhabitants. Their huts in the village are aligned in a single compact row, which, by tradition, extends in a north-south and never in an east-west direction.

The Bhoksas differ from the Tharus in their homogeneity as a community, in which there exists no class or clan system.

Remarkable is their well organised *panchayat* system. Each *panchayat* has jurisdiction over a large number of villages. The chairman (*takhat*) of a *panchayat*, whose office is hereditary, is very powerful. The *panchayat* controls practically all aspects of their social life. Continuity and change of custom and tradition are strictly controlled by the *panchayat*.

The Bhoksas practise a religion which is basically animistic, but now much overlaid by Hinduism.

The Dotiyals and Bajhangis show few if any Mongolian features, and closely resemble their Indian neighbours across the border in Kumaon.

The Kamaras and Bhujels are slave castes. When they were emancipated in 1927 they adopted a new caste name and now call themselves Shiva Bhaktas. They intermarry with the Ghartis, a shepherd clan of the Magars.

The original inhabitants of Sikkim are the Lepchas or Rongs who settled in Sikkim since the 13th century. They came from the Assam hills. They are primarily animists, but some features of Tibetan lamaism have overlaid their basic religious beliefs. In the Darjeeling area many of them have become Christians. Being very superstitious, they spend much of their time and resources appeasing evil spirits, and are also reputed to deal in witchcraft and in the casting of spells. Their professional exorcists, who may be male or female, are called *mun*. They also have an extensive knowledge of the jungle, of its wild life and vegetation, and especially of its herbs and poisons. They have a myth which curiously resembles that of the Kadar in Kerala: they believe that they are descended from a brother and sister who later married. They reside in the Kunchenjunga. This mountain as well as the ancestors are now regarded as deities.

In physical appearance the Lepchas resemble the Gurkhas. They are mainly farmers. Wherever possible they practise shifting cultivation and sow rice and maize. Plough cultivation is only a recent innovation among them. They keep a few cattle, goats, sheep and pigs. The Lepchas claim that originally they had been hunters, and they still supplement their food by jungle produce. Some work at present as stone breakers or carpet makers. Very few are employed in Government service.

The Lepcha dialect belongs to the Tibeto-Himalayan section of the Tibeto-Chinese language group. It is the only language of this group which has a pronominalised verbal formation. Grierson believes that this is due to a Mundarian influence.

The 35,070 native Lepchas, including the Bhutiya and Tibetan-Dukpa, who overran Sikkim in the sixteenth and seventeenth centuries, represent now only 21 per cent of the population. About sixty per cent of the population in Sikkim consists of Nepali Hindus who are called Tsong. Until 1961 they did not enjoy the same status as the Bhutiyas and Lepchas, and they are still debarred from settling in the fertile valleys of the north. The relations between the three population groups are not friendly; the Lepehas have not only lost much of their land to the Bhutiyas who prefer to occupy the higher regions, but also to the Nepali settlers who ruthlessly cut down the forests from which the Lepchas derive their livelihood and prepare paddy plantations. The Lepchas have thus been all along the losers against the Bhutiyas as well as the Tsongs.

The situation was aggravated by the more than 7,000 Tibetan refugees who since 1959, the year when the Chinese occupied Tibet, have migrated into Sikkim. They are now mainly employed as road workers, but they, too, want a permanent settlement in northern Sikkim. So far they are still treated as refugees with no right for a permanent home in Sikkim.

The original settlers of Bhutan, at the east side of Sikkim, are the Bhutiya Tephoo who immigrated into Bhutan from Cooch Bihar. But around A.D. 1500 a major invasion of Tibetans occurred; they soon assumed the rule in Bhutan and themselves became Bhutiyas. This indigenous population retains all the characteristics of the Mongoloids. Their faces are broad and flat, the eyes small and oblique, the mouth large, noses short and low. The Bhutiyas profess to be Buddhists, but this is only a thin veneer over the animism which is their real belief. Polyandry is generally practised though recently the King of Bhutan has abolished it legally. The chief amusement of the Bhutiyas is polo. The British learnt the game from them.

In more recent times many Lepchas have settled in Bhutan. And in the southern regions Nepali Hindus settled down and now form 25 per cent of the Bhutanese population. The country has also received immigrants from Assam and Arunachal Pradesh, like the Akas, Abors, Miris, Daflas, Mishmis and others.

BIBLIOGRAPHY

Drew, Fr.: *The Jummoo and Kashmir Territories.* Delhi, 1971.
Gaukovsky, Yu. V.: *The Peoples of Pakistan.* Moscow, 1971.
Gorer, G.: *Himalayan Village.* 2nd ed. London, 1967.
Hermanns, M.: *The Indo-Tibetans.* Bombay, 1954.
Karan, P.P. & Jenkins, W.M.: *The Himalayan Kingdoms.* New York, 1963.
Lawrence, W. R.: *The Valley of Kashmir.* Srinagar, 1967.
Randhawa, M. S.: *The Kumaon Himalayas.* Delhi, 1970.
Robertson, G. S,: *The Kafirs of the Hindu-Kush.* London, 1896.
Shashi, S. C.: *Himachal.* Delhi, 1971.
Swinson, A.: *North-west Frontier.* London, 1969.

CHAPTER IV

Nomadic Tribes in the Plains of Northern India

GENERAL CHARACTERISTICS

IN THE plains of northern India live a number of nomadic tribes who so far could not be persuaded by Government and social welfare agencies to settle down and become stable and steady breadwinners. They are passionately nomadic, and since foodgathering and hunting in the jungle, in the traditional manner, is often impossible, they have switched over to the rather dangerous, but still exciting life of 'foraging' in the fields, villages and towns of northern India. This has gained them a bad reputation and in the British times some of them were branded as 'criminal castes' and held under close police supervision. Since independence this stigma has been taken from them, but the watch over them by the police has not relaxed much, and this for good reasons.

These nomadic communities of tribal origin must be distinguished, however, from the other types of vagrant communities which are most probably of low-caste Hindu or Muslim origin. The nomadic life of the latter communities is more the consequence of the occupations they follow. There are certain occupations catering to rather rare or occasional needs which cannot be carried out unless those who follow them wander about searching for customers and clients in a comparatively wide area. To these belong the mimes, musicians and drummers, jugglers and acrobats, but also travelling artisans like smiths, knife grinders, mill-stone makers and repairers, basket makers and bamboo makers. In India, where each occupation tends to force those who follow it into a separate caste or at least into the endogamous sub-division of a caste, these occupations are consequently performed by human groups which have no choice but to be fully nomadic, however sedentary their former way of life might have been. The chance of earning a livelihood in one of these particular occupations became, by force of the caste system, their permanent and established way of life—forcing them to continue their once accepted occupation and thus condemning them to a perpetually unsettled life.

There is still a third group of people leading a more or less nomadic life and belonging to the 'criminal castes', since 1952 classified as 'ex-criminal castes' or 'denotified castes', that are also known for their criminal activities, but have taken to a life of crime for other reasons. They probably had been uprooted in the continual wars fought in northern India and deprived of earning their livelihood by honest means or, as professional soldiers, found themselves jobless after the British had restored order and peace in the country. Unable to earn a living as farmers or artisans, these discarded soldiers often turned criminals. They are thus not primitive foodgatherers, but more like degraded Rajputs, Jats and members of other martial castes, generally of higher social rank and belonging to a superior cultural category. Even in the pursuance of their criminal activities they display a higher intelligence, more involved techniques and a strong spirit of adventure often coupled with a certain chivalry. Their daring and cunning are obviously far beyond the mental capacity of the simple foodgatherers. This third group will not be discussed here, as it is not a tribal group.

Vagrant Tribes

Here we are concerned merely with foodgatherers who have partly drifted into—often petty—thieving because there was nothing else left for them to collect and to forage. They are forced by the prevailing adverse circumstances to practise subsistence thieving, that is, taking their minimal daily requirements from the land or its lawful owners: grass for their animals, fuel, fruit, vegetables, grain for themselves, and of course the proverbial 'stray' chicken. In a general way they consider the entire world a public domain. Stealing is not considered a misdemeanour as long as it is limited to the taking of bare necessities, and not in larger quantities than they need at the moment. These tribes are practically aborigines and primitives, though in their dealings with the castes and peoples of northern India they may have lost their tribal character to a large extent, retaining only the nomadic and foraging habit. Their different racial origin is still clearly recognisable though it cannot yet be scientifically defined due to the almost complete absence of anthropometric evidence. Moreover, a large amount of miscegenation has been going on for a long time between these tribes and the local Hindu and Muslim population. They have received a considerable admixture of non-tribal blood owing to the sexually accommodating attitude of their womenfolk. They are generally undersized, dark of complexion, with curiously infantile features and gracile bodies. It is not impossible that they were originally Negritos whose blood of course has now been much diluted by admixtures.

It also appears that sections of these tribes or castes have split off from the original communities and adopted the settled life of cultivators and field-labourers. Thus, the same tribe may have a branch in one region entirely devoted to settled and ordinary village life, while in another part of the country it is still in the nomadic and foraging stage.

One such caste is that of the Bawariyas or Bauris (884,133 in 1961). Their main centre is in West Bengal (501,269), Orissa (250,914) and Rajasthan (83,104). But they are also found in Punjab (41,770), in Uttar Pradesh and in Andhra, where they are called Bavuri. It is a particularly varied community. In physical appearance the Bavuris are distinctly separated from the agricultural castes, even in Punjab where they claim to have come long ago from Mewar and Ajmer.

The Bawariyas are subdivided into several sections most of which have taken to cultivation and, though indiscriminate in their diet, are not regarded as untouchables by their neighbours. But there is at least one section that still earns its living by the noose. Other sections are vagrant and petty thieves. Along the Jumna, however, their reputation is much lower, and they are treated as outcastes.

On the whole, they are fairly well Hinduised, though they have still retained some forms of worship of their own. They admit members of the higher castes into their community on payment of the cost of a feast, or merely by a ceremonial dinner with the members of the tribe.

The Bawariyas living in the eastern regions of the upper Ganges valley seem to belong to a racially different tribe. They claim to come from Baisvara and invite the Panvar Brahmins of their former habitat to act as priests for them. They claim Rajput descent and have clan names which are identical with those of the Rajputs. But their dark complexion and different racial features do not permit a genetic connection with their present neighbours or even with the local hill tribes. The claim of Rajput descent is nowadays often made by Hinduised aboriginal communities and must not be taken very seriously.

A similar tribe is that of the Aherias (4,765 in 1961), residing in Rajasthan and the Delhi area. They are split into two sections. One of these is engaged in hunting and reed-work, and is at least temporarily settled down to life in the outskirts of the villages. It is law-abiding and submissive. The other section is composed of mat-makers and collectors of jungle produce who, however, under this guise are all potential burglars. At least in former times they were notorious for the well-planned gang-robberies they effected, usually in places far away from their homes. They managed to collect a large body quickly from many different settlements, and to melt away imperceptibly as soon as the coup was accomplished. In the present day they are said to use the railway and organise expeditions far away in Bengal or elsewhere. The caste has no endogamous or exogamous divisions; and the conversion of one of its members to Islam makes no difference to his social status.

The Bahelias (28,892 in 1961) are another such tribe originally almost exclusively occupied in hunting and bird-catching. The tribe has its centre mainly in Uttar Pradesh and West Bengal, while in Bengal it cannot easily be distinguished from the Bawariyas. In Bihar the Bahelias are also known under the name of Bhula whom Risley considered a sub-caste of the Dosadhs. But in present times the two tribes do not keep any contact. In the Ganges valley the Bahelias are often regarded as a sub-caste of the Pasis, and in the west they are claimed to be Aherias. In fact, all these tribes and castes are culturally and racially similar and it is difficult to keep them apart.

In spite of their occupation of fowling, the Bahelias are not counted among the impure castes, perhaps because they have adopted a low form of Hinduism and observe the orthodox Hindu feasts. They employ Brahmins as priests and are served by them without difficulty. A few Bahelias have embraced Islam. In recent times most Bahelias have been residing in villages as daily labourers, as traders or domestic sevants. Only a small minority of the tribe is still vagrant.

The same can be said of the Mahtams, a hunting caste in the Sutlej valley, now partly in Pakistan. Only a section of them still live as hunters, while most of them are settled cultivators and field labourers, industrious and law-abiding, even a trifle dull. Today, more than half of them are Sikhs; of the other half a large portion has been converted to Islam.

In the sub-montane tract of the Punjab, there is another community of the same name which appears to have no genetic connection with the Mahtams in the Sutlej valley. This community is really a sub-caste of the Banjaras and made its way from the east, whereas the hunting Mahtams reached the Sutlej valley coming from Rajasthan. This is not an isolated case.

The Sahariyas of Bundelkhand and the neighbourhood are another of the vagrant castes. They go under various names, such as Sahariya, Sehariya, Sehria, Sahariva, Saur, Sonr, Sor, Sosia. In 1961 they numbered 208,437. Though they have no tradition of having immigrated from any other part of the country into Bundelkhand, their name and origin are commonly traced back to the Savara tribe, now residing in the south Orissan hills. The name Savara was in the past applied by Sanskrit writers to any of the Dasyu tribes in central India. Racially the two tribes seem to be similar, both have a dark complexion and their features are similar, but culturally the Sahariyas of Bundelkhand are different. They do not wander about the country more than is necessary to give them a good supply of jungle produce which they sell for their livelihood. Their criminality is confined to petty thefts and an occasional gang-robbery. They profess Hinduism, but chiefly worship the local deities without employing Brahmins for the performance of their rites. They are sub-divided on totemistic lines into a number of exogamous clans.

The Lodhas (43,268) in West Bengal and Bihar also claim descent from the Savaras. They speak a mixture of Bengali, Oriya and Mundari and are mainly nomadic foodgatherers in the jungle tracts of Midnapur. In the plains their occupation is field-labour. They have exogamous totemic clans and in eight of the enumerated nine clans they observe rules of avoidance of the totem. Two instances of mourning for the dead totem by bathing and throwing away earthen pots are recorded.

The Lodhas have the reputation of a criminal tribe. It is obvious that economic necessity has brought them to this state. They are predominantly a foodgathering community, though a section of them has recently taken to agriculture. The forests in which the Lodhas live have been almost denuded of game by the cultivating castes in need of fields. The Lodhas being attached to their jungle life continued to collect jungle produce and to hunt and trap game, but could not support themselves any more in the thinned-out forests. Other forests became private property and hunting and collecting in these areas was suddenly declared a crime [P.K. Bhowmick, p. 277].

A similar tribe is that of the Turis (109,484) of Bihar and West Bengal. On physical grounds Risley considered them to be a Hinduised offshoot of the Mundas. They still speak a dialect derived from Mundari. Like the Mundas, they have a large number of exogamous totemic septs some of which bear Munda names. The Turis are mainly cane-workers living in the outskirts of the Hindu villages.

The Dharkars (41,662) of the southern Ganges valley were also once a forest tribe, but have settled in villages and employ Baiga priests or, at best, the Ojhas, degraded Brahmins or probably priests of non-Aryan origin. They are considered a rather restless and uncivilised community. They live as labourers, cultivators, blacksmiths and snake charmers.

In this group belong also the Rajwars and Musahars of Bihar and the east of Oudh. They are now labourers of low caste, but are of aboriginal descent. The Rajwars (196,307) are the higher of the two, and employ degraded Brahmins for their ceremonies. They have retained a good deal of their tribal organisation but have settled down to cultivation and field service. Some of them have acquired holdings as tenants and, since the abolition of landlordism, as owners. According to their own traditions, they belong to the same stock as the Musahars, but their social rank is higher.

There has been a good deal of controversy about the Musahars (in 1961 their number was 1,098,517). Their name is said to mean 'rat-eaters' a habit the caste still retains, and this is one of the reasons why the Rajwars who abstain from this diet consider themselves above the Musahars. But the etymology of the word is doubtful. No doubt both castes are of aboriginal stock, but it is uncertain whether the descent is from the Mundas through the Bhuiyas, or from the Dravida-speaking tribes through the Cheros.

The Musahars do not yet observe the ordinary Hindu restrictions about food and behaviour, and have retained much of their aboriginal form of worship as also their tribal subdivisions. Occasionally they invite Brahmins for their religious ceremonies, but for most of their rituals they do not seem to require the Brahmins' priestly aid. The Musahars are divided, like so many other similar tribes, into a settled and a nomadic section. The settled section lives in villages, does menial jobs and works in the fields, while the nomadic one haunts the jungles and collects forest produce which is sold in the villages. The agricultural castes of Bihar give an interesting reason for their habit of employing Musahars to watch their crops in the fields, namely, that they alone are able to exorcise the older gods who have been driven away by the plough and resent the intrusion of the alien peasantry. They obviously connect the Musahars with these older gods and thus acknowledge that the Musahars are the oldest settlers in the area.

West of the habitat of the Musahars, in Bihar, Oudh and the districts of Uttar Pradesh lying south of the Jumna, are found the Bhars (196,307), who, in their physical appearance, bear definite signs of their descent from a similar dark race. But they now hold a higher social rank than their neighbours. The Bhars have a tradition claiming the former ownership of the land on which they now labour as servants. They point out many old forts and reservoirs as witnesses of their former greatness. But Rajputs invaded their land after their defeat by the Muslims and subjugated them. This is possible. At present the tribe appears to be of rather unsettled habits. Its favourite occupation is breaking up fresh land; when a village area has been fully brought under cultivation, the Bhars are inclined to abandon it for the nearest jungle to be brought under cultivation. In West Bengal the Bhars enjoy a higher social status than in Bihar and Uttar

Pradesh. There they employ Brahmins as official priests in their ceremonies while in Bihar and Uttar Pradesh they use no official priests at all.

The Bagdis (numbering 1,096,885 in 1961), are another tribe of doubtlessly former aboriginal type which has settled in Rajasthan, Madhya Pradesh and West Bengal. Their features and dark complexion betray their aboriginal origin, but it is impossible to trace them back to any particular racial group. The Bagdis speak the local dialects and profess a Hinduism with many elements of nature worship. Their official priests belong to their own caste. Socially the caste is considered to be very low; they accept food from all Hindu castes. They admit recruits from all superior castes, even Kurmis. Another proof of their aboriginal origin is that their endogamous sub-sections are again divided into exogamous totemic septs. Their traditional occupation is agricultural labour. In the past they were also palanquin bearers. They also accept employment as hewers of wood, porters and dam builders. Most of them are landless.

In western Bengal and adjoining Bihar, along the Jumna and in Oudh, resides another caste partly of settled and partly of nomadic habits. It is the Bediya caste (43,812 in 1961). 4,380 of the Bediyas are returned as belonging to the scheduled castes, while the rest is returned as a scheduled tribe. The caste is split into various functional sub-sections. Some of these specialise as acrobats and conjurers, others as hunters and fowlers, while quite a few earn their living as snake charmers. The more respectable members of the caste have settled down as cultivators.

The Bediyas appear to be a vagrant offshoot of the Maler tribe and thus belong probably to the Dravida-speaking group of tribals in north-eastern central India. In present times the Bediyas also earn their living as makers of fish-hooks and articles such as combs, needles, thread and tape; others make anklets, bracelets and necklets of zinc, or sell jungle medicines. In the north they have a bad reputation for thieving. They are Hindus. Some of them have been converted to Islam, but the Mohammedans do not accept them fully. Socially they are a very impure Hindu caste.

In western India, in the Khandesh region of Maharashtra, but also in Madhya Pradesh and even in Sind, the Pardhis (7,132 in 1961) are a very picturesque nomadic tribe. They are divided into many sub-divisions, with special functions and peculiarities. Thus the Phansi-Pardhis are snarers and trappers of bird and beast. The Chita Pardhis train and sell cheetas for hunting. One sub-section, the Takankar or Takia, make and repair grinding stones. Other subsections are the Advichincher, the Langoli Pardhis, the Shikaris, etc. In the Khandesh they are occasionally also employed as village watchmen. They profess a low form of Hinduism bordering on animism.

They are of medium stature, dark-skinned and very hardy. The men are inveterate and skilled hunters. They use bullocks as decoys and hide behind them when approaching their game. Sometimes they employ shields in place of bullocks. They carry all their belongings and tents on bullocks from place to place. They wander in gangs of varying strength numbering even a hundred and more. But they also commit dacoity and robbery, house-breaking, sheep-stealing and thefts of crops. When interfered with, they often use violence.

A vagrant ex-criminal tribe of undoubtedly aboriginal type, like that of the Pardhis, is the Mang-Garudi tribe (10,740 in 1961), not to be confused with the Mangs or the Garudis with whom they have nothing in common but the name. They roam about mainly in the Deccan and Mysore State, but are also found in Berar and Madhya Pradesh as also in Gujarat.

Like the Pardhis they travel with their families, animals and all their property, encamping at some distance of, but within easy reach of, a bazaar or good-sized village. For shelter they build temporary grass huts.

A gang of them may sometimes number up to eighty and even more individuals, and is headed by an elderly man who acts as their spokesman and conducts all business with outsiders. The Mang-Garudis earn their living ostensibly by begging, performing conjuring tricks, and trading in barren buffaloes which they claim to render fertile. The women collect and sell firewood, beg and prostitute themselves. Men, women and children are alleged to be habitual and incorrigible thieves and pilferers.

A similar vagrant tribe, found in the Deccan and in the adjoining southern tracts, is that of the Kaikadis (1,946 in 1961). In Andhra and Kanara they are known as Korwas or Korachas (15,326). They have many sub-divisions, each of which is again divided into four clans or *gots*. Each sub-division has its peculiar customs of dress, habits of living and ways of earning a living.

With the exception of a very small number who have adopted agriculture for their livelihood, and those who have settled in the villages as musicians, mat weavers, basket and brush makers and the like, the Kaikadis are a nomadic tribe. They travel over the country in more or less large gangs, accompanied by their women and children, with their cattle, goats, dogs and other animals, and all their property. They live in temporarily constructed huts, at some distance form the villages but in the vicinity of water. Each encampment has its leader, who is sometimes a woman. The headman's word is law. The Kaikadis are much addicted to dacoity, house-breaking and even highway-robbery; in these activities the men are ably assisted by their women. They worship a female deity, and feast her with much drinking.

Further south in Andhra, Mysore and Tamilnadu there are similar tribes and castes leading a nomadic life and indulging in petty crime, which, however, they do not consider as such as it is rooted in their traditional way of life as simply foraging and collecting food for their daily needs. They hold that they have a right to subsistence in this manner and if they are unable to collect sufficient food they are forced to take from people who have it in abundance. They do not steal from each other and distribute their earnings and the results of their pilfering among themselves with strict impartiality.

Vagrant Occupational Castes

Owing to the great variety of these castes and the uncertainty of their origin it is not easy to classify them. It seems likely, however, that some of these vagrant castes are not of tribal origin, but originally belonged to one of the many low castes or even to the untouchable communities. Their nomadic way of life is either a matter of personal or communal preference, or it is merely conditioned by the nature of their occupation. Mimes, drummers, jugglers and acrobats, but also knife grinders and the makers and sellers of querns or mill-stones must by necessity lead a nomadic life. Mat and basket makers also seem to be more or less forced into this type of wandering around. Though certain functional castes, especially the workers in bamboo, may be of tribal origin, superficial anthropological evidence seems to suggest that most of the castes of this type belonged originally to an untouchable or at least to a low Hindu caste. Other evidence which supports this assumption is that most of the untouchable or low castes still carry out these functions, though not exclusively, but rather as supplementary occupations. The vagrant castes, however, have specialised in their peculiar occupations and practise them exclusively so that they are forced of necessity to wander from place to place to earr a living.

MIMES, DRUMMERS, JUGGLERS, AND ACROBATS

The northernmost occupational caste of this type is that of the Bands or Bhagats, the minstrels of Kashmir. They combine the profession of singing and acting with that of begging. They are great wanderers and migrate as far as Punjab where they like to perform to Kashmiri audiences. The Bhagats are Mohammedans, with the exception of one group, the Akangam company. The Bands are much in demand in the wedding season, and in a year of good harvest they make a fair living on the presents of the villagers. Their orchestra consists usually of four violins with a drum in the centre, or of clarionets and a drum or two. Their acting is good and their songs are very popular. A company may have invested a lot of money in its wardrobe, and the robes and dresses, with jewellery and other properties, may amount to several thousand rupees.

The Kashmiri Bhagats are cheerful and good-humoured, in contrast to the dull and gloomy behaviour of the Kashmiri peasants. They can be recognised by their long black hair and peculiar dress. They usually marry among themselves.

A similar caste in Punjab is that of the Bahurupias, the 'caste of many disguises'. They are really a functional sub-division of the Mahtams, and specialise in the performance of dramas and plays of mainly a religious or mythological content. There is no doubt that the knowledge which the average villagers have of Hindu religion and mythology is largely due to this type of performances which are still very popular in the villages.

In the Ganges valley, on the other hand, the Bahurupias are regarded as a sub-caste of the Banjaras. They take brides from the Nats, another wandering tribe, but do not give their daughters in marriage to them. As the Mahtams are connected with the Labanas of Punjab, a genetic link of the Bahurupias with the Banjaras is probable.

This caste has a higher social status than that of the Bhands or buffoons who, like the jesters of old, ply their trade among the mansions of the great. They are given a surprising freedom of speech and often appear very offensive in the manner in which they criticise their betters. In Punjab the caste is recruited largely from the Mirasis whose name is sometimes retained as an alternative to that of Bhand.

The Qalanders are nomadic Muslim showmen and acrobats in north India. They live in tents and carry their belongings on bullocks from place to place. Sometimes their entertainments include performing bears, fighting monkeys and snake-killing mongooses. They also display quail and partridge which they have trained for fighting.

The Bhavaios of Gujarat are an acting caste performing comedies and dramas at weddings or other festivals before any village audience paying for it. A company is often attached to a certain village as part of the establishment, and from this village they also visit other places in the neighbourhood. They have the tradition of having once held a higher position in the north, but are now a purely local institution, and their full strength has never been recorded.

The Gondhalis of Maharashtra are itinerant ballad singers, and dance a special set of figures in honour of a goddess at weddings and private entertainments.

The ceremonial drummers of a village or temple all over India usually belong to one of the local low castes, and their wages are paid at harvest time in kind. However, there are others who are more strictly professional on this instrument, and wander about for their living.

The Dafalis, for instance, and the Nagarchis (403) of the Ganges valley are Muslims, with a sort of religious flavour about their performances. While they collect alms they may occasionally be asked to exorcise evil spirits by their music.

The Dholis (4,934) of Rajasthan, like the Bajanias (671) of

Uttar Pradesh, are Hindu functional castes, recruited from the village menial and scavenging castes, wandering from village to village.

The Turaihas (2,071) of Uttar Pradesh blow horns; *turhi* being the name of the trumpet in their language.

There are numerous castes of jugglers, tumblers, snake-charmers and the like, each with a different name, but all connected, at least in upper India, under the general term of Nat or Bazigar. It is difficult to state how far the term Nat is the designation of a caste or a function. In Punjab, for instance, Nat is usually held to be a caste, and Bazigar the branch of it which takes to juggling and tumbling. In the Gangetic region, again, the Bazigar is a sub-division of the Nat, while the terms Badi, Sapera, Kabutara, denote different performances. Further to the south, the Dombars or Domaras of Andhra are probably identical with the Kolhatis of the Deccan; both share the occupation and traditions of the Nats in the north.

The Nats, as a caste, are strongest in Madhya Pradesh (2,539), Uttar Pradesh (1,843) and Bihar (497) and number altogether 5,092 individuals, while the Bazigar are strongest in Punjab (5,085) and Delhi (386). They number 5,498 individuals in all.

Except in Punjab, they physically resemble the aboriginal races specially in central India and, indeed, a good many of the clan names suggest that their original home was among the tribals of eastern central India. They have generally a short stature and a black skin, but the face is no more so broad and the nose narrow—obviously through an intermixture with other races. It is said that they sometimes kidnap children whom they train to follow their profession. They are divided into different sub-divisions of various social status. Such distinctions are strictly maintained, though most of them admit members of higher castes into their community on payment of a caste feast and after a ceremonial initiation.

In addition to their acrobatic and similar performances, the members of these castes supplement their livelihood by the manufacture of horn articles, by hunting the wild pig and by prostituting their women. They hold themselves above the Doms and Chamars, but generally are not averse to eating vermin or carrion like them.

They are not by any means all criminal, though most are credited with the propensity to break into houses and steal fowl and cattle when the opportunity occurs. The small section of the Gopals, for instance, in the Deccan are notorious cattle-lifters.

In some of the Nat sub-castes only the men perform. In a few sub-sections the women do not prostitute themselves to outsiders though their sexual morals are generally more lax than in other Hindu castes. The Nat women are experts in tattooing. Their clients are the girls and women of the villages, and their services are eagerly sought after. In the south tattooing is done by the Koracha women, another division of the Nats. The Nats are said to possess a good knowledge of roots and herbs, and to be adept in the preparation of medicines. The villagers place much faith in their recipes for aphrodisiacs, philters and the means for procuring abortion. They also sell charms and amulets. There is a certain and constant demand among the village population for all this. The Nat women also attend to the needs and ailments of women.

Another caste of this type in Punjab is that of the Dums, Dumnas, Mahashas or Mirasis (95,609), who are most probably of Dom origin. They are the minstrels and genealogists of the lower castes. Their women sing and dance in the presence of other women. The Dums attend weddings and funerals, where they recite the genealogies of the wedded pairs or describe the brave deeds of the dead man's ancestors. They also have a brand of jokes and anecdotes with which they amuse their clients. If their fees are assured their language is suave and complimentary; but if they are not given their dues they spout out of their well-stocked memory old half-forgotten scandals and gibes directed against the unfortunate family which they honour with their company.

BAMBOO WORKERS

The making of mats, brushes and weavers' combs is an occupation asscoiated with a nomadic life, not only in India but wherever these gypsy tribes have established themselves, and generally connotes an inclination towards burglary or at least towards petty larceny. The girls of these castes, moreover, are usually engaged in satisfying the sexual pleasures of the lower classes and even those of the upper who dare to run the risk of excommunication from their caste. There is a more or less definite line drawn, however, in India between these castes and those, equally low and impure, who devote themselves exclusively to working in bamboo, a plant which in several cases has become almost a deity of the whole tribe, and is worshipped accordingly at the annual caste gatherings.

Most of the cane-workers of eastern and northern India belong to the Dom caste. But the sub-divisions which have taken to this work are generally settled on the outskirts of villages, not wandering like the rest, and give themselves the name of Bansphoras (15,604), Basors (126,105), Bansors, Bansos, Bansodis, in token of their profession. In upper India they admit outsiders into their community after payment of a fee and a ceremonial initiation. In Bengal the Bansphoras are said to descend from the Patnis, the fishing section of the Doms.

In Bihar and in the eastern districts of Uttar Pradesh, we find the Moghiyas, who are also Doms; their name is probably derived from the old kingdom of Magadha. They are pure nomads, or at least were so until a short time ago, wandering about in gangs which were often, during the absence of the adult males in jail, under the leadership of a woman. They pretend to follow the usual occupation of the vagrant tribes—the weaving of mats, basket making and the like. But these are often only a cover for less lawful practices, and the Moghiyas are reputed thieves and cheats.

MAT AND BASKET MAKERS

Mat and basket making and similar callings also seem to necessitate a nomadic life, or, on the other hand, a propensity for a nomadic life can be satisfied by basket and mat making. Often these occupations are a cloak for less reputable means of livelihood among which fortune-telling is one of the more respectable. Most of these castes admit recruits from higher castes, and they indeed now and then attract unruly individuals from such castes or men who have formed illicit connections with women of the caste, some of whom appear to be specially attractive even to those far above them in rank. The offspring of such high-caste connections might form a new sub-division of the caste; thus the caste is much sub-divided, and the general tie between the sub-divisions is rather loose.

The Kanjars (47,242 in 1961), for instance, of upper India (Rajasthan, Uttar Pradesh) have a section which is still in the jungle or hunting stage, living on any fruits or roots which their women can collect. They are clever in trapping birds, squirrels and any kinds of animals that come their way and all of which they eat without discrimination. Other sections, however, have settled near the villages and make their living by the manufacture of weavers' brushes, winnowing fans, baskets and the reed-mats (*chattai*) used for their own tents and the tilts of the peasants' carts during the rains. They also cut querns like the Khumras, and make leaf-platters like the Baris, and stretch the skins of small animals for drums. With an iron-shod spud they dig out snakes, field-mice and lizards from the mud walls of the houses, and eat them all. They are said to reserve a certain number of their girls for marriage within the community while prostituting the rest. As a rule, they haunt the Jumna valley and east Punjab, but gangs are found also in central India and they occasionally filter into south India where they enjoy a reputation even worse than in the north.

As in all castes of this description, the women enjoy a position of much authority, owing allegedly to the frequent absence of their husbands in jail. If the husband's enforced absence is for a long period, his wife is permitted to form a temporary connection with another member of the caste to bridge the interval. Most of the castes are Hindus of a low type, worshipping with preference female deities. Brahmins do not serve them.

A small caste of this type, the Bantar (44,555 in 1961), is found in Bihar and Bengal. They make baskets and thatch houses for the villagers. A few of them work as field labourers. The Bantars keep pigs and eat pork. Socially they rank low. As far as their religion is concerned they are completely Hinduised.

The Thoris in the Rajkot division of Gujarat are few in number (73). They are probably an offshoot of the Waghris, a larger nomadic tribe from the north. The Thoris make and sell bedsteads and mat-work, and wander about in small tents, using the donkey as their means of transport.

A similar caste in central India is that of the Bargundas in the former Ratlam State. In 1961 they numbered 4,943. Their main occupation is the making of mats, brooms, etc., of date palm leaves and baskets of palm (*kajur*) sticks. The local population treats them as untouchables. From the dialect they speak among themselves they must come from Tamilnadu, but their Tamil is not pure, being mixed with Kanarese or Telugu. They are not able to state how, when and from which particular place they came. Old persons state that it was twelve generations ago that they arrived in Ratlam State.

The Bargundas eat every kind of flesh except beef. They are experts in catching large lizards which they eat. They worship the lower orders of the Hindu pantheon and believe in evil spirits which they greatly fear.

TRAVELLING ARTISANS

There are a few small castes which may be fairly termed travelling artisans rather than gypsies, since there is no stigma attached to them personally nor is their calling held to be a mere cover for criminal means of gain.

The Saiqulgars or Shikligars (7,424), for instance, are a Muslim caste who travel throughout the open season grinding knives and scissors, and at other times plying in the cities. A sub-division undertakes the care of razors. In old times the Shikligars were the armourers and polishers of weapons, but they are now in sadly reduced circumstances.

Their Hindu counterpart is called Ghisara; they are probably from the Deccan or south India. They are a short, wiry race, with a dark skin, high cheek-bones and thick lips. They are a migratory people moving with their wives and children, carrying their materials and tools in carts.

The Khumras are another small Muslim caste of upper India whose function is to quarry and sell querns or mill-stones for domestic use. They are hewn at the quarry and hawked about on pack-animals. The roughening of the face of the stone after it has been used for a long time is the work of another caste in central India and the Deccan, the Takaris or Takankar, a sub-division of the Pardhis. While the Khumras are honest people, the Takaris are said to utilise the time they spend squatting on the premises where they are employed, in finding out the exact position of certain property of the household that could easily be 'removed' by a nocturnal visit.

Then there are various nomadic blacksmith castes. One of these is the Gadolya Lohar caste. The Gadolyas are a traditionally nomadic group in western Rajasthan, primarily occupied as blacksmiths, with cattle trading as a subsidiary occupation. They move in carts, therefore the name Gadolya. With the progressive development of the iron industry they find less and less employment and their income is dwindling.

They live in small kindred groups. Three persons are required for the management of a smithy: One to work the bellows, the second to do the hammering and the third, the most skilled one, to give proper shape to the article. The management of a smithy is the job of a household. The bellows is served by old women or children. The hammering of the hot iron is done by men or women, while the proper shaping of the article is the job of a skilled worker, usually the head of the family. The methods of production may not have changed for many generations; they have been handed on from father to son, without any improvement nor any desire for it. The working unit is the nuclear family, rarely including additional kin, i.e., the wives and children of married sons or widowed parents.

THE SO-CALLED CRIMINAL CASTES

In upper India a number of so-called criminal castes are in existence which claim Rajput descent. It is possible that, after the defeat of the Rajputs by the Muslims, some groups of them, dispossessed of their land, were unable to earn a living by cultivation or as soldiers in the armies, and took to a life of crime. During the almost continuous wars in north India and the struggle for supremacy there was no authority to check these lawless groups which pilfered the countryside. After the British had taken over the rule of India, however, they were determined to stamp out these anti-social bodies and to introduce law and order. The British administration was at that time confronted mainly with two well organised bodies of criminal pursuit, the *Thugs* and the *Pindaris*. They had to be exterminated in specially organised campaigns.

Finally, the various displaced and vagrant communities were

also to be tackled. Various special laws had to be introduced to meet these dangers to public safety legally. In 1871 the Criminal Tribes Act was promulgated which was amended later several times, the last time in 1924. It placed certain communities under strict supervision and restricted their free movement. However, the fact of being branded with the designation 'criminal tribe' had often very tragic consequences for a whole community and especially for those individuals who were keen on leading an honest life. For, all members were indiscriminately placed at the mercy of often very unsympathetic and oppressive officials. Instead of weaning the real criminals among them from a life of petty thieving, they often drove, by the despair of wounded feelings, innocent members of such communities into a life of rebellion and serious crime. After India became independent the Criminal Tribes Act was rescinded in 1952 by the new Indian Government. They are now called 'Denotified Communities'.

The Sansis (59,073 in 1961) are one tribe of this type. They claim Rajput descent. According to their traditions their ancestor was the Rajput Sansi who had two sons, Behdoo and Mahla, who in turn had twelve and eleven sons respectively. In fact, there exist in north India the Sansi caste as well as the Bediya (10,311) and Mala (4,506) castes. Each of these castes is sub-divided into various sections though always pursuing similar occupations. According to their traditions, the Sansis were expelled from Rajputana by Muslim invaders in the 13th century. Dispossessed of their homelands, the Sansis first migrated to Punjab and other regions eking out a living by being shepherds. field-labourers and genealogists for the land-owning Jats. It is claimed that the great Sikh leader Ranjit Singh was a Sansi.

The nomadic habits and rather frequent indulgence in marauding and cattle-lifting, petty thieving, etc., made them soon suspect to the British officials who, especially in the troubled times after the 'Mutiny', made strenuous efforts to restore internal peace and a semblance of order and lawfulness in India. The Sansis, as 'vagrants', fell under the category of 'criminal castes' and were treated strictly according to the letter of the law. They were deprived of their human rights merely due to the fact of their descent from the Sansi community and often forced to a life of crime. This has happened also in more recent times and even some Rajputs like the famous, robber-king, Man Singh, became dacoits because they were prevented by a cruel fate from earning their living by honest means.

But though many members of the community may have led a reputable life, the caste as such certainly deserved its bad reputation. Highway dacoity and cart robbery were Sansi specialities. But they also indulged in house-breaking, tent thieving, looting of encampments and isolated homesteads, cattle and sheep lifting, thefts of all sorts including standing crops and other agricultural products. They also took to railway thieving.

In all this they were ably assisted by their women who sold roots and herbs, but at the same time spied out likely homes yielding a good booty. In contrast to the practice of the Nats, the Sansi women were not given to prostitution and were very staunch in the defence of their male relatives when trouble was threatening.

While parts of the caste are settled in the north and earn a living by cultivation or field labour, another part is still a wandering tribe with no steady habitat. Sansis can be found practically all over India. They travel in gangs of various strength, with their families, animals and all their belongings. They never put up in towns or villages; they shun all habitations, temples, rest-houses (*dharmshalas*) and the like. Each gang is headed by a so-called Naik or Sarganah. He is socially their leader and directs all their enterprises. His authority rests mainly on his capabilities.

The Sansi women hold a good position in the community. They enjoy much influence in the tribal councils in which they can speak freely, bear witness and give advice. This would be unthinkable in Rajput society. The status of the woman in the tribal council is the more important as owing to the natural aversion of the Sansis in applying for the protection of the law, these councils practically regulate all affairs and disputes of the community. Moreover, a woman can inherit property; she can divorce her husband and remarry. Sansi society, further, discourages polygamy and permits it only in the form of levirate and sororate. The custom of paying a bride-price is frowned upon by the Sansis.

Socially the Sansis are organised into various endogamous sub-sections, which are split again into exogamous clans and hundreds of sub-clans. A sub-clan (*dera*) was originally simply a temporary encampment under the control of a leader. Some clans, owing to marital unions with members of lower castes, have an inferior social status and find it consequently difficult to get their daughters married into the higher clans, and to acquire brides for their sons.

The Sansis stand in a curious relationship to the Jat tribe, each family of which has its Sansi genealogist. The word of the Sansi is accepted as final when a question arises in connection with pedigrees. It is not easy to trace this important functional attachment between the Jats and the Sansis unless some real racial connection is assumed.

The Sansis profess a religion which is basically Hinduism, but it is of the most simple type, and they feel bound to call in outside spiritual aid only in cases where the ghost or demon of the locality has caused serious illness or bad luck. A few Sansis have been converted to Islam, more have become Sikhs, but one large section asserts its Rajput origin and keeps aloof from the rest of the tribe. It appears that recent anthropometric studies of the Sansis support this claim to some extent [Sher Singh Sher (1965), pp. 24–30].

In physical appearance the Sansis do not indeed differ much from the Rajputs and Jats of north India. The men are of wheatish brown colour, but never dark. They are of medium height, strong, wiry and agile. Their women are often slender, good-looking and well-formed.

The small vagrant tribe of the Haburas (2,466), along the upper Ganges and Jumna, claims descent from the Chauhan Rajputs. It is more likely that they are a sub-division of the Sansis. They resemble the parent tribe in the high status of the women and the propensity to thieving, but seem to be more Hinduised in their customs. The unmarried girls enjoy considerable sexual freedom. Like many of the criminal tribes in northern India, the Haburas, too, have a strong mixture of Gujarati in their dialect. This would suggest a south-western origin and a probable Rajput connection. In any case, the Haburas display a notable audacity in their criminal exploits.

Another criminal caste, originally from Punjab, but at present settled and operating in many parts of India, is that of the Chapparabands, also known as Fakir coiners. They are specialists in forgery. Many of this caste have settled down in the Bijapur District, but travel all over India. They are all Sheikh Muslims, and ostensibly live by begging. But some have taken to cultivation and a few earn their living as village watchmen. On the whole, however, it is only their womenfolk that work in the fields and stay at home, while the men often absent themselves for months while on their expeditions. They usually work in gangs from three to ten. Though traditionally manufacturers of counterfeit coins, they are not great adepts in this craft and are able to pass on their crude products only to the more backward and simple villagers.

Another caste with criminal inclinations, likewise claiming Rajput origin and nomadic in habits, are the Mianas of Kathiawad and Cutch. Their central place is Malia, a former princely State. From there they used to make long journeys to Sind as also to Ahmedabad and all over Kathiawad. In the past they seem to have been seafarers and great pirates.

The Mianas, though originally Hindus, were some centuries ago converted to Islam. Though they hold certain Pirs in esteem, their mode of life is still much akin to that of the Rajputs. In appearance they closely resemble the Sindis. They are a handsome, virile-looking race, tall, with long wavy hair, well-kept bushy beards and aquiline features. Their skin colour is swarthy. Their women are known for their good looks and loose morals. Though a few have accepted employment in the police force or do farm-work, the majority of the Mianas do no honest work. If their movements were not checked and controlled by the police, they would still be what they were in past: confirmed and desperate freebooters and dacoits, addicted to daring highway robbery, cattle lifting, house-breaking, thefts of all kinds, kidnapping of women, etc. But the present close supervision through the police will force them to change their criminal habits.

Another well-known wandering tribe in India which, at least until recent times, subsisted by organised robbery and thieving is that of the Bhantus (7,903). They are found in north and central India, though sections of the tribe reside also in the east and extend their operations as far as Pakistan.

The Bhantus, too, claim Rajput descent and consider Chitorgarh their mother-city. Their tradition runs that they were dispersed when the Muslims took Chitorgarh, and thus were forced to leave their homes and accustomed manner of life, to live in the jungles or to become wanderers.

But in fact the Bhantus seem to be an offshoot of the Sansis, Haburas, Kanjars, Karwal Nats and Jats. But nothing definite can be stated in the absence of anthropometric evidence. The Bhantus are divided into thirty-six gotras or clans, which are exogamous, and differ in the observance of customs relating to worship, marriage, burial, etc. The clans are not totemistic.

The Bhantus have a good physique and are reputed to be good runners. The women are strong, handsome and gifted with exceptionally strong voices. They lead their nomadic life in gangs, consisting of about a dozen families. Usually they camp away from the villages. Their system of internal administration is communal; all disputes are settled by a council of elders. Discipline is strict, and morality, excepting offences against property, rather high. Incest is severely punished, and sexual promiscuity is not tolerated. Divorce is permitted, but frowned upon.

Their religion resembles that of the lower Hindu castes; they mainly worship female deities, and never visit Hindu temples or employ Brahmins in any ceremony. They also venerate their ancestors.

Among themselves they speak a kind of thieves' slang, mutilating the words in order to make them incomprehensible to outsiders. Their raids used to be well prepared and rehearsed. A gang would usually consist of some thirty to forty men. If resistance was shown they were merciless. They were not averse to torture and rape. The plunder was at once buried; after the excitement had died down, it was dug up and disposed of by the women. The receivers were usually goldsmiths.

It may be added that in 1926 a large gang of Bhantus with their wives and children were resettled in the Andaman Islands. They indeed abandoned crime altogether, earning their living by cultivation while some Bhantus found employment in saw-mills and as coolies. Their conduct is now above reproach.

The Sanaurhiyas, or Chandravedis, another nomadic community of predatory pursuits, often declare themselves as Sanadh Brahmins. They are a composite social group, recruited from all sorts of castes, but now bound together by the usual caste regulations, including one prohibiting all crimes of violence. They commit thefts by day only. Their headquarters are at Bundelkhand, but they are mostly on the move in disguise with a few of their more wealthy members established in the chief towns to act as receivers of the goods obtained on the journey.

All these castes, with the exception of the Sanaurhiyas who claim to be Brahmins, keep up a pretence of Rajput descent and have caste divisions or gotras like the Rajputs. Their marriages are arranged according to these sub-divisions among the Rajputs, while birth and death ceremonies are likewise governed by Rajput customs with local variations.

The Waghris of Gujarat (109,583 in Gujarat, altogether over 200,000), obviously identical with the Baghris or Bagdis of central India, claim kinship with the Sansis of the Punjab. This may be correct, for they are very similar to the Sansis in physical appearance though their racial stock is somewhat modified by the admixture of local blood [S. Fuchs, p. 127 ff.]. According to their own traditions the Waghris came to Gujarat via Rajasthan. From Gujarat they later spread over Madhya Pradesh and the northern Deccan. Though adopting everywhere the local languages, they have retained remnants of Gujarati in their present forms of speech.

They are sub-divided according to their various main occupations, and where they are numerous, are also divided according to areas. These sections are endogamous. The Waghris are still great hunters and bird snarers. They also keep fowl and rent fruit trees and other productive trees by the year, selling the crop. Several sub-sections, like the Kankodias and Talabdas, have taken to cultivation. Others are cattle dealers and sellers of stick brushes for cleaning the teeth (*datania*), or drummers during the wedding season. Most of them wander during the fair season, though some groups have now more or less permanently settled near villages and in the slum areas of the big cities like Ahmedabad and Bombay, buying and selling old clothes and other things. When travelling, they are under a headman, in gangs from five to ten families, with their animals and property, staying only two or three days in one place. They have their own priests or clan-elders (*Bhuvas*) who perform all ceremonies for them and regulate general social matters. It is worthy of note that they have a sort of confession which is resorted to, especially when a husband is doubtful about the fidelity of his wife.

The Waghris, though not quite in the range of criminal castes, have a bad reputation as thieves. In north Deccan, too, this caste is credited with a good deal of offences against property. In the towns and cities they are permanently under police supervision.

CONCLUSION

The overall analysis of the nomadic tribes in northern India suggests that they fall into three main categories: (*a*) one group belongs to a basically primitive foodgathering and hunting stage of culture; (*b*) the second group belongs to a more advanced culture of jungle dwellers and primitive cultivators, akin perhaps to the Doms, and the aborigines of north-eastern India in their past; and (*c*) a third group which probably belonged to originally predatory nomadic tribes, immigrants from central Asia, such as the Jats and Rajputs. And even the travelling artists and artisans seem to have adopted their respective occupations more because they allowed them the freedom of unrestricted wandering than the necessity of earning a living in this peculiar manner.

It can be well assumed, in general, though for lack of anthropometric evidence it cannot yet be proved scientifically, that racially the nomadic tribes of the first category are all of a comparatively short stature with an infantile and gracile body form, a dark skin colour, and highly developed hunting and collecting instincts and abilities. These racial characteristics would suggest a genetic connection with the Pygmies of Africa or the Negritos of Asia. But unfortunately their racial constitution does not run to type, as they received generous admixtures from the present-day village population of northern India due to the promiscuity of their womenfolk.

The social organisation of these tribes bears all the characteristics of typical foodgatherers and primitive hunters. They practise kinship exogamy in marriage. Premarital sex relations are easily tolerated. Their marriage ties are loose; women and girls sell their favours to outsiders in most groups as a matter of course. Several families, usually related by kinship or affinity, wander together in close cooperation and social intimacy. They are headed by an elderly man or woman whose authority is far from absolute. Each family is free to break away from a gang and to join another one.

Their basic economy, too, is that of foodgatherers and primitive hunters. They still hunt with primitive weapons and use the trap and the noose; they collect foodstuff in the jungle, but also from the fields which do not belong to them. Deprived of their original hunting and collecting grounds, they consider themselves justified to beg, to steal and to pilfer, to deceive and cheat, even to break into houses and barns and to rob travellers and helpless persons. Usually they are averse to wounding and killing human beings and resort to violence only to escape detection and imprisonment. Their methods of deception and stealing are rather unsophisticated and simple.

By religion these tribes are Hindus; but Hinduism sits very lightly on them. They have a special preference for a female deity which they worship under various Hindu disguises, but they also venerate and fear evil spirits. Of ancestor worship they have little or nothing. It might appear that they have no moral principles at all, but this is not so. Within their own community they observe a fairly good ethical standard; they live peacefully and amiably together; they do not steal from each other; they submit to the authority of their leader; they help each other unstintingly. But the outside world they regard as their enemy against which any stratagem is permitted. They find themselves in a constant state of war against the world and use every means, fair and foul, which helps them to survive.

The tribes of the second category are generally more advanced in culture. Racially they seem to belong either to the aboriginal tribes still surviving, especially in the eastern and southern parts of north India, on the slopes of the Himalayas and the jungles of the Vindhya mountains and their promontories. But in eastern north India an old race is supposed to exist, the Doms or Domars, with a culture, at least in some aspects, superior to that of the aborigines in north-eastern central India. This race had been conquered and enslaved at an early date, probably by the Aryan and central Asian immigrants whose descendants are the present-day cultivating and land-owning castes of eastern north

India. In course of time the Doms had been reduced to a class of landless labourers and serfs and subjected to a merciless economic exploitation and social degradation. The racial position of the Doms is not at all clear, nor do the anthropologists know in what way, if at all, they are related to the present-day aborigines of north-eastern central India. In physical appearance both groups are similar though the Doms are of lighter build, less pigmented complexion and more long-nosed. Before their spirit was broken through incessant and profitless toil for their exploiters, they must have been a strong and numerous race because so many castes trace their origin back to the Doms.

In material culture they must have been well versed in the cultivation of grains and garden products, but also in leatherwork and weaving and in the manufacture of bamboo and reed articles. Their descendants have retained many of these traditional skills.

The nomadism of these tribes is not as pronounced as that of the tribes of the first category; they move around but in a more restricted range. Often they have a permanent residence to which they return seasonally. In some tribes only the male members move while the women remain stationary.

The social structure of the Dom-descended tribes is more of a territorial type, with village kinship exogamy, rather loose sexual morals, polygyny and some sort of a fraternal polyandry. The tribes descended from the aboriginal tribes have retained to a large extent an original totemistic clan organisation, pronounced father-right and a well-organised and disciplined village organisation with headmen, officials, priests and professional healers and shamans.

In religion the nomadic tribes of this category are at least nominal Hindus, with a strong preference for mother goddesses and nature spirits, bloody sacrifices and magic practices. The mat and basket makers venerate with special fervour a jungle deity incorporated in the bamboo.

The nomadic tribes of the third category are all one in claiming high-caste descent; most of them want to be counted among the Rajputs, a few trace their origin back to Brahmins.

This claim cannot easily be substantiated; still, it is obvious that these tribes belong to a race different from the first two categories. They are taller, of lighter complexion, with longer faces and noses. They thus conform more to the local farming and land-owning population.

In social organisation they seem to have adopted, or retained, the clan organisation and territorial divisions of the Rajputs. They are more Hinduised and stricter in the observance of Hindu food and behaviour regulations than the other nomadic tribes. Those individuals and communities which lead a life of crime are more daring and violent, more cunning and cruel, but at times chivalrous and generous towards the poor. They have a strong feeling of injustice being done to them in ancient or present times and often justify their lawless behaviour in this manner. But it is obvious that they originally belonged to the restless, predatory nomadic races of inner Asia who could not adjust themselves to the dull life of peaceful farmers and found, moreover, manual work below their dignity. Many members of these tribes have joined the army or police force, but the strict discipline of these services is against their turbulent nature. However, the successful reformation of the small group of Bhantus deported to the Andaman Islands where they were given land for cultivation proves that even the most inveterate criminal and nomadic tribes can be settled and pacified under favourable conditions by sympathetic social workers.

BIBLIOGRAPHY

Anderson, K.: *Tales of Mansingh, King of Indian Dacoits*. Bombay, 1961.

Ayyangar, A.: *Report of the Criminal Tribes Act Enquiry Committee, 1949–50*. Delhi, 1951.

Baines, A.: *Ethnography*. Strassburg, 1912.

Bhargava, B. S.: *Criminal Tribes*. Lucknow, 1949.

Bhowmick, P. K.: *The Lodhas of West Bengal*. Calcutta, 1963.

Blunt, E. A. H.: *Social Service in India*. London, 1946.

Bonington, C. J.: 'The Bhantus, A Criminal Tribe in India', *Census of India 1931*, Vol. I, Part III, pp. 36–44. Delhi, 1933.

Briggs, G. W.: *The Doms*. Mysore, 1953.

Census of India 1931, Vol. I, Part II. Delhi, 1933.

Census of India 1961, Vol. I, Part V–A (i). Delhi, 1966.

Census of India 1961, Vol. I, Part V–A (ii). Delhi, 1966.

Crooke, W.: *Natives of Northern India*. London, 1907.

Das, A.K. et al.: *Handbook on Scheduled Castes and Scheduled Tribes of West Bengal*. Calcutta, 1966.

Fuchs, S.: 'Anthropometric Analysis of the Waghris' in P. G. Shah: *Denotified Communities in Western India*. Bombay, 1967, pp. 124–45.
Gunthorpe, E. J.: *Notes on Criminal Tribes*. Bombay, 1882.
Hutton, J. H.: *Caste in India*. Oxford University Press, 1951, 2nd ed.
Katiyar, T. S.: *Social Life in Rajasthan*. Allahabad, 1964.
Lawrence, W. R.: *The Valley of Kashmir*. Srinagar, 1967.
Majumdar, D. N.: *Race Realities in Cultural Gujarat*. Bombay, 1950.
Misra, S. C.: *Muslim Communities in Gujarat*. Bombay, 1964.
Pfeffer, G.: *Pariagruppen des Pandschab*. Freiburg i. Br., 1970.
Rahelia, S.P.: *The Gaduliya Lohars of Rajasthan*. New Delhi, 1968.
Shah, P. G.: *Denotified Communities in Western India*. Bombay, 1967.
Sher Singh Sher: *The Sansis of Punjab*. Delhi, 1965.
————: *The Sikligars of Punjab*. Delhi, 1966.
Turner, A. C.: 'Some Ethnographic Notes on Miscellaneous Castes and Tribes', *Census of India 1931*, Vol. XVIII, Part I, pp. 588–618.
Vakil, D. F.: 'The Burgundas', *Census of India 1931*, Vol. I, Part II, pp. 45–7,
Waterfield, H. G.: 'Note on Moghias', *Census of India 1931*, Vol. I, Part II, pp. 33–6.

CHAPTER V

The Tribes in the Central Area

General Characteristics

THE ABORIGINES of central India are spread out in loosely connected groups all over the central belt of the Indian peninsula, from Gujarat across Madhya Pradesh, Bihar, Maharashtra and Orissa to West Bengal. They form the largest part of the tribal population of India. Their main strength is concentrated in the adjoining corners of four States: Madhya Pradesh, Bihar, Orissa and Maharashtra.

Some of the tribes, like the Gonds and Bhils, are very strong in number and run into several million individuals; they are spread over a large area and have reached a fairly high standard of culture. Though politically unawakened, they form a mass of people which one day may become politically influential. Other tribes are very small, numbering just a few thousand individuals, often very primitive in culture and unsteady, shy, passive, self-retiring and submissive. There are about a dozen main tribes while more than two hundred smaller and less important tribes live alongside or are interspersed between the main tribes, enjoying their protection or being exploited by them.

Racially as well as culturally these tribes have considerable variety. Their physical and cultural differences cannot be explained merely as local peculiarities or due to influences from alien neighbours; these differences are of a more significant and fundamental nature.

It is difficult to unravel the knotty problem of their origin because no written documents exist about their ancient past. Nor are their own traditions about their original homes and migrations very reliable. Not even the ancient Hindu scriptures, which indeed often refer to the indigenous population, can be more relied on; often they are too vague in their references or distort their descriptions by mythical interpretations and by their racial and religious prejudices. So far it has been largely impossible to identify the tribes mentioned in the ancient scriptures and to connect them, with any certainty, with present-day primitive tribes of central India.

Even prehistoric research has not yet been very helpful. One reason is that fieldwork in the prehistory of this region is still in an initial stage and sporadic; and another is that the early history of the present-day aborigines in central India is too little known to connect them with the available prehistoric evidence. More knowledge about early migrations of the tribes is vital.

Almost all the larger tribes believe themselves to be the original settlers, if not of the tracts they now inhabit, at least of one within a comparatively short distance. They also claim, in their traditions, that in the past they had occupied a much larger area than they are holding now in present times, and in most cases they support their claim by evidence such as that of ancient forts, names of places and castes, and by similar forms and objects of worship. They hold themselves to be the true *adivasis*, the first occupants and original owners of the land. However, prehistory and archaeology seem to suggest that these claims are not justified (cf. Chapter I). Most of the tribes are comparatively recent settlers in the tracts they are now occupying.

The Economic Situation

It can safely be stated that by tradition and choice all the more important aboriginal tribes are agriculturists. Even those individuals among them who follow other occupations pursue them only to ultimately buy a plot of land and to end their life as farmers. However, at least in the past, hunting and collecting wild-growing vegetables and fruits in the forests was a substantial supplementary part of the food supply for all these tribes.

Their traditional method of cultivation was the primitive and superficial shifting cultivation—burning the jungle and sowing the seed in the fertile ashes. To increase the land revenue, the former British Government as well as the native rulers invited many non-tribal farmers into the jungle areas. They had no qualms of conscience if they thereby deprived the original tribal settlers of their land. The latter themselves often played into the hands of their land-hungry competitors by their half-nomadic and unstable manner of life, by their wasteful and indifferent methods of cultivation, by their easy-going habits, their lack of foresight and thrift, excessive drinking, and by their borrowing of money at high interest, etc.

In areas where tribal land-owners are not protected by special Government legislation, this process of land dispossession is still going on. Slowly, but inexorably, the tribals are squeezed out of their land holdings and reduced to the status of field servants and daily labourers, or forced to emigrate to the tea gardens of Assam, or to seek employment in the industrial centres, usually in the lowest grades of unskilled labour.

Most of the tribals must have been primitive cultivators already at the time when they arrived in central India to settle there permanently. They have been dependent on the cultivation of land ever since, and in spite of all industrial developments, agriculture is likely to remain the prevailing pattern of their economy for quite some time to come.

The greater part of the tribal population in central India lives in the hilly jungle areas where much of the land is in the Reserved Forests. In fact, they preferred these tracts as more suitable for their traditional manner of cultivating—shifting, or slash-and-burn cultivation. But in 1867 shifting cultivation was prohibited by law because it did much damage to the forests. Shifting cultivation is now permitted only in Baiga Chak (Mandla District), Abujh Mar (Bastar District) and in a few forest ranges in Bilaspur, Surguja and Raigarh districts. It is however practised surreptitiously in many other places.

Even when the tribals have given up or been forced to abandon shifting cultivation, their subsequent method of cultivation has been through old, traditional and primitive methods, with crude implements, poor quality seeds, poor working animals, without the knowledge or practice of manuring or crop rotation. Consequently the yield and the value of the crops produced by them is very low. Soil erosion, lack of fencing round the fields, and paucity of irrigational facilities further reduce the yield.

Some sections of the Bhilala, Gond and Korku tribes, living in closer contact with the non-tribal farming castes, have learned from them better methods of cultivation and have consequently much improved their economic conditions. Some tribes in Chota Nagpur, notably the Mundas and Oraons, seem to have had from the first a better knowledge of farming, and even some form of irrigation. But also among these tribes wealthy farmers are rare, and the vast majority of people eke out a living scarcely above the level of starvation. In times of drought they suffer terribly and incur debts which they can scarcely ever repay as the rate of interest is so exorbitantly high. On the whole the tribals have been extremely adverse to close contacts with non-tribals and preferred to withdraw to relatively isolated tracts, on hills and into jungles whenever non-tribal farmers invaded their habitats and usurped their most fertile lands.

Poorer still than the agriculture of the tribals is their husbandry. The cattle population in the tribal areas of central India is quite high, but the breed of cattle reared by them is usually very poor. In the traditional economy of shifting cultivators plough animals were not required, and cattle served only as suppliers of food and pack animals. Of greater economic importance for them was the rearing of pigs and poultry, which is still a common feature in the tribal villages all over the eastern and southern areas.

Most of the tribal communities supplemented their subsistence by the collection of jungle produce and by hunting. Unfortunately, during their shifting cultivation period much of the valuable forests in central India have been damaged. To protect the devastated forests, the Government took over their management. Of the total forest area, the largest part has been declared Reserved Forests, another part as Protected Forests and only a small part as Unclassed Forests. In the Reserved Forests all private rights and concessions have been abolished, while in the Protected Forests the local population has only retained certain restricted privileges in regard to firewood and grazing cattle. Thus the jungle does not yield them the important subsidiary subsistence it did in the past.

Besides doing agriculture and selling forest produce wherever possible, fishing and hunting provide extra food in some parts. In some areas the tribals have taken to cattle-grazing as a primary and, more often, as a subsidiary source of income. Elsewhere they engage themselves in many other jobs to supplement their income, such as serving as agricultural labourers within or without the village they live in, working in the Forest Department or under forest contractors, in constructing and maintaining roads, and as labourers in mines and collieries. Central India is rich in mining and industrial potential and with the progress of industrialisation in the rural areas, more and more tribals in search of employment will be attracted to such places and jobs. So far the employment of tribals in mines and factories is not high; in the coal mines of Parasia (Chhindwara District), for instance, only 1,200 tribals were employed; in the manganese mines in Balaghat District about a thousand. The steelworks at Bhilai gave work to 250 tribals only. They are mainly unskilled labourers with low wages. But they show ability, strength and industriousness. A redeeming feature in this type of employment is that tribal labourers are treated exactly like their non-tribal co-workers. But among the tribals the percentage of absenteeism is very high. At Parasia, for instance, a tribal labourer works only 235 days on the average in a year. They absent themselves for frequent visits to villages, celebrating, drinkings and dancing, or just idling. Most tribals do not like to work more than what is necessary to earn enough for their daily needs. The idea of saving is alien to all except the acculturated tribals.

The economic situation of the tribals in central India is consequently rather unsatisfactory for reasons that are inherent in the traditional culture of the tribals, in the encroachment of land-hungry and exploiting outsiders on their habitats, in their own weaknesses, such as extreme conservatism, improvidence, excessive love of drinking, etc., and in a faulty or unimaginative treatment by the Government.

Even more deplorable is the lot of the nomadic hunters and food collectors whose hunting grounds are daily getting more restricted so that they eke out an increasingly precarious subsistence.

The Government of India is making strenuous efforts to alleviate the hard lot of the tribal population. In 1958, about

750 million rupees were set aside for this purpose, though eventually not even half of this amount was spent. Still, schemes of irrigation, of reclaiming waste lands are inaugurated, assistance for the purchase of livestock, fertilisers, seeds, implements, etc., is provided and cattle-breeding and poultry farming are introduced. Roads are built, loans given, free housing sites granted, dispensaries opened and mobile health units sent to tour the tribal areas. Legislation extends relief for indebtedness, bondage and land tenancy.

Hand in hand with this economic assistance goes a generous planning for the education of the aborigines. It has been well recognised that mere school education is not sufficient. The tribals need as much social and communal education. The adult tribals, above all, must be actively associated with the formulation and solution of their own problems.

Government maintains several tribal research centres (at Ranchi, Nagpur, Chhindwara, Poona and Ahmedabad, for instance) to study the aboriginal problems scientifically and to advise the officials and social workers through experts. Government also employs a host of social workers and development officers while semi-official and private agencies, too, are active in tribal welfare work. Most prominent among these is the Bharatiya Adim Jati Sevak Sangh, the strongest semi-official body with branches all over India; it is so powerful that it gets a lion's share of the funds earmarked for the uplift of the tribals.

However, all these schemes fail in one important respect: the social workers and development officers have not been able to gain the full confidence and active cooperation of the aborigines. One reason is that they usually belong to the very people whom the aborigines hold responsible for their economic and social plight. They also frequently show little understanding of the tribal mentality and often publicly express their feeling of superiority and their contempt for the primitives.

Only recently the head of all the Government welfare schemes for the tribals deplored the lack of proper personnel with a spirit of service and devotion and also the absence of a right policy in dealing with the tribals. Moreover, Government and private agencies have largely failed to train leaders among the aborigines themselves and have enlisted the help of outsiders too exclusively.

As for school education, much has been done to promote

literacy, but on the whole the educational facilities for tribal children are still woefully inadequate. Above all, too little is being done to provide a higher education to the more talented tribals and to train an elite. Complaints are also heard that private agencies active in the educational field frequently pursue their own communal interests to the detriment of the tribals. But the schools managed by the Christian missions seem to flourish, with the result that the tribals who have been converted to Christianity have a higher rate of literacy. They have also the greatest number of high-school and college students. Under the Five-Year Plans, increased educational facilities are provided for tribal children by way of scholarships, free tuition, books, etc., and by way of clothing and midday meals.

Social status is an important factor for establishing the mental equilibrium of the individual as well as of a whole community. Social prestige is a powerful stimulant for human ambition and drive. This axiom holds good also for the aborigines of central India. In the past they have been living apart and keeping to themselves. But gradually they are coming into ever closer contact with the non-tribal population of India, which is predominantly Hindu. The aborigines are thus necessarily drawn into the still all-compelling Hindu caste system.

The tribes of central India react differently to this social adjustment. Some tribes, like the Bhils and Gonds, Bhilalas and Minas, have decided to adopt Hinduism and aspire to the social rank of Kshatriyas (Rajputs). They, therefore, observe the social rules and taboos of the high-caste Hindus with anxious correctness and avoid any lapse that could create the slightest suspicion of unorthodoxy.

We may see in this a retrogressive step, as the tribals are adopting a way of living which the better-class Hindu population is just outgrowing. It leads also to tribal disintegration. Since not all the members of a tribe can live up to the required standard of behaviour, the tribes of this category often split into two sections, a Hinduised 'upper' section and a tribal 'lower' section. Examples of such dichotomy can be found among the Gonds (Raj-Gonds and Jungli-Gonds), Korkus (Muasis and Paharias), Bhilalas (Bara Bhilalas and Barelas), Raj-Banshis and others.

Another group of tribes has also accepted the Hindu way of living with its set code of caste rules and taboos. But due to a lax observance of these rules (especially the food taboos on beef and pork, and drinking alcohol) Hindu society has relegated them to the status of outcastes and untouchables. Tribes belonging to this category are, among others, the Nahals, Agarias, Kols, Pardhans, Ojhas, Nagarchis, Ganras and Pankas.

Certain small tribes still absolutely reject any large-scale acculturation and in their extreme conservatism and attachment to their old ways of living will rather die out than change their form of culture. Such tribes are, among others, the Baigas, Korwas, Birhors, Juangs and Kamars. They are still outside the Hindu caste system and want nothing more than to be left alone.

A fourth and perhaps most important group is formed by those tribes who live in more compact and numerically strong communities. They have developed some degree of tribal consciousness, and meet non-tribals on a more or less equal footing. They refuse to be completely absorbed by non-tribal culture and society. In central India the tribes of Chota Nagpur belong to this group.

On the other hand it is a curious fact that the aborigines of central India had in the past no strong tribal solidarity. Even such important tribes like the Bhils and Gonds have not and never had an organisation comprising all the members of the tribe; they rather live in small groups gathering only a small number of village communities in a certain area as a social unit. The Bhil tribe in particular is broken up into many unconnected sub-sections which even bear different names and have partly mixed with non-tribal communities.

This absence of tribal solidarity is certainly one of the main reasons why the tribals of central India, in spite of their numerical strength in certain districts, are politically so powerless. Other reasons are doubtlessly their general backwardness, their lack of education, their indifference to larger political issues and to affairs beyond their immediate concern.

Unfortunately, even those few tribal representatives who have succeeded in getting themselves elected to the legislative assemblies and to parliament are often either alienated from tribal culture and have adopted a strongly non-tribal outlook and mode of living (graduates, landlords, local chiefs), or they are so inarticulate and inexperienced in their new and strange surroundings that they cannot play an effective part in political life. No wonder that such representatives are hardly able, or scarcely try, to defend the interests of their tribal compatriots on the political platform.

Some degree of tribal consciousness and the existence of a tribal leadership can so far be found only in Chota Nagpur. Even there it is of recent date. But the tribal leaders in these areas have raised the demand for a separate state in which they would be left to themselves, could rule and govern themselves and be rid forever of any interference by non-tribals. The motives for this demand are clear: a nostalgic desire for a return to a happy past, aversion to outsiders exploiting them and interfering with their traditional way of living, and a desire for working out their own fate.

Unfortunately, the Jharkhand movement in Chota Nagpur and Orissa, as this movement is called, will always remain an unrealistic dream. The present political rulers of India view it with alarm and reject it as anti-national. Moreover, the part of India where the tribals want to establish their own state is of tantamount importance for the industrial progress of India. It is rich in coal and iron ore, and recently at least two of the giant steel factories (at Rourkela and Bhilai) have been built there.

Other factories, dams and hydro-electric projects are planned in the same area. These important industrial concerns would fit badly into a tribal state; they would on the contrary attract a large influx of non-tribal labourers and naturally shatter the isolation of the tribal population, as the latter forms itself into a welcome labour potential for these industries.

In the general breakdown of all their traditional values and traditions the aborigines of central India find their ancient religion and world outlook inadequate. While in the past their religion formed the basis of their mental equilibrium and gave them inspiration and strength in their daily life and strife, this is no more so. Their old religion cannot give a satisfactory answer to the many new problems and difficulties that beset them. Therefore, they are on the look out for a new and adequate religion.

The Hindu religion certainly presents itself as the most attractive choice. And Hinduism can muster a formidable force of, mostly informal and voluntary, missionaries among the tribals. Not only Hindu fellow villagers, but also employers, traders, money-lenders, and in particular social workers and many Government servants act as propagators of the Hindu religion. No wonder, therefore, that the Census of India 1961 when recording the religion of the 'scheduled tribes' lists only three categories for their religion: Hindus, Christians and, under 'other religions', Muslims, Jains and the members of the various tribal religions. Only those tribals fall into this category who officially declare themselves as members of a particular tribal religion, else they are returned as 'Hindus'. The number of those who declare themselves as followers of a tribal religion scarcely rises above 1.5 million.

In Chota Nagpur, where tribal consciousness was more alive and the tribal aversion to non-tribal (Hindu and Muslim) interference most articulate, large groups of tribals turned to Christianity. Christian missionary activity began in Chota Nagpur about a hundred years ago, just at the time when exploitation and oppression were most poignantly felt, and it appeared in impressive strength. Moreover, it was the religion of the British masters. Thus in the course of the past hundred years the number of Christian Oraons, Mundas and Kharias has risen to about 700,000.

Christian missionaries have in the past opened mission centres all over central and western India, but among the other tribes their success has always remained very small. In spite of occasional alarms raised by militant Hindu agencies, there are at present nowhere any mass conversions to the Christian religion, nor are they likely to take place in the future. If any mass conversions are taking place, they are to Hinduism alone.

It requires no gift of prophecy to foretell that aboriginal religion and culture are doomed to disappear from India in the near future. This disappearance of aboriginal virtues and values, and of many picturesque customs is deplorable; but an over-populated India cannot really afford setting apart large tracts of land to keep 29 million people in a tribal paradise. Naturally, the acculturation of the aborigines, their transition almost overnight from a prehistoric era to the modern industrial age, creates formidable difficulties for them and results in deep mental unrest. Here and there this disturbed state of mind already reveals itself in the rise of so-called 'messianic movements'. Such movements are also reported from Africa and the Pacific Islands among peoples experiencing similar cultural upheavals. In Chota Nagpur and in the country of the Bhils new prophets are rising—the so-called Bhagats—who promise their followers an earthly paradise and a new era of freedom from oppression.

Such prophets are not new in tribal India; about eighty years ago a certain Birsa excited many thousands of Oraons and Mundas to open revolt; and earlier still similar agitations arose among the Hos and Santals, and among the Bhils. The emergence of new religious prophets today is a signal that a dangerous situation is developing which the Government should not ignore. In the past, these agitations have often resulted in revolts which had to be suppressed by force. The aborigines of central India will not be able to retain their ancient ways of living. They are bound to lose their tribal character and will be absorbed by the new national culture which is in the making. It is to be wished that public and private agencies exert themselves to the utmost to help the aborigines pass this critical state of transition with as little physical suffering and mental heartbreak as possible.

The aboriginal tribes of India are classified as such because of certain characteristics which distinguish them from the rest of the Indian population. Most noticeable is the comparatively low standard of material culture. But also in social structure and religion they differ from the Hindus and Muslims of India. Though even in the central area the aborigines show great variety in their cultural forms, they do have certain traits of culture in common by which they can be distinguished from the rest of the Indian population.

Social Structure

FAMILY AND MARRIAGE

Various are the ways of the aborigines of central India in acquiring mates. The most usual kind is the one by which the marriage is arranged by the parents of the marrying parties. Marriage by capture is now rare, but it must have been more frequent in the past. The Hos of Singhbhum and the Savaras still practise this form of marriage, as also the Khonds; the Baigas, Gonds and Khonds perform a mock-fight during their wedding ceremonies. Marriage by trial was an established form among the Bhils; in recognition of his courage or bravery a Bhil received the right to select a girl as his wife without paying a bride-price. Among the Bonda Gadabas a girl tested her suitor by burning him with a stick.

But marriage by paying a bride-price is still the most common form of marriage. Another popular way of acquiring a mate is by service. The bridegroom has to serve his prospective parents-in-law for a certain number of years. The wedding takes place when the service is at least partly completed; the wedding expenses are paid by the bride's father. Marriage by exchange—two families exchanging daughters—is also quite frequent. Marriage by mutual consent and subsequent elopment is the usual form of marriage among the Bhilala and Gadabas, while marriage by intrusion—a girl entering the house of her lover and disclosing her intention of living with him—is also practised though not frequently.

In the choice of mates the preference for cross-cousins is very marked among the Gonds and Baigas. Levirate, a man marrying the widow of his deceased elder brother, and sororate, a man marrying his wife's younger sister, are practised by quite a few tribes in central India.

In marked contrast to Hindu custom, pre-marital sex relations are openly tolerated by those tribes that have youth dormitories; while other tribes frown upon such liberty, they may nevertheless be quite lenient in punishing such relations in their own community. Among all these tribes, however, pre-marital sex relations end with the pregnancy of the girl who in such a case is quickly married off, not always to her lover.

Though most of the tribal marriages in central India are monogamous, polygyny is prohibited by no tribe. On the contrary, it is regarded as a sign of wealth and increases a man's social prestige. Polyandry is normally not found among the tribes of central India, though it is sporadically reported in old sources relating to the Gonds, for instance. There is, however, some sort of fraternal polyandry in existence—because sex relations of a woman with her husband's younger brothers are easily condoned—among some central Indian tribes, though this is not publicly admitted.

No tribe of central India permits or even tolerates other forms of extra-marital sex relations. Adultery is usually severely punished.

Divorce is permitted by all tribes for the husband; the wife, on the other hand, may force a divorce on her husband by eloping with a lover. To make the new marriage permissible the new husband must pay a compensation; while no compensation is granted to the husband if he divorces his wife. Widow marriage is generally admitted, though Hinduised tribes aspiring to higher rank in the caste hierarchy try to prohibit it.

The family system of the tribals in central India is generally patriarchal and patrilineal. Most families are extended joint families, that is, the married sons stay together with their father in one common household.

No marriage is stable without children. A woman without children must expect a divorce or a co-wife. Children are generally welcome and treated with affection though they receive little formal education. No initiation ceremonies are performed by any tribe. Adoption is occasionally practised by childless couples.

KINSHIP ORGANISATION

Tribal endogamy is the rule among almost all the tribes; exceptions in the past were the Baigas, Gonds and Ahirs who occasionally intermarried. The same was permitted among the Hos, Santals, Mundas and Bhumij, and the Korkus and Nahals. At present, tribes of an inferior social status accept marriage partners from the superior tribes and Hindu castes. But there is no reciprocity; it is more in the form of hypergamy. A kind of territorial endogamy also exists; daughters are rarely given in marriage to men living at a great distance.

Many tribes are split into endogamous groups and sections which do not intermarry. The reason for this prohibition is generally the varying degree of Hinduisation. The more Hinduised tribal sections consider themselves superior and refuse intermarriage with the less Hinduised tribal groups. Such grades exist among the Gonds, Bhils, Bhilalas, Korkus and Mundas, etc.

Most tribes practise kinship exogamy in various degrees of

relationship. The more Hinduised a tribe is, the larger is its exogamous kinship group. Besides clan and kinship exogamy, there often also exists a kind of village or territorial exogamy which is, however, no longer strictly enforced.

Kinship relationship is of great importance in the social life of all central Indian tribes. Descent is reckoned in the male line only, the male element being predominant in all social relations of the tribes. Inheritance, too, is in the male line; and the predominance of the male line is so strong that it results among many tribes in the custom of levirate, that is, a man has the duty to marry the widow of his elder brother and to accept her children into his household. No divorced woman can take her children along; a baby at the breast must be returned to the father's family after it has been weaned. Service marriage, that is, uxorilocal marriage, is an accepted form of marriage among most tribes, but it is somewhat disreputable and after the wedding most bridegrooms try to return as soon as possible with their wives to the paternal home and village.

Relatives by kinship and affinity feel a strong mutual obligation to assist each other in all possible needs and difficulties. In fact, in times of distress a person may expect help only from his relatives. This is one of the reasons why parents are so careful in the choice of marriage partners for their sons and daughters; a marriage is more the alliance of two families than the union of two persons who love each other.

The social life of relatives is regulated by definite rules of behaviour. Rules of avoidance are to be observed which apply particularly to relatives by affinity. The social relations between parents-in-law and their daughters-in-law and sons-in-law, between brothers-in-law and sisters-in-law, are defined in minute details. This is done to prevent undue familiarity which, in a joint family, might cause serious disturbances and tensions.

On the other hand, there exists also the so-called 'joking-relationship' between certain members of the relationship, especially among those who are prospective marriage partners. Such 'joking', consisting of abuse and banter, vulgar or obscene references to sex, playing pranks, may take place between a man and his younger sister-in-law, a woman and her younger brother-in-law.

Close relatives rarely address each other by their names or by the correct terms of relationship existing between them. Husbands address their wives as 'the mother of their children', and children frequently address their father as 'uncle' and their mother as 'aunt'. This custom is called teknonymy. It is widely in use among the tribals.

Paternal uncles often occupy a privileged position, and are supposed to assist their nephews and nieces in getting married. Often it is the paternal uncle who carries the bride or the groom in the wedding procession on his shoulder.

Though many of the tribes in central India have a totemic clan organisation, clan solidarity is weakly developed. The feeling of being related is not strong among clan members. But clan exogamy is still widely observed, and intermarriage between clan members is regarded as incest and not tolerated. Even clan taboos are still observed, but they are mainly of a ritualistic nature. No person expects effective help from others on the basis of belonging to the same clan.

Relatives connected by kindred and affinity pay each other social visits, exchange presents on certain festive occasions, and attend each others' weddings and funeral feasts. Among the Gonds the Nat relatives, related by affinity, act as masters of ceremony on important occasions, such as the celebration of the solemn pig sacrifice (Laru kaj) or the re-admission of a relative into the community after excommunication.

Political Organisation

Each tribe in central India has a political organisation of its own, though often in a rather rudimentary form. The tribal solidarity is only weakly developed; the basic political unit is the village community or the clan. Sometimes several clans are united into a phratry, and village communities into a federation of villages with a common headman. In a number of tribes leading headmen had been able in the past to establish dynasties and to rise to the rank of *rajas*. But the very fact that these self-styled kings surrounded themselves everywhere with Hindu officials and eagerly adopted Hindu or Mughal customs is a proof that the institution of royalty was alien to tribal democracy. These kings ruled generally over small areas and nowhere was such a tribal prince able to unite his whole tribe under his sway.

The lowest political authority among the central Indian tribals, in consequence, is the village headman. Among the north-eastern tribes he is usually called *manjhi*. The Santals and Maler call him by this title. He and the village elders meet and talk over the village affairs. The headman is entitled to certain gifts at weddings and other feasts, and he holds rent-free land. The *manjhi* is both a civil and moral authority. In his civic functions he is assisted by a sub-headman, the *paranik*, who at least in former times looked after the fair and just distribution of the village land for cultivation. In addition he had also to provide for the welfare of guests, and he was entitled to levy contributions from the villagers for their entertainment. There is also a hereditary village priest.

In the discharge of his moral functions the *manjhi* was assisted by the *jog-manjhi*, who acted not only as the master of ceremonies at birth, wedding and funeral ceremonies, but was also responsible for the morals of the village youth.

The lowest village official is the messenger, called *gorait*. These officials, with the village priest (*naeke*) and some elders, form the village council. Over the village council is set a council consisting of the headmen of a group of villages varying in number from five to twelve. In order to show that their offices depend on the will of the community, an annual festival is held, called Magh. All the officers lay down their duties to the accompaniment of a great drinking bout of home-brewed rice beer, and a week later they are reinstalled with more drininkg.

Under this constitutional authority the traditional village life proceeds smoothly, and the villagers feel that from birth to death they are under the proper leadership ordered by their forefathers. This gives them a certain sense of security and stability.

The Mundas call their village headman *munda*. His religious counterpart is the *pahan*. A group of about twelve villages (*patti* or *parha*) are headed by a *manki* who is usually the most influential of the village headmen forming a group. The *munda* and the *pahan* are hereditary officials.

The Hos too call their village headman *munda*. In the past the whole tribe in Kolhar was divided into twenty-four *pirs* or *parganas*, headed by a *manki*. Some of the *pirs* are now sub-divided into groups ranging from five to twenty villages headed by a *manki.* In other areas the village headman is called *pradhan*, assisted by a *paramanik.*

The Hos have a tendency towards a hierarchical structure of society. Members of the families of headmen tend to intermarry among themselves, and they like to call the ordinary Hos *praja*, i.e., subjects. Nowadays those working in the mines or steel-factories and thus earning comparatively high wages insist on demanding a high bride-price for their daughters. This too leads to a certain degree of endogamy among the industrial workers, and consequently to the emergence of a new class in Ho society.

The political organisation of the Oraons is almost the same as that of the Mundas. But in addition to the *munda* and *paranik* the Oraons have a third village official called *mahato.* All these officials hold hereditary plots of land called *khunt.*

Beyond the village community the Oraons have a federal organisation of villages called *parha*, consisting of either seven, nine, twelve, twenty-one or twenty-two villages. Every year a *parha* meeting is held, called *parha jatra*, when the village communities of a *parha* settle all outstanding disputes and confirm their tribal solidarity by a big feast.

Each *parha* was originally associated with a certain clan; it had its own name, its particular territory of agricultural land, village sites, forest tracts, grazing lands, water sources and fishing pools.

Each village was associated with a particular lineage, a *bhuinhari khunt.* This lineage formed an aristocratic nucleus while the strangers who came later to settle in the village were regarded as of lower rank. The ownership of the farm land in each village was vested in the *bhuinhari khunt.*

The Maler have a rather elaborate political organisation. The village community is directed by a headman. But village communities within a radius of seven to twelve miles constitute a regional unit, presided by a regional headman or *sardar* who is also the president of the council of village headmen under his jurisdiction. This traditional Maler organisation is ignored by the modern Government administration and is therefore degenerating into a powerless institution.

The Bhumij, on the other hand, were in the early decades of the 19th century ruled by petty chieftains, called *rajas.* They proudly claimed to have exercised independent authority over their subjects for more than fifty generations. These *rajas* are rather like big landlords who claimed Rajput rank and adopted many Hindu customs, while the ordinary Bhumij retained their tribal customs.

The Gonds are divided into different ranks which usually do not intermarry. The highest rank is claimed by the Raj Gonds or the aristocracy; then follow the Dhur Gonds or common peasantry, while the Pardhans and Ojhas occupy the lowest rank and are often treated as outcastes and untouchables. The Pardhans are the musicians and bards of the Gonds, and the Ojhas their priests and soothsayers.

But the basic political unit of the Gonds is the village community. A Gond village consists of a collection of scattered hamlets (*tola*), from two to twelve in number. The village headman is called *patel*, *mandal* or *bhoi*. He is assisted by some elders of the village in settling the village affairs. Not infrequently, the Gond headman rules also over people of other tribes and castes belonging to the village but living usually in separate hamlets.

The political organisation of the Marias in Bastar District is strongly developed. The members of the tribe have a high respect for authority. The whole area of the Marias is divided into districts (*parganas*) with *a pargana manjhi* (headman). He represents his people before Government officials and other outsiders. His office is hereditary. In each *pargana* are a number of villages with a *patel* as headman. Each village consists of several hamlets (*para*) with a *mukhya* (headman) for each *para*. Each headman of the *para*, village or *pargana* has his council. The issues which the *para mukhya* cannot settle with his council go to the higher authority of the village *patel*, and on an appeal may reach the *pargana manjhi*. He is the highest authority in the tribe. The village *patel* with his elders also distributes the plots of land for cultivation each year before the monsoon sets in.

The political organisation of the Khonds is similar; their village headman is called *abbaye* or *malika*. A group of village communities is headed by a *mutha malik*, and above him there is a *sardar*. A *mutha* consists of a group of village communities varying in number between six and thirty-three.

The Porojas live in closed villages; they have a headman for each village who is appointed by all the villagers. In former times his appointment had to be approved by the landlord. Sometimes the landlord appointed a man of his own choice as headman; but without the consent of the villagers the headman was powerless. The headman decides matters under dispute with the assistance of the village council. The council meeting is held in the centre of the village under a pipal tree or a wild mango tree. The headman sits on a platform on a raised stone slab, while the council members take their seats on large stones lying around the tree. Women have to remain standing.

The Savaras have three classes of which the *gamang* is the civil head of a village. He represents his people before the Government. In pre-British times he was a real chief; the British curtailed his powers severely. He has not recovered his power since independence.

The *buya* is the religious head of the village. He is equal in rank to the *gamang*. The two classes intermarry. The *buya* may delegate his priestly functions to practical and officiating *buyas*.

The third class is that of the *parjas*. They are the subjects of the two upper classes. The upper classes will take *parja* girls in marriage, but will not give their daughters to *parja* men.

The Bhils in western central India generally live in scattered homesteads or loosely grouped hamlets. Several such hamlets are united into a village which is headed by a *patel* or *tarvi*. His office is hereditary. He is assisted by some elders in the neighbourhood. The Gujarat Bhils call their village *gam*; it consists of three to forty families living in huts widely scattered. The village headman is called *vasawo*. He has an assistant called *pradhan*.

Among the Chodhris of Gujarat a council is established in each village, with the headman as its president. Each village community is independent. But in 1949 the leading Chodhris formed higher councils (*chhora panch*) which consist of ten to twenty-seven village communities. And over these *chhora panch* is a supreme council (*mukhia panch*) whose president is the chief leader of the whole tribe. But this new organisation is not generally recognised by the older generation.

The tribal council is generally in control in all the tribes of Gujarat. It is a democratic body though influential members can often have their way in it as few dare oppose them. The Dublas, for instance, have such a traditional village council. But over the village councils of a district is a district council. Each council is headed by a hereditary president, usually the village headman.

The Gamits have only village councils which regulate the life of the community. The president of the council has two assistants. The influence of the councils is, however, gradually breaking down and Gamits who are not satisfied with the decisions of the village council may appeal to the courts.

The Naikdas have village councils; the *chhora panch* (of *taluka* level) exercises authority over all the village councils of a sub-district. The authority is strictly a tribal authority and functions side by side with the parallel institution established by the Government, a *panchayat* system which has authority over all the different communities residing in a village.

Religion

THE HIGH-GOD

The high-god of the central Indian tribes is known mainly by Aryan names: Thakur deo, Burha deo, Bara deo, Bhagwan, Dharmesh, Param deo, Narayan deo, Parmeshwar, Parmatma, etc. Only the Mundari-speaking tribes (Santals, Mundas, Hos, Bhumij, Birhors, Turis and Asurs) call him Sing Bonga (*sing* means sun, *bonga,* originally the moon, now a spirit). The high-god is indeed often identified with the sun. Sing Bonga, however, is probably originally the bright moon, but under totemistic influence he became the sun. The Mundas have still another name for him; they call him Haram, 'the Old One'.

The high-god has no wife or brother; he does not require food, like the lower deities and spirits. He is saluted at sunrise. During public sacrifices he is addressed first. The only sacrifice of homage, however, which the Mundas perform, is addressed to him. But also sacrifices of propitiation and petition are directed to him. He accepts with preference white animals (cocks, goats, bulls). The sacrificer faces the east when he officiates. In divination the high-god is invoked first, as also in thanksgiving ceremonies. In the funeral service he is mentioned as the master over life and death. He is reproached in misfortune, and called to witness in oathtaking. A periodical sacrifice is performed in his honour every third, fifth, or twelfth year. The priest officiating in this sacrifice is the head of the celebrating family, not the village priest. Yet the supreme god is in many respects a distant god, benevolent but rather indifferent to the joys and sorrows of man, or he is indeed powerless to protect them against the malice of the evil forces (*bongas*).

THE MINOR DEITIES

The minor deities of the central Indian tribes are of various types. One category could be called mountain or vegetation gods. Thus the Santals, Mundas, Hos and Bhumij venerate Marang Buru (the great mountain); the Oraons and Kharias call the same god Barnda, the Savaras and Korkus Dongar deo (hill-god). This mountain-god is mainly a vegetation and rain god (the dark moon?). He is inferior to the high-god and sun-god. The Hos venerate a forest deity, Desauli, who has his fixed abode in the village grove, and protects his clients from evil spirits, diseases and epidemics and sends rain and abundant harvests.

Each village has its special god represented in a stone slab put up in a grove or under a tree. This deity is worshipped mainly after the harvest through public worship, much feasting and drinking; sexual excesses also occasionally take place at this feast.

These tribes also worship female deities; prominent among them is the Earth-mother. Among the Mundas, Hos and Bhumij she is called Chandu Omol (the moon, wife of the sun-god). The Oraons venerate her under the name Chala Pachho—the old lady. She is a village goddess. The Gonds and Baigas call her Dharti mata or Prithwi mata—the earth-mother.

The tribal pantheon also includes house and family gods. It is further believed that the spirits of the deceased relatives take their abode in the house in which they formerly lived (*ading*). The ancestors are venerated and offerings addressed to them on special feast days. Many of the tribes perform a double burial. The second burial should be at the ancestral village. Stone or wooden monuments are erected there to the deceased relatives. The tribals also perform protective rites at the funeral against the return of the spirits.

Sacrificial victims are mainly animals, such as cattle, goat, fowl and pig. Occasionally even human sacrifices are performed. The Mundas call them *ondoka*. The victim is killed in the jungle; only a finger and some blood is taken and buried with prayers in the *ading*. The Khonds of Orissa performed until the last century numerous human sacrifices, called *mehra*. They were found necessary to increase fertility in house, stable and field. At present they have been replaced by buffalo sacrifices.

The central Indian tribes also make offerings of liquor and of morsels of food to the ancestors. They burn clarified butter and incense in these offerings. Coconuts, too, are often given in sacrifice.

MAGIC AND ANIMISM

The central Indian tribes believe that every person has several souls, such as the name, shadow, life spirit (*jiw*) and breath (*atma*). They also believe in a rebirth of some of these souls, either in the same family or outside it. Spirits not reborn or not laid to rest by appropriate rites become dangerous to the survivors. They cause sickness, misfortune or death.

The tribes also believe in the existence of many evil spirits who have never been human beings. There are also spirits animating trees, rocks, rivers and springs, hills and mountains. They may harm a human being if they are offended or if offerings due to them are omitted. If a person gets sick or has a misfortune, or rather a number of misfortunes within a short time, diviners, soothsayers, exorcists and magicians are consulted to discover what deity or spirit has been offended and how to appease it. In almost every village community shamans can be found who easily fall into a trance. The tribals believe that the gods and spirits take possession of them and speak and prophesy through them.

They are firm believers in the efficacy of witchcraft and magic. Black magic can only be counteracted by white magic. Witches are mostly women. When found out they are often killed.

ETHICS

The primitive tribes of central India are generally known for their honesty, truthfulness and generosity. This is so because they firmly believe that God has given men the order to be honest, truthful and generous; that he rewards them for their good deeds and punishes them for their sins, in this life and in the life after death.

If sins, i.e., breaches of the moral code, as instituted by the supreme god, are not punished by him, this will certainly be done by the minor deities and spirits of whom the tribals are generally much more afraid than of the supreme god. Any misfortune, sickness or death is attributed to the malice or revengefulness of a god or spirit who was offended either by a breach of the moral code or of one of the numerous rules and taboos of ritual behaviour.

Many of the tribes are known for acts of violence. Kidnapping of women for marriage, rape, murder in revenge, murder for adultery, murder in drunkenness, robbery and cattle lifting, all these are crimes of which the tribals are often accused. In areas where the tribals have been displaced and reduced to landless labourers or prevented from pursuing their old traditional way of living, or where they have been much oppressed by rapacious landlords and moneylenders, such crimes are indeed not infrequent. The Bhils, who have suffered much from the land-hungry Rajputs and from dishonest moneylenders, are known for their criminal propensities. Even now the frequency of crime in certain areas is higher than in Chicago. The Minas in Rajasthan are another example, as also some tribes in Gujarat. Sometimes there were uprisings of the tribals against their exploiters with murders, robbery and rape. Such revolts were reported from Bihar, eastern and western Madhya Pradesh, Gujarat, Maharashtra, Orissa, Bengal and Assam. Usually these revolts were quickly suppressed by the police or even the military. But such crimes are more reactions to intolerable economic and social exploitation than results of criminal propensities.

In more isolated cases crimes might be the results of religious and magic beliefs. Human sacrifices for fertility of women and fields, head-hunting, human sacrifices for beginning great and important undertakings, the building of bridges, dams, houses and places, etc, and the wide field of black magic and witch-hunting are now punished severely by modern jurisprudence, but are widely considered as justified defence actions or proper forms of punishment according to the moral code of the tribals.

THE TRIBES IN CENTRAL INDIA

ANCIENT ARYAN-SPEAKING TRIBES

It was pointed out in Chapter II that the central Indian tribes fall, according to their manner of speech, into four different categories; one group—in which the most primitive tribes are found—must have adopted Aryan speech very early; a second group comprises those tribes speaking Mundari; the third group speaking a Dravidian language and a fourth group, of either Munda or Dravidian origin, having adopted Aryan dialects comparatively recently. This latter group we may ignore and deal with the tribes individually as belonging either to the Munda or Dravidian group.

It is significant that the tribes claiming to be the oldest and earliest settlers in north-eastern India now speak an Aryan tongue. Generally they are also more primitive in material culture and in social structure. They are more addicted to a hunting nomadism and to the collection of jungle produce than the two other linguisitc groups. Their methods of cultivation are slipshod and primitive. There will be occasion to point out some more significant differences.

The fact that these earliest settlers in central India speak an Aryan dialect suggests strongly that they have adopted their present language before the Mundari and Dravida-speaking tribes arrived in the central region. This assumption is also supported by cultural evidence. Many of their tribal myths reveal that they have been subjected to considerable Hindu influence of an ancient type [S. Fuchs (1952), p. 607]. This fact has of course often been obscured in present times by a second wave of Hindu influence, strongly supported this time by Government and private welfare agencies as by modern school education.

To this group almost certainly belong also a few tribes who, secondarily, adopted either a Munda or Dravidian dialect from their neighbours speaking these languages. To these tribes belong, among others, the Birhors, Korwas and Koras, the Maler and Juangs.

Of the Aryan-speaking tribes, the Baigas are possibly the most ancient survivors who still retain a tribal conscience. They practised, until recent times, and in places (Baiga Chak) still do so, a shifting cultivation of a primitive type, using only the hoe and abjuring the plough. Analogous to the custom of some aboriginal Australian tribes, the Baigas, too, permit the marriage between a man and his classificatory granddaughter, or a woman and her classificatory grandson. Unions between direct kin are of course excluded. The Baigas, further, perform a pig sacrifice that closely resembles the famous *ashvamedha* (horse-sacrifice) of the Vedic Aryans [S. Fuchs (1960), pp. 427–449; V. Elwin (1939), pp. 403-7]. They live in close economic and cultural symbiosis with the Gonds with whom in the past they even intermarried. At present the Gonds refuse interdining and intermarrying with the Baigas, since they have ambitions of rising in the Hindu caste hierarchy.

The Kamars, a small tribe of 11,795 (in 1961) in all, are located in Chhattisgarh (Madhya Pradesh) and are thus distant neighbours of the Baigas. Described by J. Bell in 1876 as wild hunters and foodgatherers, living in caves, they are today shifting cultivators and collectors of jungle produce. Until quite recently they were without cattle and buffaloes, and only kept pigs, some goats and poultry. Their social organisation is quite simple. It is based on the local group system, though a clan organisation with some slight traces of totemism can also be found. It appears from the identity of the Kamar clan names with those of the Gonds, that they adopted totemism from the Gonds from whom they seem to have borrowed also many other customs pertaining to the important phases of life, birth, marriage and death. Hinduism, too, has made deep inroads into their cultural life [S.C. Dube (1951)].

The Pardhans (94,472 in 1961) are the minstrels, bards and servants of the Gonds. It is, however, doubtful if they are of Gond origin as they claim. At any rate, they speak a Hindi dialect. The word '*pardhan*' is of Sanskrit origin and signifies a 'chief'. In Mandla District, they are also known as 'Pathari', persons who recite the religious songs of the Gonds. They are found mainly in Madhya Pradesh and Berar. Economically they depend much on the Gonds who look down on them as social inferiors. They treat them as impure. The Pardhans eat almost any kind of food, including beef, pork and the flesh of rats and mice. They practise levirate. They are averse to hard work in the fields and prefer to earn their living as singers and musicians of the Gonds [S. Hivale (1946)].

A similar tribe are the Ojhas (less than 10,000) living in the eastern tracts of the Gond area. They act as soothsayers and minstrels of the Gonds and Korkus from whom they receive their livelihood. They lead a wandering life and do some hunting and food collecting in the jungle as a supplementary occupation. Gonds and Korkus regard them as impure and do not interdine with them. They eat beef and pork, but no vermin. They too practise the custom of levirate.

Another tribe living in the habitat of the Korkus and Bhils on both sides of the Narbada valley are the Nahals (about 25,000). In the Census of 1961 they appear as a sub-division of the Korkus. But they have a language of their own; at least remnants of it are still in existence. This language was neither Dravidian nor Mundarian. The Nahals are an impure tribe of field labourers, graziers, village watchmen and forest workers, with an old reputation for cattle-lifting and robbery. They eat any kind of food. They have totemic exogamous septs and observe totem taboos and totem worship.

The Agarias (11,761 in 1961) reside on the Maikal range of the Mandla, Raipur and Bilaspur districts. They are aboriginal iron-smelters speaking an Aryan dialect. It is not known whether they are related to the Asuras, the iron workers of Chota Nagpur. But they do not seem to have any connection with the Lohars, the iron workers of the Hindu areas. The Agarias are organised in totemic clans; totemistic beliefs and practices are still much alive among them. They even believe in descent from the totems. Their striking mythology centres around their occupation of primitive iron smelting and working. The Gonds treat them as a socially inferior and impure community [V. Elwin (1942)].

Their counterparts in Chota Nagpur are the Asuras (5,798) whose iron-smelting occupation sets them apart from the Mundas and also the Dravida-speaking cultivators though they now speak Mundari. They, too, are socially inferior to the cultivating tribes. Physically they are rather short, with heavy broad noses, thick lips, coarse features and a very dark complexion. Their totemism and mythology play an important role in their socio-religious life. S. C. Roy [(1917), p. 567] found individual totemism among them, but a later observer failed to detect it. It would have been the only instance of its kind in India.

In Orissa the members of the Pentia tribe (9,656 in 1961) are black-smiths by profession. They appear to have the same function as the Agarias in Gondawana and the Asuras in Chota Nagpur. They use the double bellows which they work by foot. In the past they were also iron smelters and dug for iron ore in suitable places. In present times they find it easier to fashion their articles from scrap iron. The Pentias are now much Hinduised, but they are still numbered among the 'scheduled tribes'. Because they work their bellows by foot, they are lower in social status than the ironsmiths working their bellows by hand.

In Orissa as well as in some regions of West Bengal there exists a caste of brass workers who are obviously of tribal origin. They call themselves Dhokra Kamar or by other names. They are itinerant artisans who stay in one village as long as they find work. Collecting broken brass utensils they turn the metal, through a process of *cirre perdue*, of lost wax process, into vessels, grain measures, toys and money boxes. These brass workers have two endogamous sections; one uses bees' wax, the other *sal* resin (Shorea robusta) for the *cirre perdue* process. Each section considers itself superior to the other. In effect, the brass workers are now a low artisan Hindu caste, though unmistakably of tribal origin. However, the Hindu brass workers do not recognise the Dhokra Kamars as their social equals.

The Juangs or Patuas (21,890 in 1961) are probably too primitive to belong to the Munda race although they speak Mundari. They inhabit the recesses of the Orissa hills and are very shy. They worship their own forest and village gods, but have no official village priests like the neighbouring tribes. Any adult member of the tribe may perform the religious ceremonies. They offer animal sacrifices and vegetable food to deities residing in the jungle, in the sky and in the earth. They eat beef and carrion. It appears that in former times the Juangs had a territorial system which was exogamous; but they have adopted the clan system of their neighbours which, however, interferes somewhat with their territorial system. Today the clans of the Juangs are patrilineal, strongly totemic and governed by the usual regulations. The Juangs are widely known for their former practice of dressing in leaves. In the past the Juangs lived by hunting, the collection of jungle produce and a little shifting cultivation. Though now forced to plough their fields, they supplement their livelihood by work in bamboo and by selling baskets, wickerboxes and winnowing fans. With the money thus earned they buy cloth, iron tools and rice.

The Pandos (92,369 in 1961) reside in the eastern districts of Madhya Pradesh. They claim descent from the Pandavas of Mahabharata fame. Their main occupation is collection of jungle products, hunting, agriculture and basketry. They prefer living in the forest areas.

The Pandos are divided into two endogamous sub-sections the Uttarhars and the Surgujias. The latter consider themselves superior in rank. Each sub-section is again divided into a number of exogamous clans, called *gotis*. They are totemistic and bear plant or animal names. There are about eighty of them. All clans are of equal social status.

The Pandos speak a dialect of their own; it is Chhattisgarhi Hindi with an admixture of Korwa and Oriya words. They are short in stature, of light to dark brown complexion with scanty body hair.

The Korwas (67,062), too, speak a Munda language. But they are mainly food-collectors and hunters, and very primitive and indifferent cultivators. They trade in forest products, honey, bees' wax and stick lack. They live in Surguja. Jashpur and Palamau districts (former native states). Physically they are very dark, have heavy flat noses depressed at the root, thick lips, heavy jaws and some measure of prognathism. Totemism is not strong in the tribe. They worship a goddess, Khuria Rani, who demands the sacrifice of many goats and buffaloes.

The Maler (55,634 in 1961), now speaking a Dravidian language and living in the upper parts of the Rajmahal hills, have, like the Juangs originally, no exogamous clans and observe only kinship exogamy. Marriage is forbidden within the third degree on both sides. Sexual morals are strict in theory but lax in practice, particularly in the dormitories in which the unmarried of both sexes sleep. Marriage is usually by bride-price in which a pig is sacrificed. A menstruating woman is under a variety of taboos which also apply to her husband, who thus shares the pollution of childbirth.

The Maler are very reluctant to accept the amenities of civilisation and have so far managed to preserve a large amount of independence. They grow various crops by slash-and-burn cultivation. Maize is their most important crop; its cultivation is regarded as a sacred activity and is accompanied by many rites and sacrifices. They also subsist on game and the wild products of the jungle.

Each village has a hereditary headman, who is at the same time its religious leader, and one or more priests, a shaman and a diviner. The sun is regarded as the supreme deity but receives no cult; many other deities have shrines and cults and are believed to help them if the proper offerings are performed [L.P. Vidyarthi (1963)].

There is a more Hinduised section of the Maler, called Mal-Paharias, living in the lower levels of the Rajmahal hills (61,129 in 1961). They speak a closely allied dialect of the Kurukhi language or a corrupt form of Bengali. Since long in contact with the people of the plains, they employ more advanced methods of cultivation, using ploughs and bullocks to till the small tablelands of the plateau. They raise substantial dry crops. But many have no fields and take employment as field labourers. Prolonged contact with the Hindu population has led to the adoption of many Hindu customs, such as child marriage, polygamy and the usual food taboos. They cremate their dead. Their religion is a low form of Hinduism with many remnants of their old tribal religion.

The Koras (21,013), though now speaking a Dravidian language, might have originally belonged to the pre-Dravidian races as they always preferred a nomadic and foodgathering life. Even now they have retained their nomadic habits to a large extent, being employed largely in digging and road-work, for which reason they might be described as an earth-working caste.

Another such tribe are the Birjias (4,029 in 1961), found in the Palamau District of Bihar. Some have now settled as cultivators in the valleys of the south, but the bulk still live in groups of two or three families on the spurs of the highest hills. They practise shifting cultivation, planting the seeds in small holes dug in the ground with a pointed bamboo stick. They wander from hill to hill and supplement their diet by roots and herbs, and barter jungle produce for grain, salt and tobacco.

THE MUNDARI-SPEAKING TRIBES

The Mundari-speaking tribes have been variously designated by anthropologists as pre-Dravidians, Kolarians, Dravidians, Australoids, Nishadics, and Austrics. It has been admitted by several anthropologists, like A.C. Haddon, S.S. Sarkar and P.C. Basu, that the Mundas differ racially from the Dravidian-speaking tribes, like the Oraons, for instance.

At present the principal home of the Munda languages is Chota Nagpur, the plateau and the adjoining areas. It is believed that the Munda languages once occupied a larger part of north-eastern India and that also tribes which racially did not belong to the Mundas adopted this language.

The racial origin of the Mundari-speaking tribes is still an unsolved problem. R. von Heine-Geldern attempted in a series of articles to prove that though the Munda tribes were racially and culturally mixed, their dominant type was Mongoloid, that this component was brought to India by the Neolithic Austro-Asiatics who came from the east, that the Austro-Asiatics were the bearers of the shouldered celt, and that they had been strongly influenced by the Austronesians, with the result that the Austro-Asiatics produced in India the megalithic elements of the eastern variety and a blend between the two characteristic forms of adzes—the shouldered adze of the Austro-Asiatics and the quadrangular adze of Austronesians.

This theory was called into question by several critics. D.N. Majumdar, for instance, maintained that the general physical make-up of the tribes in Chota Nagpur did not suggest a Mongolian infusion, that it was hard to assert a general miscegenation on the basis of a few stray cases of Mongoloid features, and that the various Munda tribes could easily be affiliated to the same proto-Australoid stock as the other tribes and might not be independent races or even types. In 1943, G.T. Bowles questioned the linguistic and racial links of the Munda tribes with the Mon-Khmer peoples and languages. Finally, A. H. Dani asserted that the archaeological evidence available in India hardly justified the assumption of a link between the Austro-Asiatics and Austronesians on the basis of certain adze forms and the megaliths.

However, these critics have not been able to disavow convincingly the assumption of an eastern origin of the Munda tribes. The existence of tribes in Assam (the Khasis) and on the Nicobar Islands, speaking similar languages, is too strong a proof for the eastern origin of the Munda tribes. Majumdar's argument, moreover, overlooks the fact that the Munda tribes lived for centuries in close contact with the pre-Dravidian tribes and also with the Dravida-speaking Oraons, and that consequently racial mixtures and mutual cultural borrowings may have taken place, thus to some extent blurring the original racial and cultural differences.

It is, therefore, safe to assume that the Munda race constitutes a different and independent population group.

One of the most important tribes of this group is undoubtedly the Munda tribe (1,014,689 in 1961). At present the main stock of the Mundas is found in Bihar, particularly in Chota Nagpur. They are a vigorous and fast-growing tribe. While in 1931 Bihar returned 474,207 Mundas, their number had grown in 1941 to 530,676 and in 1961 to 628,931.

The traditions of the tribe do not give us any reliable information about the origin of the Mundas. They relate some relatively late migrations in Bihar and the adjoining states, but it has not been possible to identify the places and regions which are mentioned in these traditions. They also relate that the Mundas migrated several times to other regions because of the Oraons who in the time after their arrival began to multiply exceedingly so that the Mundas felt crowded and moved away. A Munda legend also records a sanguinary struggle of the Mundas with the iron-smelting Asuras, earlier settlers in Chota Nagpur. The Asuras were defeated and had to leave their land to the Mundas. They retreated to the western parts of Chota Nagpur.

The name 'Munda' is a Sanskrit word and means 'headman'. It is a honorific title given by the Hindus and it became the tribal name. How the Mundas originally called themselves is unknown, perhaps Ho, now the name of another tribe, because 'hor' means 'man' in Mundari.

The Mundas are primitive cultivators. Their staple crop is rice, but as secondary crops they grow other grains, millets and pulses. Each farmer is as far as possible self-sufficient, growing all the varieties of foodstuff that he requires to feed his family. This is getting more and more difficult, for Munda families are large and adult sons want their own fields. Land scarcity has been the great problem for the Mundas since the beginning of the last century. The land scarcity was still more aggravated by the inroads of Hindu and Muslim cultivators, producing better crops and ready to pay higher taxes. Much valuable land was given away in misplaced generosity to Hindu priests and courtiers by their own *rajas* and chiefs, and later more land was lost in the Land Settlements of the British administration. But the individual Munda farmers too were responsible for the loss of their land, by their own improvidence, excessive drinking, excessive expenditure for social celebrations, religious feasts and for the appeasement of evil spirits.

The Mundas, however, did not meekly submit to the loss of their land. Between 1789 and 1832 they revolted seven times in the hope of regaining their lost land and of expelling the hated foreigners, Hindus, Muslims as well as British officials.

All their revolts were suppressed by the more powerful weapons and the better strategy of the British army. Finally, the Mundas put their trust in a messianic leader, Birsa Bhagwan, who posed as their saviour and promised to deliver them from the yoke of the foreigners and restore their pristine independence. This messianic movement also failed and Birsa Bhagwan died in June 1900 of cholera while in jail awaiting his trial for an armed revolt.

Disappointed after so many failures, large numbers of Mundas turned for help to Christian missionaries who at this time appeared in Chota Nagpur. Today 197,976 or 19.50 per cent of the Mundas are Christians.

As is customary among large tribes in general, the Mundas too are split into three different sections: (1) the Bhumij Mundas, who are held to be highest in rank because many of them are in the possession of large lands and have in their society some *rajas* and estate owners. Some of them have been able to intermarry with Rajputs. (2) The second class is formed by the members of the ordinary Munda tribe; and (3) the third class by the Khangar Mundas, whom the two upper classes regard as impure because according to old traditions their forefathers once ate unclean meat. But most probably the degraded status of the Khangar Mundas is due to intermarriage with a member of an inferior tribe.

Besides these three sub-divisions, there are a number of others which are equally endogamous; but they are of equal social status. Each sub-division is split into a number of exogamous septs which are totemic. Totemic rites and taboos are not strictly observed. The reasons for this are disputed; it could be that totemism had declined among the Mundas, or, as is also possible, the Mundas had originally no totemism, but had adopted it later, probably in Chota Nagpur. This adoption was however incomplete.

The highest object of veneration for the Mundas is Sing Bonga, the supreme god represented by the sun. But their most important and most venerated deity is the mountain god (Marang Buru). The priests (*pahan*) are members of the tribe.

The Hos (499,144 in 1961), also called Larka Kols, consider themselves the highest of the Munda tribes. 'Ho' is a Munda word meaning 'man'. In former times the Hos intermarried with the Mundas and also with the Santals and Bhumij, with whom they share a number of clan names. Their main habitat is the Singhbhum District, a region of Chota Nagpur more fertile than other districts. For this reason the Hos have always fiercely defended their territory against any intruders from outside. In this they have succeeded better than the rest of the Mundas.

The Hos are generally short of stature and dark complexioned. They have short, broad and flat noses, small and dark eyes, wavy to curly hair, scanty beard and hair, a narrow chin, medium sized lips and small, finely developed ears. Agriculture is their mainstay though their methods of cultivation are still primitive. For lack of land many Hos are forced to work in mines and steel factories recently opened in their areas. Their social structure conforms to that of the other Munda tribes, though totemism is weakly developed. The Hos speak a Munda language. They, as well as the Mundas and Birhor, have youth dormitories, or at least had them in the past.

The Kols (128,471 in 1961), from whom the early ethnographers of north-eastern central India coined the term 'Kolarian', by which they meant the Mundas as well as the Dravida-speaking tribes, reside today for the most part in the Mirzapur District along the Ganges, in the Jabalpur and Mandla districts of Madhya Pradesh and in the Baghelkhand tracts of the Vindhyas. The whole tribe is now largely Hinduised and has lost not only its Munda idiom, but also its former social structure and tribal religion. Outside the Munda area the Kols have adopted plough cultivation and differ little from their Hindu neighbours except in a more frequent practice of sorcery, and in the propitiation of the local gods in preference to those of the Hindu pantheon.

The Kols have both a territorial and a clan system side by side. If their clans were ever totemic they have lost this character completely. In the eyes of the Hindus the Kols form a low caste, employed mainly as farm labourers and village servants, at the most as tenants on the fields of their landlords.

Still more advanced in the process of Hindu acculturation and of much higher social rank than the Kols are the Kharwars (111,097 in 1961), probably because a number of local chiefs belong to this tribe. They have managed to be accepted into Rajput society by paying very heavy dowries for Rajput brides. The Kharwars appear to have spread from the south-eastern part of the Chota Nagpur plateau northwards and down into south Bihar. Here their rank seems to depend much on their possession of land. Those who hold large estates claim to be Rajputs, and the middle classes employ Brahmins for religious functions. But for a few and important tribal ceremonies which they have retained, they call in priests (*baiga*) belonging to any of the local tribes, even Korwas. Only few of them speak the tribal language; most of them have adopted the local dialects of Hindi.

The Bhumij (307,779 in 1961) are another branch of the Mundas. They have spread from the central home of the race to West Bengal and the districts of Manbhum and Singhbhum. The tribe is almost entirely Hinduised, except in the western parts of their habitat where the Munda language is still current and they even intermarry with the Mundas of the uplands and often call themselves by that name. But the farther away they have settled from Chota Nagpur the more they have abandoned tribal religion and the Munda language. The land holding class in particular has adopted Hindu customs of a strictly orthodox type; they treat Vaishnava ascetics with special reverence. In the wealthier families, the practice of calling themselves Rajputs or Kshatriyas and dropping their ancestral connection altogether is growing. The less advanced Bhumij, however, still worship their old tribal gods and employ their own village priests (*laya*) on all occasions. But even the Hinduised Bhumij permit divorce and widow marriage though this goes against the custom of the Hindu high castes.

Of equal or even higher rank are the Cheros (31,404 in 1961), probably because they are even more completely Hinduised than the Kharwars. They have the same tradition of having been expelled from a kingdom of their own in the south of Bihar. They were the last to leave the plain for the plateau, and are accepted as a respectable Hindu caste. A small section in the interior, however, still keeps to the jungle and breeds tussar moths, a source of income which makes them impure to their Hinduised caste fellows. Long periods of settled life, combined with frequent intermarriage with Rajput families and others, have in fact made the land-holding body of the Cheros a different and distinct community, claiming the rank of Chauhan Rajputs. A dynasty of Chero chiefs ruled in Palamau for over two centuries. But the totemic septs of their primitive section prove their connection with both the general Munda race and, perhaps more specifically, with the Kharias.

The latter (224,781 in 1961) believe that they came up to Chota Nagpur from the Orissa State of Mayurbhanj. The Kharias have three sub-divisions, the Hill, Dhelki and Dudh Kharias. The Hill Kharias, especially those who remained in Manbhum, are among the most shy and unsettled of all the Munda tribes. They were so shy that in the past when a stranger settled within sight, they moved off, a tendency welcomed by their neighbours who then occupied their sites. They practise a crude form of shifting cultivation and are adepts in the collection of honey and bees' wax, which they barter for salt, tobacco and grain. They hunt with bows and arrows, sticks and spears. Their Hindu neighbours believe that they possess exceptional powers of magic, applicable against both man and beast. Their language is a dialect of Mundari.

The Turis (113,291 in 1961), in Bihar and West Bengal, are now practically an impure functional caste engaged in the making of baskets, mats, brushes and other bamboo articles. They also do farm work. On racial grounds Risley considered them a Hinduised offshoot of the Munda race. Moreover, they speak a dialect derived from Mundari, and have a number of totemic, exogamous septs bearing Munda names. Their religion, too, is similar to that of the Mundas; they venerate the Munda deities Baranda Deo and Bura Deo. They act in many villages as priests (*pahan*). But they also worship the Hindu gods and many have joined the Shiva-Narayan sect. They interdine with Mundas and Oraons, but refuse to eat beef and abstain from liquor.

The Bhuiyas (156,878 in 1961) are a widely distributed and populous tribe, found mainly in Orissa, but also in Bengal, Bihar, Madhya Pradesh and other states. Since *bhuiya* means 'land holder', various tribes might have assumed this title, and it consequently does not signify a tribe in the proper sense of the word. But S. C. Roy stated that the Bhuiyas are rightly included among the Munda tribes on cultural grounds, although racially they do not differ much from the Dravida-speaking tribes either. They, too, have a hill section and a much larger Hinduised plains section.

The Pauri or Hill Bhuiyas have village, but no clan, exogamy, in fact they have no totemic septs. They have, however, the youth dormitory system of the other Chota Nagpur tribes. They are mainly foodgatherers and primitive cultivators. In the past the Hill Bhuiyas were much dreaded for their sudden raids into the plains.

Most of the Bhuiya sub-sections in the plains, however, have managed to gain a comparatively high social status and rank with the Rajputs as one of the dominant cultivating castes. They are nearly completely Hinduised and rigorously observe all restrictions concerning food and social intercourse with other castes. But they still have their own tribal priests and venerate the old tribal gods in sacred groves, besides the Hindu gods for whose worship they employ Brahmins. Where traces of totemism are found in the social divisions of the Bhuiyas of the plains, they are not accompanied by exogamous restrictions, which suggests a borrowing rather than a survival of totemism.

They practise polygamy, and allow widow marriage and divorce. In contrast to the Hill Bhuiyas they have no dormitory system and marry off their children when they are quite young.

The largest of the Mundari-speaking tribes is that of the Santals, who call themselves, like the Mundas, 'village headmen'—Manjhi. In 1961 they numbered 3,154,107 individuals. In fact, after the Gonds, they are the largest tribal community in India. The Santals are the most easternly of the Munda tribes, spread over parts of Bihar, Bengal, Orissa and Uttar Pradesh. For about a century, they have been rather restless and ever in search of land for cultivation. Their exploitation by Hindus and Muslims and an unsympathetic land administration by the British led in the middle of the last century (1855) to the so-called Santal rebellion which took the British over a year to suppress and resulted in much bloodshed. The eastward movement of the Santal expansion is still in progress. Many Santals have found employment in the tea-gardens of Assam and the Terai.

About their origin little is known; but racially and linguistically they seem to belong to the Munda tribes. Since the tribe is so large and spread over a vast area, it is not surprising that rather conflicting statements are made about the racial and cultural features of the Santals. Physically, they possess very primitive traits; they have short, broad, flat noses with a sunken root, thick and protruding lips, a dark complexion, and wavy sometimes curly hair. Their social organisation is definitely totemistic. Originally the Santals had twelve clans which in the course of time were sub-divided into numerous sub-clans (*khuts*) which are, however, not always totemic.

Though rather good cultivators today, they still take a great interest in hunting and faithfully perform a ceremonial hunt once a year. They still worship their tribal gods, especially the Sun-god and a mountain god. Each family, moreover, has its own domestic god and in addition a secret god whose name is known only to the head of the family, never to the women of the house. The name is handed on from father to the eldest son only.

Akin to the Santals is a small tribe called Mahali (27,233), which is at home in Chota Nagpur (chiefly in the Manbhum and Ranchi districts) and in West Bengal. Judging from the names of its sub-divisions, the tribe is merely a branch of the Santals. Forced by economic necessity to do menial jobs and to make baskets for sale, which the Santals consider as degrading, they were outcasted by them and thus became an independent tribe. In Bihar they speak Mundari, in Bengal a corrupt form of Bengali. The Mahalis profess a Hinduism strongly intermixed with tribal elements. They still offer sacrifices to the god of the mountain and to the snake. One subdivision, however, has advanced well into the religion of the plains people, and Brahmins readily perform their religious ceremonies. For the sake of prestige they abjure any food considered impure by the Hindus.

Another such caste is that of the Majhwars, Manjhis or Majhias (27,476), who in all appearance are a mixed tribe originating from the Gonds, Mundas and Kawars. In Mirzapur, they have Gond clans, in Surguja and Raigarh clans of the Santals and Mundas. But they are strict in the observance of the totem taboos and even show reverence to their totems.

The Pahiras or Parhaiyas (12,268), too, resemble the Santals in physical appearance. Their daily life is devoted mainly to foodgathering and hunting. They have totemic clans though the clans are not exogamous, provided that the two families concerned have separate graveyards. This proves that the territorial system is stronger among them. The totem taboos are not strictly observed.

The Korkus (204,524 in 1961) are the most westernly of the Mundari-speaking tribes. They live in middle Madhya Pradesh, mainly in the central parts of the Satpura mountains, and are widely separated from the main block of linguistically related tribes. They have four endogamous sub-divisions, further divided into totemic exogamous clans. The names of the clans are taken mainly from those of plants, but animal totems and totems of inanimate objects, too, occur. They observe scarcely any totem taboos, but are strict in the observance of clan exogamy. They still remember some myths about the origin of these totems. The outlay of the Korku village is striking; each hamlet consists of at least two rows of hutments which face each other over a wide courtyard. The houses do not stand alone as is usual in tribal areas, but are attached to each other in a row, so that there is space for a garden or courtyard behind the row of houses only. In former times the Korkus were certainly shifting cultivators, but are now forced to use the plough. They are fairly industrious cultivators, though they like to supplement their diet by the collection of jungle fruits. They earn their livelihood also by cutting and carting timber in the forest. The Korkus are of strong build, dark skin and heavy features; in appearance they resemble the Mundas closely. In addition to the locally venerated Hindu gods, the Korkus worship their own gods. Shamanism is very common among them, and they believe strongly in the evil efficacy of witchcraft. In their creation myth the horse appears as the great enemy of the human race. It repeatedly destroyed the clay figure which God had moulded. Only after several attempts God succeeded in breathing life into it and making it human.

Another Munda-speaking tribe, separated from the original stock, is that of the Gadabas (65,779 in 1961) in southern Orissa, and northern Andhra Pradesh. Their women's dress is distinctive. It consists of a small piece of cloth, woven by themselves on a primitive loom of hand-spun jungle fibre. The cloth is woven with stripes of red, blue and white. The Gadaba women wear enormous earrings made of brass wire. They eat beef like other hill tribes. They cremate their males; women and children are buried. They erect stone slabs as memorials to the dead.

Their chief deities are Ganga Devi or Takurani, Eswara or Mouli, Bhairava, and Jhankara is the god of land, rainfall and crops. The worship is done in a sacred ground surrounded by a circle of boulders. They sacrifice she-buffaloes to Eswara, and pigs, goats and pigeons to Ganga.

Though the Gadabas of Orissa are considered locally to be a branch of the Porojas, and their sub-divisions seem to confirm this view, G.A. Grierson in his Linguistic Survey classes the Gadaba language with the language of the Savaras, as southern Kol-Kherwari, a Munda dialect. The tribe, however, has no tradition of migration from the south.

There remains the Savara tribe (428,383 in 1961) of which the greater portion is now found in the Orissa hills and the adjacent wild country in Bihar and eastern Madhya Pradesh. The ancient geographers Pliny and Ptolomy mentioned tribes of similar name, the ancient Suari or Sabarae, as residents of the south Ganges valley. If the present Savaras could be identified with these ancient tribes, they would once have possessed a considerable dominion in the north of their present habitat. Some writers believe that the Savaras of old were the dominant branch of the great Mundarian family pushed aside by other tribes in the north and the east and by the Gonds in the south, and that at one time they stretched right across central and eastern India [G. A. Grierson (1927), p. 14]. It is curious to find even in the present day small pockets bearing the name Savara in the very north of Madhya Pradesh and Bundelkhand, with no traditions of migration or former importance. The Maler of Rajmahal who call themselves also Sauria are likewisc believed to have some connection with the Savaras. Be this as it may, the isolated group in the north-west has lost all trace of its primitive religion and language, and is simply a low caste of the ordinary Hindu type. Another section of the Savara tribc which had settled in western Bengal is gradually detaching itself from the main tribe and getting progressively Hinduised.

The Savaras belong linguistically and culturally to the Mundari-speaking tribes with whom they share many elements of culture. Most remarkable is the fact, however, that Savara society in the south of Orissa is, in sharp contrast to all the neighbouring tribes, lacking any higher structure. The one essential social unit is the extended joint family, descended from a common male ancestor; beyond that the southern Savaras have neither totemic clans nor a territorial system. Even their endogamous divisions are often vague and disregarded. This is what V. Elwin (1955) found in the Ganjam and Koraput districts of Orissa. But H. Risley and R.V. Russell found that the northern Savaras had totemic clans. H. Risley also mentions that the Savaras of Orissa have no clans. This lack of a clan system among the Orissan Savaras can be explained only as a loss, because all other Munda tribes have a totemic clan system.

The wilder Savaras have functional classes, such as the agricultural or the metal-working, the weaving and the cane-working classes, and Elwin has found, among the Hill Savaras of Ganjam and Koraput, divisions into an aristocracy and a proletariat, and divisions by villages. The Savaras in the southern boundary of their habitats seem to be inclined to separate themselves from tribal fellows and to try to merge in the Kapu, or farming caste.

Elwin (1950) has made a detailed study of the Bondos, another Munda tribe. Their origin and racial affinities are obscure, but Elwin believes that they must have come from the north-east. The Bondos are close neighbours of the Gadabas. They have a complicated and confused social system of clans, phratries and village communities, of which the only strict exogamous unit is the village community. According to Elwin the system of phratries is the original system of social organisation for the Bondos, and it is a relic of a genuine dual organisation with patrilineal descent. It is totemic.

THE DRAVIDA-SPEAKING TRIBES

Of the Dravida-speaking tribes of the Chota Nagpur plateau, the most important is that of the Oraons (1,444,553 in 1961) or Kurukh who, as their traditions maintain, came long ago from the Karnatic. The word 'Oraon' is probably derived from *horo*, man, a Munda word, as is also Kurukh, from *koro*. According to their legends they once held a large portion of south Bihar, but were driven out by the Muslims and had to find themselves a new home. They split into two groups, one following the Ganges to the Rajmahal jungle, the other, much larger one, going up the Son and occupying the north-west corner of Chota Nagpur. The main portion of the tribe is now settled in this area, covering the districts of Ranchi and Palamau. But as their language, which is akin to Kanarese, indicates, they must originally have come from the south and gradually displaced the Mundas from many of the areas on the Ranchi plateau which they now inhabit. Due to land scarcity a large number of Oraons have emigrated to Assam and the Jalpaiguri tea gardens, and even to the Andaman Islands. After living in close contact with the Mundas for many generations, the Oraons have dropped many of their original customs and adopted those of the Mundas. But in racial features they still differ from the Mundas. They are a short-statured, broad-nosed and dark-complexioned people. They have generally dolichocephalic, narrow heads and often a projective jaw. The lips are thick and the nose is depressed at the root. They are more hairy than the Mundas.

In their religious practices the Oraons are more conservative. They have their own priests, called *naya*, very like those of the Mundas. According to tradition, it was the Oraons who introduced the plough into the plateau and took to regular cultivation. They regard the Mundas as the earlier settlers, and where the two are in the same place, the Oraons yield precedence to the older tribe. Their methods of cultivation are more advanced compared with those of the Mundas and other tribes of the region.

The advance of the land-hungry cultivating Hindu and Muslim population and the system of land administration so alien to their traditional one, have been detrimental to the prosperity of the Oraons, who are steadily losing ground before the superior cultivating castes which prey upon the less educated tribes, gradually dispossessing them of their lands and homes.

The Kawars, Kanwars or Kaurs most probably also belong to the Dravida-speaking tribes though at present they speak a corrupt form of Chhattisgarhi Hindi. Their main concentration is in Surguja, Raigarh and Bilaspur districts. In 1961, their number was 91,828. The name of the tribe is really a honorific title, meaning a 'headman'. The Kawars live in the plains and are cultivators.

They have several endogamous sub-divisions whose social status depends on their degree of Hinduisation and possession of land. The Tanwar, for instance, to which most of the big landlords belong, claim Rajput status. But this claim is not recognised by the Brahmins and Rajputs of the region.

Each section is divided into a number of exogamous clans which are totemistic and named after plants and animals.

The Nagesias (46,903 in 1961) are another originally Dravida-speaking tribe of eastern Madhya Pradesh. Cultivation and field labour are their main occupations. A few thousands of them have found work in the tea-gardens of Jalpaiguri District in West Bengal. These latter speak a Sadri dialect. Their main god is the sun. They also worship the tiger.

The largest and most widely-spread of the Dravida-speaking tribes of central India is that of the Gonds (3,986,677 in 1961) whose name comprises most probably a number of racially and culturally diverse communities. Some authorities trace the name 'Gond' to *konda*, the Telugu word for 'hill', as in the case of the Khond or Kandh tribe. The Gonds certainly cover the hilly country from Orissa westwards and northwards, with a strong concentration in the Satpura mountains and north of them.

It has been found that their language is akin to the Kanarese rather than to the neighbouring Telugu, but they have little or no tradition of their former wanderings. At the present time, however, the greater part of the Gonds have stopped speaking their original language and now use local (mostly Aryan) dialects. While in 1931 of the then slightly over three million Gonds 1,720,790 spoke their trial language, in 1961 the number of Gondi-speaking tribals dropped to 1,232,886 persons.

The Gonds are sub-divided into numerous sections some of which might be even of different race. They have two aristocratic sub-sections, the Raj-Gonds and the Khatolias. The Raj-Gonds claim a higher rank because they form the land holding section of the tribe. It appears that already by the fourth century A.D. a group of Gonds pushed up the Narbada and Kaimar rivers where they became progressive and wealthy farmers and were gradually being transformed into Nagbansi Rajputs. When the Gauli dynasties in this area declined, the Gonds established themselves as rulers. The zenith of their rule was from the sixteenth to the beginning of the eighteenth centuries, when the Marathas under Bhonsle overran their country and completely dispossessed them of their power except in the hill fastnesses, which held out against all invaders.

From the Kaimar the Gonds passed eastwards into Baghelkhand and the hills along the south of the Ganges valley. Here they are known as Majhwars or Majhis, meaning 'headmen', like the Mundas. In the former Chota Nagpur states the Gonds hold their land on communal tenure, a fact which seems to indicate that they were in possession before the princes assumed power.

All the northern and central Gonds are more or less Hinduised. The upper classes, descendants of the former chiefs, and the chiefs formerly holding petty states, claim to be Rajputs, and have for generations inter-married with families of that caste whose circumstances were in need of reinforcement from some landed class better off than themselves. Underlying the prevailing beliefs, however, are the old tribal worship and customs, and while Brahmins are consulted about auspicious days and invited to perform certain religious ceremonies, the efficacy of the tribal priest and exorciser, the so-called Pathari, Pardhan or Ojha, in practical dealings with the supernatural world, is everywhere acknowledged.

In the south-east of the Gond country, from Chhattisgarh to Orissa, the tribes are much less Hinduised and prefer life in the forests. The Marias, for instance, are such a tribe. They reside in the Bastar District and in the adjoining Chanda District. Their population is about 11,000 in over 150 villages. The exact number of Marias is not known, since in the Census of India 1961 they have been lumped together with the Gonds. They speak a Dravidian dialect similar to Gondi.

The Marias are probably the wildest of the Gonds. As anthropometric data are not available, it cannot be stated whether they are really a part of the Gond race or whether they are one of the earlier indigenous tribes whom the Gonds have assimilated. The Marias are divided into two sections, the Hill Marias and the Bison-horn Marias. The Hill Marias are the least influenced by the outside world and have retained most of their original cultural and religious traditions and customs. Most of them live in the picturesque Abujhmar hills. They are very shy and shun contact with outsiders. Wherever possible they practise shifting cultivation. They disdain the plough. Before the monsoon starts, the village elders assign the available field plots to each family of the village. Hunting and fishing, and the domestication of pigs, fowls and goats provide additional food.

The Bison-horn Marias live south of the Indravati river. They are mainly foodgatherers and live for most of the year on jungle produce, especially the *mahua* flower and the wild mango. They have a characteristic wedding dance for which they put two bison horns into their well-decorated head-gear, hence their name.

Another Gond sub-tribe is that of the Murias. They too live in the Bastar District. They are a vigorous tribe. Their number was about 78,000 in 1931 but in 1951 it had risen to over 100,000.

Their tribal name 'Muria' has been derived from *mur*, the Palas tree. But this is a doubtful etymology; it is more likely that 'Muria' means 'aboriginal'. The Murias are prosperous and industrious cultivators. They prefer paddy cultivation. They supplement their subsistence by hunting and the collection of forest produce. *Mahua* liquor plays a major role in their religious and social life. Their social life centres around the *gotul*, the youth dormitory, in which the young boys and girls of the village gather in the evenings to sing, dance, make love and for other social activities.

Akin to the Gonds and living in the Bastar District (Jagdalpur Tehsil) and the adjoining District of Koraput in Orissa are the Bhattras (72,304 in 1961). Over 60,000 of them are found in Jagdalpur alone. The word 'Bhattra' means 'a servant'. Most of the Bhattras are village watchmen or daily labourers, the rest are farmers. Formerly they practised shifting cultivation, but at present they all use the plough.

Their affiliations are confined to smaller territorial units called *parganas*. They commonly marry only within a certain *pargana*. They have three sub-groups, the lowest of which has mixed considerably with the Murias. But the Bhattras seem to be racially different from the Murias.

More to the south live the Koyas (220,207 in 1961). 'Koya' denotes a hill-dweller; it is not exactly the name of a specific tribe. The real Koyas are probably the Gutta or Racha Koyas, while the other names are usually taken from their occupation. Thus the Kammara Koyas are hill-dwelling blacksmiths, the Gampa Koyas basket-makers, the Musara Koyas brass-workers, and the Oddi Koyas are their priests. The Linga Koyas are Telugu Saivas.

The Koyas are primarily plough cultivators whose main crops are irrigated wet-rice and millet. They possess fairly large herds of cattle and goats. Hunting and fishing and the collection of jungle products are important subsidiary occupations. They eat beef and prepare alcoholic drinks from the juice of the Palmirah and arraq distilled from Ippa flowers. The Koyas do not use tobacco so much for smoking as for chewing.

The Koyas have no overall political institution or authority uniting the whole tribe or even its endogamous sections. The largest political unit is the *samutu*, a juridical unit consisting of ten to twelve villages under a headman (Samut Dora) with two assistants. Each Koya village has a headman (Pinna Pedda) who is assisted by the village council. When he dies his heir is usually elected as successor by the assembly of the village elders. If the heir is unfit for the office, being a minor or for any other reason, a regent is selected to officiate for him. The Pinna Pedda is different from the Government-appointed Kula Pedda or patel (village headman) responsible for the village to the Government.

As regards the social organisation of the Koyas, the Gutta or highland Koyas are divided into five exogamous phratries, and the Gammu or lowland Koyas into four such phratries of equal social status. Each phratry has its own set of deities worshipped annually exclusively by the male members of the phratry. A Gammu village consists of several hamlets each occupied more or less by a kinship group.

Among them cross-cousin marriage is preferred. Descent, inheritance and succession are strictly patrilineal. The Koyas speak a dialect of Gondi.

East of the Koya region are found two tribes, the Konda Kapus and the Konda Doras. The Konda Kapus, numbering 29,823 in 1961, are divided into two sections—the Pedda Kondalu residing in the hills and the Chinna Kondalu living in the lowlands and dominated by the Telugus. The Pedda Kondalus have retained their hill customs; they have totemistic clans, named after animals like the snake, the tiger, the tortoise, etc.; they marry with preference the father's sister's daughter, while the Chinna Kondalus follow the Telugu system and marry the mother's brother's daughter. But both sections intermarry and interdine, and both eat beef.

The Konda Doras (103,437 in 1961), in north-eastern Andhra and southern Orissa have taken to the plains and now follow Hindu customs. They are cultivators and labourers. Though they eat beef and carrion, they are not treated as untouchables. They talk Telugu. Though some of them are wealthy and even employ tenants under them, the majority are poor and heavily in debt. They are much addicted to drink, opium and gambling.

The Halbas (130,123 in 1961) also came originally from the Bastar District; they have settled in large numbers all around the District of Bastar. The greater the distance from their former jungle home, the more strongly they disown their connection with the Gonds. They claim to be an independent Hindu caste.

In the time of Gond rule in these regions some Halba chiefs obtained grants of land for their war service. These *zamindari* families now feel themselves superior to the ordinary Halbas.

They take Halba girls in marriage, but marry their own daughters only to other *zamindari* bridegrooms.

The Halbas are excellent cultivators. Those who own no fields must work as field servants. They do not accept other occupations than field and forest work.

Socially they are divided into two endogamous sections, the 'pure' and the 'mixed' Halbas. Both sections have exogamous clans which are partly totemic. The Halbas of Bastar District still venerate their totems which consist of animals and plants. They will not kill and eat their totems and they mourn them on their death.

But other clans have territorial or occupational names, an indication perhaps that they admitted members of other castes into their community. The family mores are not very strictly observed; pre-marital and even extra-marital sex relations are easily condoned. Divorce is easy. Cross-cousin marriage is the rule. Widow marriage is permitted.

Of all the Dravida-speaking tribes the Khonds or Kondhs (840,601 in 1961), with a number of sub-divisions, come next in importance to the Gonds. The main body calls itself Kui. The etymology of both Kui and Khond is uncertain. Kui is the name of the language which they speak; it is a mixture of Tamil, Telugu, Kanarese and Oriya. There are regional differences.

The tribe is much divided and by no means uniform in its structure or habits. As usual, the Khonds are divided into a hill section (Kuttia Khonds and Dongria Khonds), relatively untouched by Hinduism, and a plains section which is adopting both the language and the religion of the Hindu peasants.

The plains section is again divided into various endogamous groups, such as the Poroja Doars, Konda Doars, Jatapu Doars, Muka Doars, etc. One section, formed by owners of large estates, is called Raj Khonds. They are superior to all the other sections and marry only among themselves. But even artisans and menials who serve the Khonds now claim to belong to the tribe. There are thus Khond blacksmiths and potters, as there are Gond blacksmiths, minstrels and drummers.

The Khonds practise a primitive type of agriculture; all Khonds are keen hunters. They are skilled bowsmen, but also experts in throwing the axe. They have a great attachment to their fields once they have wrested them from the forest. In the past they held all the village land in common. Their religion is strongly concentrated on the fertility of the earth, in particular on the growth of the Kumkum plant (vermilion). About a hundred years ago the Khonds attracted a good deal of notoriety due to their practice of human sacrifice (*meriah*) on a large scale. It was suppressed by the British Government with great difficulty. The Khonds now sacrifice buffaloes in the place of human beings, but they complain that the earth goddess is not pleased with this substitution and consequently the crops suffer.

The various marriage forms include marriage by purchase, by service, by mutual consent, elopement, capture, and by selection from the Dangari Basa. Since the Khonds practised female infanticide in the past on a large scale, they were obliged to take their brides from outside tribes. Now the marriage laws are controlled by the exogamy of their totemic clans. The clan names are usually those of animals (tiger, cobra, tortoise, more rarely of the monkey, bull, cow, dog, bear, iguana, goat, lizard, peacock and vulture), but also of plants (pumpkin), of stone and the sun. The Khonds have the institution of boys' and girls' dormitories.

The Porojas (169,216) are not easily defined as a tribe or caste. They are divided into seven sections each of which speaks the language of the (aboriginal) landowners whose fields they cultivate as tenants or labourers. They are much attached to the land and are hard workers. Their name derives probably from the Sanskrit word *praja,* which means 'subject' or 'tenant'. True to their name, they adapt themselves in language and custom among the 'scheduled tribes', but it is doubtful if they are a tribe at all.

The Jatapus (73,595) may originally have been Khonds, but they are now an independent and a much Hinduised tribe. Those residing in the hills still speak Kui, while those living in the plains prefer Telugu. The Jatapus now observe the Hindu rules relating to marriage and food, but they have not yet given up their old tribal gods to whom they sacrifice animals through priests of their own community. Their main god is called Jankara (sun-god). In the hills they observe a totemic exogamous clan system, while in the plains they have also adopted the Telugu *intiparlu* territorial system.

The Hill Reddis (3,132) or Reddi Doars are a partly

detribalised group of shifting cultivators, living in the hills on both sides of the Godavari gorge. Though they bear the name of an important Hindu cultivating caste in Madras State, they do not seem to be an offshoot of the caste. Today they speak Telugu. Lower caste Hindu ideas and practices are spreading among them as a result of the strong Hindu penetration of the area in the last hundred years. This is especially so in the river valley where timber contractors employ the Reddis as labourers. So far the spread of Hinduism among the Hill Reddis has resulted in a growth of tribal consciousness and solidarity [C. von Fürer-Haimendorf (1945)]. It has not split the tribe into two sections, as elsewhere.

The Kolams (43,788) have their habitats more in the north, in the Wun taluk of the Yeotmal District. They speak a Dravidian language, closely allied to Gondi, with admixtures from Kanarese, Telugu and Tamil. They also speak Marathi. They do not intermarry with the Gonds, but consider themselves an independent tribe.

They are industrious rice cultivators, but like to supplement their crops by hunting of which they are very fond. Their settlements are well laid out in straight rows within a square fixed by pegs at the four corners. The planning is done by the village priest or diviner.

The Kolams have no sub-divisions, but are divided into exogamous clans. In the Adilabad District the Kolams have clans which are grouped after the manner of the Gonds into phratries with 7-brother, 6-brother, 5-brother and 4-brother clans. But these phratries have no mythological sanctions as among the Gonds. In Maharashtra the Kolams have Maratha sept names, and in the Telugu plains they have house-names or *intiperulu* like their Telugu neighbours.

Kolam girls seem to use the privilege of intrusion (*gharghusi*) more often than other tribals. The bachelor caught in this manner has to accept the girl. Widows are debarred from using this manner of acquiring a mate. Nor can widowers be wooed in the same way. A widow can only remarry a widower. Divorce is permitted.

Of a peculiar type are the Andhs (60,261), a cultivating and hunting tribe of the same area in which the Kolams reside. Their racial features resemble those of the Gonds in their dark complexion, thick lips and prominent cheek-bones. But they state that their forefathers formerly lived more in the north of their present habitat.

They are now practically a Hindu caste, but allow cross-cousin marriage, permit widow marriage and divorce. On the other hand, they prohibit levirate. They worship the local Hindu gods and the usual village deities.

THE TRIBES OF WESTERN INDIA

From a purely geographical point of view western India, with Rajasthan and Gujarat in particular, but also western Madhya Pradesh and Maharashtra, is different from central India. But also the tribes of this western area appear to be racially and culturally different from the tribes in central and north-eastern central India. Of course, some of the western tribes have spilled over into central India and mixed with, or at least influenced or been influenced by, the tribes of central India. Though ethnographers of an older generation (H. Risley, R. V. Russell and Hiralal, even S. B. Guha and E. von Eickstedt) have assigned these tribes to the so-called 'Kolarian Group', there is no proper justification for this classification.

The tribes of western India may belong rather to three different groups: (1) to a group of nomadic, mainly animal-breeding culture, with a warlike tradition, possibly of inner-Asiatic origin, somehow closely related to the Rajputs and usually claiming descent from them. To this group belong tribes like the Jats of northern India, the Ahirs, Gujars, Minas and Meos of Rajasthan, the Mers, Bhavods and Rabaris of Gujarat. Of these tribes only the Minas still fall under the category of 'scheduled tribes'. The other communities are now either completely assimilated by Hindu society or are sufficiently advanced in their culture as not to require any more special protection and assistance from the Government.

(2) The second group is formed by the numerous tribes which go under the name of Bhils. Some of the Bhil sub-divisions have now become independent tribes. To the Bhil group belong the Barelas, Bhilalas, Dhankas, Dublas, Gamits or Gamtas, Mankars, Mavchis, Pathias, Rathias, Tadvis, Talavias and Vasavas. The Girasias (62,492 in 1961) in Rajasthan are perhaps the

northernmost Bhil group. Though many Bhil tribes claim that they are the descendants of mixed Bhil and Rajput ancestors, they have also the tradition of fierce opposition to the Rajputs who gradually usurped all their fertile land leaving them only the barren hills. The Bhils differ from the other two groups also by a totemic organisation of their society. Totemism is absent in the other groups.

(3) The third numerous population group of western India, now largely Hinduised and only partly tribal, bears the name of Kolis (over 3.5 million). This group, divided into many different tribes, is spread over Rajasthan, Gujarat, Maharashtra, Madhya Pradesh and even Punjab and Andhra Pradesh. Many communities still call themselves Kolis, though others go under different names, such as Barias, Bhalias, Gedias, Chhodras, Khants, Kotwals, Naikdas, Patelias, Patanwadias, Takardas and Talabdas. The Koli group, too, has been linked with the Kols and related tribes and castes of north-eastern India. Possibly this was done more because they bear the same name than for any reasons of racial and cultural homogeneity. In fact, no convincing evidence for a genetic connection between the two populations can be found. On the contrary, they show differences of racial type and cultural forms. Though this might be due to a different geographical environment and to contact with different peoples, it is more likely that they are genetically different in race and culture.

As mentioned before, of the first group only the Minas are still a 'scheduled tribe'. The Minas (1,134,499 in 1961) have a Mohammedan branch, the Meos (318,000 in 1965). They are also called Mewatis. They were converted to Islam in the eleventh century and thus became separated from the Minas who had remained Hindu. Both tribes had in former times a bad reputation as daring robbers and plunderers. They went on these raids not only to enrich themselves, but to display their manliness and boldness. The Mughal rulers and the British administration were scarcely able to control their criminal propensities and they had to use draconic measures to suppress them. Finally they succeeded; the Minas and Meos have become peaceful farmers. But they still take pride in the daring exploits of their forefathers and they venerate as semi-divine heroes those who lost their lives in their high-spirited forays. Their bards sing about them and the Minas and Meos remember their glorious past with nostalgia.

Both tribes claim descent from the Rajputs. But it is more likely that their forefathers came along with the Rajputs or other invaders from inner Asia, as an inferior people following and serving the leading invaders as soldiers or in other capacities. It could also well be that they took wives from a local population and mixed with the common people while their leaders married the daughters of high-class people. Even today both tribes accept outsiders into their fold. However, the Minas do not intermarry with the Meos any more.

The Minas are divided into twelve exogamous clans (*pal*). The Meos likewise have twelve *pals*, but only six of them have the same names as those of the Minas. Both tribes have now other clans as well.

Minas and Meos permit widow-marriage and practise the levirate. They allow divorce. The Minas cremate their dead, while the Meos bury them. The Minas employ the village Brahmins for the performance of religious ceremonies and observe the customs and share the religious beliefs of the local Hindu population.

The Meos are only imperfectly converted to Islam. They dress like the local Hindu castes, drink liquor, occasionally worship Hindu deities and celebrate Holi and Diwali. But they circumcise their male children and at their marriages a Mohammedan official functions, though the preparatory steps are taken by Brahmins.

Both tribes are now agriculturists though they are not as good in farming as the local Hindu cultivating castes. The Minas have two classes—a class of landlords and farmers, and a lower class of watchmen (*chaukidars*). There is even a third section, the Dhedia Minas, who eat beef.

Semi-aboriginal tribes such as the Jats, Ahirs, Gaulis or Goalas, and in Gujarat the Mers, Bharvads and Rabaris cling to their nomadic, animal-breeding past still more. The latter tribe is engaged in the breeding of camels. A. Baines [(1912), p. 103] calls them 'derelicts of a Scythian inroad'. All these tribes have the reputation of being robbers and cattle-lifters if given an opportunity. They worship with preference *matas* (mother goddesses). The Bharvads have the peculiarity of celebrating marriages only at long intervals, of ten, fifteen or even twenty years' duration. They are believed to possess powerful spells and charms. While the Mers and Rabaris claim descent from the Rajputs, the Bharvads, Gaulis and Ahirs derive their origin from the race of Krishna.

The second main tribal group in western India is that of the Bhils. It is a numerous race (3,744,786 in 1961), spread over western Madhya Pradesh, Rajasthan, eastern Gujarat and northern Maharashtra.

Their racial origin is still a mystery. The Bhils have completely lost their tribal language and, except in the more remote regions of their habitats, also their original religion. They have adopted Hindu beliefs and practices, and even their myths and folktales seem to have been borrowed. The name 'Bhil' is generally derived from the Dravidian word for 'bow', as also in the toddy-tapping Billavas of Kanara. Whether this etymology is correct is another question. But it is certainly appropriate to call the Bhils 'bow-men', as until very recent times they were seldom seen without this weapon.

E. von Eickstedt classifies the Bhils as Gondids, with the Malids as a sub-section of the Veddids. B.S. Guha calls them Proto-Australoids, to which category he also assigns the Veddids. Even if this classification is correct, it tells us little about the racial history of the Bhils, when they arrived in India, where they lived before they settled in their present habitats, what their exact relations are to the tribes in the eastern and southern neighbourhood. A more intensive study of their physical traits and a comparison of these with the corresponding traits of the other so-called Proto-Australoid tribes may help to solve the problem. But the hope is not great because the Bhils were always much exposed to outside influences of a racial or cultural nature. And while these influences may have affected the Bhils in one particular manner, the influences and changes which their supposedly Proto-Australoid neighbours in central and north-eastern central India experienced may have developed in quite a different manner so that today even the most penetrating anthropological and cultural comparison may fail to recognise the original common origin of both tribal groups.

Like many other tribes, the Bhils, too, are divided into a tribal hill and a Hinduised plains section. The Census of India 1961 enumerates the following Bhil sub-divisions: Bhil Garasia, Dholi

Bhil, Dungri Bhil, Dungri, Garasia, Mewasi Bhil, Rawal Bhil, Tadvi Bhil, Bhagalia, Bhilala, Pawra, Vasava and Vasave in Gujarat and Maharashtra, Barela, Bhilala and Patelia in Madhya Pradesh. Most of the sections still belong to the tribal, but some to the Hinduised divisions. However, even the so-called Hinduised Bhils do not seem to have reached a high status in Hindu society and culture. They are comparatively poor farmers, and many have lost their lands and now work as labourers.

The tribal Bhils cultivate the hilly sites often much eroded and with a poor soil. They live also by the collection and sale of jungle produce and by forest and field labour. They are fond of the *mahua* tree (Boswellia serrata) the flowers of which they collect for food and the distillation of a strong liquor. Since the Bhils have been driven into tracts which are scarcely suitable for cultivation, even by the methods adopted by the agricultural castes, in bad years the Bhils were often forced to dacoity, crop raiding and cattle-lifting. These activities have earned them a bad reputation. It was their custom to work in large gangs which after committing a robbery dispersed quickly and without a trace. They were greatly helped in the past by the partition of the land into many territories belonging to different petty kings and *rajas*.

The Bhils have no organisation uniting all sub-sections into a tribal community. They have no real tribal consciousness; each sub-section lives its own life and cares nothing for the other. Each sub-section is again divided into exogamous clans which at least in former times were totemic. The taboos associated with the totems have now largely disappeared. They still have clan headmen.

They call their principal deity Bhagwan, but also worship a number of local deities, among whom Wagh deo, or the tiger god, is prominent. They erect large stone slabs as memorials for their dead, after the fashion of the Rajput monuments common in western India. The image of a man on horse-back is carved on these slabs, flanked by a woman carrying a waterpot on her head. They drive epidemics out of their villages by means of diminutive carts. They also employ exorcists to disclose the cause of a disease and to appease the offended spirits. Often they are shamans who fall into a trance with ease and, while in this state, prophesy and disclose the activities of witches.

Among some Bhil sections fire-walking is a notable rite of their religious ceremonial.

Some of the eastern Bhils, in Khandesh especially, have been converted to Islam. These are called Tadvis—headmen. But they are rather half-hearted about the observance of the Mohammedan tenets, and the women in particular keep to their old tribal practices.

In former times the Bhils seem to have occupied a large part of the country north and west of their present habitats, and were driven out by the Rajputs under pressure of the Muslims. Even now, their former claim to the land is acknowledged ceremoniously in some places on the occasion of the enthronement of a Rajput chief.

The Bhils may be related to the Chenchus, Reddis and other aboriginal tribes in the south and south-east of their habitat, and they may be both pre-Aryan and pre-Dravidian. Originally hunters, fishermen and food-collectors, they later acquired primitive cultivation and absorbed at different times both different racial strains and different cultural influences. From the Rajputs or Gujars they received their present language and their cultivation methods, while the cultivating castes gave them their religious ceremonies, their wedding and funeral rites and so on.

Strong evidence can be found for the assumption that the Bhil tribe was reinforced by occasional accretions of fugitive Rajputs who have left their marks on certain clans of the Bhils, especially in southern Rajasthan. In fact, most tribes in the area claim to have intermarried with the Rajputs in the past. The connection of Rajputs with Bhils is said to have resulted in the formation of a special tribe, the Bhilalas. In other regions, however, the Rajputs were implacable enemies of the Bhils whom they hunted down and killed mercilessly until the last century, taking the best lands from them and pushing them back into the barren stony hills of western India.

The Bhilalas, whose numbers cannot be ascertained as they are recorded under the category of Bhils, are divided into two sections: the Bara Bhilalas (Great Bhilalas) and the Chhota Bhilalas (Small Bhilalas) or Barelas. The Bara Bhilalas are almost fully Hinduised, while the Barelas have retained many tribal features of the Bhils. Physically they appear to be taller and of a lighter complexion than the Bhils. They are hardworking farmers and not as poor as the Bhils. Related to the Barelas are the Rahwa-Bhilalas who reside in the jungles east of Baroda. The Barelas have no closed villages: small clusters of huts are dispersed all over their hills. A Barela homestead has a peculiar outlay: the spacious house for the family has a veranda on the east side. Facing the veranda at a distance of a few yards is the stable, usually somewhat smaller. The Barelas have a clan system like the Bhils, observe clan exogamy, but do not observe any totem taboos. A popular form of marriage among the Barelas is by elopement; a boy and girl who love each other and want to get married disappear for some time from home. When they reappear, they are considered married, though the tribal council has later to settle the problem of the bride-price and other gifts.

Akin to the Bhils and Bhilalas are the Dhankas (169,664 in 1961) residing in Gujarat as well as in Maharashtra. They are found mainly in the Panchmahals, in Broach and in Baroda districts in Gujarat and in West Khandesh. Physically they do not differ from the Bhils. Their name 'Dhanka' is commonly derived from *dhanushyakas*—'holders of bows'. But today they are by occupation farmers and field labourers: some are wood-cutters in the forest. The Dhankas derive their origin from the Rajputs, and they have a myth to this effect. But it is more likely that they are a Bhil sub-section. The tribe is divided into three sub-divisions which do not intermarry. The Tarvi section considers itself the highest; it invites Brahmin priests for marriage and is more Hinduised than the other two sections. The Dhankas live mainly in joint families; a marriage is usually arranged by the parents, but marriage by elopement is not at all rare.

Similar to the Dhankas in physical appearance, social habits and occupation are the Patelias (38,743) who live in the same region as the Dhankas. The Tadvis and Pavadas, two Bhil sections which got separated from the main stock, reside now in the Satpuras of Khandesh.

The Gamits or Gamtas (253,248 in 1961) now call themselves an independent tribe, but originally they were Bhils. They are found in north-western Maharashtra and south-eastern Gujarat. They form five endogamous sub-divisions. They are primitive cultivators and forest labourers. In former times the test for a boy that he was marriageable was that he had to be able to climb a palm tree. They permit widow-marriage and polygamy. While they had no real caste organisation in the past and no headmen, they have comparatively recently introduced tribal councils and tribal headmen. The tribal councils are quite powerful and tolerate no deviation from the accepted regulations. The reason is that the tribal leaders are anxious to maintain a respectable social status in the Hindu caste system.

Another important tribe in the area, where the three states Rajasthan, Madhya Pradesh and Gujarat meet, are the Naikdas. In 1961 they numbered 105,940 souls. In the past they were a rather turbulent and restless race, and the British had to suppress their revolts and raids on several occasions by force of arms. But finally their warlike spirit was broken and they have not disturbed the peace now for quite some time. They are very conservative; and still much attached to their primitive mode of cultivation and their dependence on the jungle for their livelihood. Modern conditions and a stricter control of the forest have forced them to work under the forest officers to cut and transport timber, instead of working the jungle on their traditional wasteful plan. They pay homage to the mother goddess and to Hanuman which are the main Hindu deities that they worship. They do not engage the services of the Brahmins; on the contrary, they are much averse to them.

The tribe is divided into four endogamous sections, the Unchas (i.e., Hinduised 'upper ones'), Nichas (i.e., tribal 'lower ones'), Choliwalas (whose women wear a blouse) and Kapadias. These divisions are each further divided into several endogamous lineages tracing their (patrilineal) descent from not more than four or five generations.

At some distance from the Naikdas there is a small tribe of the same name, the Nayaks. They do not seem to be related to the Kolis, although closely connected with the Dhodia tribe. They are only found in the south-eastern part of Gujarat where they live near the forest. The Dhodias of the open country pay them respect at all formal ceremonies, though they do not interdine and intermarry with them. The Nayaks are more conservative than the other tribes of this kind and have preserved many of their old customs. They are accomplished drummers, and are often invited by the other tribes for weddings and other festivals.

The Dhodias or Dhundias (i.e., 'hut-dwellers') in Gujarat, who have been just mentioned, are probably of Koli origin, but settled now in the plains, mainly in southern Bulsar District, from Chikli Balsar eastwards through former Bansda and Dharampur states to the western portions of Khandesh. The tribe is gradually passing from the status of landless labourers into that of tenants and small-land holders. In social rank they are higher than the Dublas.

The Dhodias (254,146 in 1961) have no endogamous subdivisions. But they have exogamous clans which they call *kul*. They allow widows to remarry. A poor boy may acquire a bride by serving her father from one to five years. The dead are buried if they are poor but cremated if the heirs can afford the expense.

In most Dhodia villages one family provides the headman for several generations. The headman receives high respect, but has to listen to a council of elders. More serious matters are decided by larger gatherings of tribals often held on the occasion of a funeral feast.

The Koknas (or Koknis, Kuknas), were 322,890 in number in 1961. One-third of them live in south-eastern Gujarat and two-thirds in western Maharashtra. Their name would indicate that they came originally from the south, the Konkan. They speak a mixed dialect of Gujarati and Marathi. It is believed that they were driven northwards by the great Durga Devi famine (A.D. 1396 to 1408). They differ little in physical appearance from the Koli tribes. They practise a primitive mode of cultivation, but own proportionately more fields than the other tribes in the area.

They practise widow marriage, polygamy and service marriage. They cremate their dead, but do not employ Brahmins for their religious ceremonies. Divorce is frequent.

The village councils keep order and peace in the villages, see that the tribal laws and regulations are observed, and fine and punish offenders according to the seriousness of the offence.

The Dublas (288,146 in 1961), living in the same area, are socially of an inferior rank. For a long time they have been the dependents and tenants of the land-owning castes and are still in a state of practical serfdom on the farms of their masters. Enthoven says that they have about twenty clans, but a recent monograph on the tribe [P. G. Shah (1958)] maintains that thtey have nowadays no 'definite ideas of clans'.

Being so dependent on their Hindu masters, they have themselves adopted many Hindu customs. They dress like the Hindus, abhor beef, worship Hindu gods, employ Brahmins for their ceremonies and treat them with great respect. They cremate their dead. But they eat meat, are fond of hunting quails and lizards, and drink liquor, often in excess.

They, as also the other tribes in western India, worship in Hindu temples, but they also have their own shrines under a tree near the village. They also venerate their ancestors and erect memorial pillars of stone and wood for them. They have shamans and diviners whom they consult when sick or in misfortune and who indicate to them how to propitiate the offended deities.

The Chodris (143,515 in 1961), now mainly in the Surat District of Gujarat, have the tradition of a former home more in the north, in southern Rajasthan, from where they were evicted along with some Rajput clans by the Muslims. Like the Dhodias, they are small farmers who till their lands industriously, though using the old traditional cultivating methods. In the past they had the reputation of being great marauders, though at present they are very peaceful and steady workers. The Chodris have no temples, but worship their gods either in caves or on hill tops, or else place stones for them under trees in the village. They have shamans who are very influential and are much consulted in sickness. They have four sub-divisions which are endogamous. They still observe the custom of bride capture as a legitimate form of marriage.

The three or four small tribes of the northern Sahyadris are almost contiguous to those just mentioned and are possibly of the same race. But they have no tradition about their origin. The lowest of these tribes, the Katkaris or Kathodis (138,197 in 1961), seem to have lived in former times in south Gujarat. Their name is supposed to be derived from *catechu* (Accacia catechu) which they extract from forest trees.

They are found in the hilly regions of the Deccan of Western Ghats, ranging from Thana in the north to Ratnagiri in the south. They are still mainly a nomadic jungle people, collecting, hunting and fishing in the forests of these hills. The Government made strong efforts to settle them down and turn them into farmers, but did not have much success with them. Wandering is in their blood, and when the jungle fruits ripen they get restless and gladly leave their fields to roam in the jungle.

They live in local groups of ten to a hundred and fifty individuals. The entire tribe is divided into two endogamous sections, Sone and Dhor, of which the Sone Katkaris ('the pure ones') are the more settled. Many of them are employed as field labourers, while others extract *catechu* from the *khair* tree, collect fuel and other jungle produce which they sell in the villages and markets. They also cut trees and make charcoal. The thinly forested hills do not yield sufficient food for them and thus they are often forced to supplement their livelihood by committing petty thefts in fields and houses. But they no longer possess the daring to commit serious robberies.

They are slight in build and of medium height. Their complexion is brown to very dark, with deep-sunk eyes, a shallow nasal bridge and full lips. In both sexes the hair is often curly. Their physical appearance would link them rather with the south Indian tribes.

Their society is divided into exogamous septs. Some surnames of the septs bear the names of animals, trees and other objects. They are rather lax in the observance of their food taboos. Originally they were probably a totemic tribe, but lost much of their totemism due to the influence of their Maratha neighbours whose language they have also adopted.

They venerate their own gods and have their own rites of worship; they do not employ Brahmin priests. The tiger is an object of special regard. The other tribes keep at a distance, not only because the Katkaris eat anything however impure, and do not care for personal cleanliness, but especially because of their reputation as powerful sorcerers.

The Warlis (341,690 in 1961) whose name means 'uplanders' are supposed to have come from the region above the Ghats. They are now resident along the coast, but still in the forest, in the north-eastern part of Thana District. According to their own tradition they came originally from Kanara. This could be true because of certain customs which distinguish them from the Bhils, making them resemble the south Indian tribes more. In appearance they are superior to the Katkaris, and quite industrious cultivators, generally working as tenants of landlords who exploit them mercilessly. Wherever possible they also collect jungle produce.

They have four endogamous divisions and two hundred exogamous clans (*kul*). Among the clan names some refer to animals, others to trees and their products, and still others to titles, occupations, localities and so on. But they observe no totem taboos nor do they show special respect or reverence towards the animals, trees and other objects after which they are named.

They venerate, by similar rites, some of the Katkari deities, especially Vaghoba, the tiger god, whom the lower Hindu castes also worship. The Hindus regard the Warlis as slightly less impure than the other tribes; they may visit the houses of at least those Warlis who breed cattle.

Socially the third tribe, the Thakurs (159,372), is graded still higher by the Hindus, though the Thakurs are hardly distinguishable from the other tribes of the District. They might be somewhat cleaner and more fastidious in their eating habits. They speak Marathi and have also in other aspects adjusted themselves better to their Maratha neighbours. As owners of land and cattle they are better off than the other tribes in the District. But they still prefer to settle in villages of their own.

They have two endogamous divisions, and had originally three exogamous septs to which more were added later. They observe certain taboos relating to animals and trees, probably relics of a former more vigorous type of totemism. They are patrilineal and patripotestal. On the whole they hold the same tribal beliefs and worship mainly mountain and tiger gods. But in their domestic rites they employ the Deshasta or Maratha Brahmins.

In former Bansda State, in Bulsar District, a small tribe similar to the Katkaris can be found. They call themselves Vitolia, Kotwalia or Barodia (8,838 in 1961). The Vitolias are treated as untouchables by the rest of the population, probably because they eat all kinds of animals, except the dog, even cats and donkeys. They live by plaiting bamboo baskets and winnowing fans and selling them in the market. They appear to have no headmen and no distinct clans. They allow polygamy and widow-marriage. The deceased members of the tribe are cremated, and memorial stones (*khatran*) are erected under a tree. The Vitolias worship Samla Deo and Kakabana, the small-pox goddess.

Similar in social status, occupation and behaviour are the Kolghas, also called Kolchas, Dhor or Tokre Kolis (30,000 in 1961). They reside in the southern Surat District, and are hereditary servants, labourers and wood-cutters. They are treated as impure people whose touch defiles. They have no headmen, and when any disputes have to be decided there is a meeting of the whole tribe living within a certain area. They are much Hinduised, cremating their dead, worshipping Hanuman and the smallpox goddess, Kakabalia. But they still belong to the tribal population of Gujarat and keep aloof from the untouchable castes, especially the Bhangis (sweepers) whom they will not even touch.

BIBLIOGRAPHY

Amir-Ali, Hashim: *The Meos of Mewat.* Delhi, 1970.
Archer, W. G.: *The Blue Grove: The Poetry of the Uraons.* London, 1940.
Baines, A.: *Ethnography.* Strassbourg, 1912.
Biswas, P. C.: *Santhals of the Santhal Parganas.* Delhi, 1956.
Bradley-Birt, F. B.: *Chota Nagpore.* London, 1910.
Chapekar, D. L. N.: *Thakurs of the Sahyadri.* Bombay, 1959.
Culshaw, W. J.: *Tribal Heritage.* London, 1949.
Das, A. K. et al: *The Malpaharias of West Bengal.* Calcutta, 1966.
Datta-Majumdar, N.: *The Santal—A Study in Culture Change.* Delhi, 1956.
Dave, P. C.: *The Grasias.* Delhi, 1960.
Doshi, S. L.: *Bhils.* New Delhi, 1971.
Dube, S. C.: *The Kamar.* Lucknow, 1951.
Elwin, V.: *The Baiga.* London, 1939.
————: *The Agaria.* Calcutta, 1942.
————: *Bondo Highlander.* Bombay, 1950.
————: *The Religion of an Indian Tribe.* Oxford University Press, 1955.
Enthoven, R. E.: *The Tribes and Castes of Bombay.* 3 vols., Bombay, 1922.
Forsyth, J.: *The Highlands of Central India.* London, 1919.
Fuchs, S.: 'Another Version of the Baiga Creation Myth', in *Anthropos.* Fribourg, 1952, vol. 47, pp. 607–19.
————: *The Gond and Bhumia of Eastern Mandla.* Bombay, 1960.
Fürer-Haimendorf, C. von: *The Chenchus.* London, 1943.
————: *The Reddis of the Bison Hills.* London, 1945.
————: *The Raj Gonds of Adilabad.* London, 1948.
Glatter, A.: *Contributions to the Ethnography of the Chodris.* Wien, 1969.

Grierson, G. A.: *The Linguistic Survey of India. Introductory.* Calcutta, 1927.
Grigson, W. V.: *The Hill Marias of Bastar.* London, 1938.
Ghurye, G. S.: *The Mahadeo Kolis.* Bombay, 1957.
Hivale, S.: *The Pardhans of the Upper Narbada Valley.* Bombay, 1946.
Hoffmann, J. and A. van Emelen: *The Encyclopaedia Mundarica.* 13 vols., Patna, 1930 ff.
Karve, I.: *The Bhils of West-Khandesh.* Bombay, 1961.
Lokanathan, P. S.: *Socio-economic Conditions of Primitive Tribes in Madhya Pradesh.* New Delhi, 1963.
Naik, T. B.: *The Bhils.* Delhi, 1956.
Nath, Y. V. S.: *Bhils of Ratanmal.* Baroda, 1960.
Orans, Martin: *The Santal.* Detroit, 1965.
Punekar, V. B.: *The Son Kolis of Bombay.* Bombay, 1959.
Roy, Sarat Chandra: *The Mundas and their Country.* Calcutta, 1912.
————: *The Oraons of Chota Nagpur.* Ranchi, 1915.
————: *A Note on Totemism amongst the Asurs, J.B.O.R.S.*, III. Calcutta, 1917, pp. 567–71.
Russell, R. V. and Hiralal: *The Tribes and Castes of the Central Provinces of India.* 4 vols., London, 1916.
Save, K. J.: *The Warlis.* Bombay, 1945.
Shah, P. G.: *The Dublas of Gujarat.* Delhi, 1958.
————: *Naikas—Naikdas.* Bombay, 1959.
————: *Tribal Life in Gujarat.* Bombay, 1964.
Sengupta, S.: *Social Profiles of the Mahalis.* Calcutta, 1970.
Vidyarthi, L. P.: *The Maler.* Calcutta, 1963.
Weling, A. N.: *The Katkaris.* Bombay, 1934.

CHAPTER VI

The Tribes in Eastern India

THE EASTERN area of India, in the sense in which it is taken here, comprises the States of Assam, Meghalaya, Arunachal Pradesh, Nagaland, Manipur and Tripura, as also West Bengal and the union territory of Mizoram. This area is separated from Bhutan by the Himalayan range and from upper Burma by the Patkoi mountains. On the north-west it is connected with the plains of Bengal. The country is mountainous, with two fertile plains divided by the Khasi-Jaintia hills. Situated between the eastern Himalayas, southern Tibet, China, Burma and Bengal, this area has received immigrants from all these countries. The rugged topography of the country has kept the larger portion of the hill tribes in comparative isolation until modern times, with all their traditional habits and institutions more or less intact.

RACIAL HISTORY

The racial history of this easternmost portion of India is extremely complicated. A great number of races have invaded it from all directions. And there was an almost continuous migration of the tribes and peoples within the area which has not yet come to an end in present times.

The first inhabitants appear to have been a Negrito race. The occurrence of curly or even kinky hair in connection with a short stature and strikingly Papuan profile suggests, in the opinion of J. H. Hutton, the survival of some submerged Negrito strain.

Next came the Khasis and Syntengs (or Pnars), the Wars,

Bhois or Lyngnams, tribes that now inhabit the recently formed State of Meghalaya. They numbered 314,161 in 1961. Linguistically these tribes belong to the Austro-Asiatic or Mon-Khmer group. Their origin can thus be traced back to southern China. Through their language they form a link between the Munda tribes further west and the tribes in Indo-China. They also resemble them culturally; they have, for instance, stone monuments to their dead ancestors like the Mundas and Hos of Chota Nagpur and, on the other side, like the tribes of Indonesia. The Khasis and Syntengs are remarkable for their strong muscular development, especially of the leg. They are rather fair, often of ruddy complexion, but have flat round faces and the epicanthic fold.

Linguistically, the aborigines of Nicobar Islands (13,993 in 1961) near the coast of Burma also belong to the Mon-Khmer group. Needless to say, there are also tribes of the Mon-Khmer linguistic group in Burma, such as the Palaungs and the Was in upper Burma, as also the Mons or Talaings of Pegu.

The Khasis and Syntengs are now separated from their tribal cousins in north-eastern central India through the Aryan-speaking Hindu castes, mostly Bengalis but also people from northern India who entered Assam in the beginning of the Christian era from the west and ever since continued to infiltrate and take possession of the fertile lowlands and river valleys. They brought Hindu culture and social organisation at a very early date to Assam. They have formed the dominant classes in Assam, with various degrees of intermixture, while the bulk of the population has remained Indo-Chinese.

The next immigration into this country was that of the Bodo group (*Bodo*—meaning Bhot, Tibet). The Bodo group is now chiefly found along the northern bank of the Brahmaputra, from the western boundary of Assam to the Darrang District. The Bodos formerly also possessed land far to the east and south, and in the southern direction they still form the main population of the Cachar hill tract, received—as tradition relates—as a dowry from Tripura in the balmy days of Bodo rule.

The Bodos were undoubtedly of trans-Himalayan origin, but it is still uncertain by which route and stages they reached the Brahmaputra valley. They are supposed to have risen to power first in the north-east of the valley, and eventually advanced down the river and spread across it as they approached the plains.

Today the Bodos are a sturdy, independent, and remarkably clannish community of labourers. They have none of the objections of the hill tribes to seasonal migration, and frequent the tea-gardens of the upper valley in large numbers.

The Bodo group includes, first of all, the eastern sub-Himalayan tribes such as the Monpas (c. 20,000) the Daflas (36,128), the Hrussos or Akas (c. 1,000) between the Dafla country and Bhutan, then the Miris (163,211), Galongs (879), Abors (14,042), Minyongs (c. 17,000) and Mishmis (20,462).

South of the Brahmaputra are the Rabhas (113,397), the Garos (252,635), the Lalungs (61,059), the Dimasas or Hill Kacharis (68,405), the Bodos or Plain Kacharis (with the Sonwals 235,192), who in Goalpara call themselves Mech (6,830). The Mikirs (120,953) reside in the north-east of the north Cachar hills. The Tripuris (189,799) who occupy the hills south of Silhet are also of Bodo stock. They have the same Mongoloid features and a complexion varying from olive, and with a ruddy tinge, to dark brown.

The Daflas, in particular, live to the east of Kameng and the west of Subansiri. They call themselves Bangni, which means 'man'. Since the time of Aurangzeb they had the reputation of being an independent and aggressive tribe. They enslaved those whom they made prisoners on their frequent raids. The Apa Tanis especially suffered under their aggression. But today they are quite peaceful, and live in economic symbiosis with the Apa Tanis exchanging cotton and other goods for the Apa Tanis' cloth and rice. They are also excellent cane-workers though they otherwise lack artistic talent.

The Daflas have decidedly Mongoloid features and speak a language closely allied to the Miri dialect.

The Hrussos or Akas (which means 'painted', as they paint their faces with black marks) live between Bhutan and the Daflas. They are keen traders with the Bhutanese and the tribes in their own neighbourhood, and thus fairly prosperous. In the past they often raided the plains, but now they are peaceful and progressive.

Dalton [(1872), p. 22] believed that the Miris, Galongs, Abors or Padams, together with the Mishmis, Akas and Daflas, are all one common race, but they have their differences in language, economy, social organisation and religion. Whatever the case might be, the Miris can be divided into two sections: the hill Miris and the Miris of the plains. The latter are offshoots of the Abors and are regarded by the common people as runaway slaves. But some of their clans have settled in Assam for ages. It is most likely that they came from the north and settled on the banks of the Brahmaputra and its estuaries and affluents, and cultivated the alluvial flats of that river. Physically they display strong Mongoloid characteristics, but are tall and of a strong build. They are unclean in their habits; it is alleged that they never bathe, and take all kinds of food objectionable to the principles of the Hindus.

The Abors or Padams live just north of Dibrugarh, west of the Dihang river. They are also called Adis. 'Abor' is actually a misnomer. In Assam it means 'savage and warlike'. They are a tall race, with marked Mongoloid features and an olive complexion. Like the Miris, they have a deep and sonorous voice. Many of them are disfigured by goitres. Men and women have a peculiar hair-cut: around the crown of the head they comb their hair over a knife and chop it off with a piece of wood.

The Minyongs are neighbours of the Padams and live on both banks of the Siang river. They number about 17,000. Formerly a warlike and raiding tribe, an activity which brought in many slaves, they are now peaceful.

East of the Siang river, in the easternmost corner of Arunachal Pradesh, is the home of the Mishmis. They are divided into the Idus and Kaman Mishmis. The Idus entered their present habitats about five hundred years ago, coming from Burma. They are closely related to the Padams. In the past, they were notorious for their harsh treatment of strangers. Now they are quite friendly. They are keen traders, but indifferent cultivators.

The Kaman or Miju Mishmis live in the upper reaches of the Lohit river. They are said to have come from the Kachin hills of Burma. While the Idus Mishmis cut their hair short like the Abors, for which reason they are also called Chulikattas (crop-haired), the Kaman Mishmis wear their hair long. They regularly come down to the plains for cane-cutting at which they are expert. They are fond of opium and tobacco. The Mishmis are light to dark brown in skin colour, their faces are flat and broad, their nostrils wide and their eyes covered with the epicanthic fold. In 1961 their number was 20,462.

The Rabhas, the westernmost representatives of the Bodo group, in West Bengal and Assam, are related either to the Garos or the Kacharis. In fact, they are often said to be Hinduised Garos or Kacharis. This is borne out by the language they speak, which is a link between the Garo and Kachari languages. But they are gradually giving up their own language for Assamese. Like many other tribal groups, the Rabhas live on agriculture. Many work as field labourers. In earlier times they must have been hunters; for even now they perform a ceremonial hunt three or four times a year. Before the hunt they worship the forest deities. Fishing is still both a sport and an economic pursuit for them.

The Rabhas are divided into two sections one of which is more conservative and pure, while the other is largely Hinduised and has adopted many customs of the Bengalis. In fact, there are more sub-sections among them, but they are not yet endogamous. Though largely Hinduised and celebrating all feasts in the Hindu fashion, the Rabhas still consider themselves a people set apart from the Bengalis.

The eastern neighbours of the Rabhas are the Garos, who also belong to the Bodo group. They live in the westernmost part of Assam, south of the Brahmaputra. But they have migrated to the districts of Goalpara and Kamrup in Assam, and the Mymensingh District of present-day Bangladesh. Owing to the persecution by the Muslims in the then East Pakistan about 100,000 Garos returned to India in 1964.

The Garos claim Tibetan origin. But about their history little is known. Their language belongs to the Tibeto-Burman linguistic group. They are certainly physically and linguistically closely related to the Kacharis. Physically they are rather short in stature, of dark complexion, round faced, with a small nose. Compared with the Khasis, the Garos are economically backward. In the past they were regarded as ferocious raiders and head-hunters who could only be effectively pacified through the occupation of their country in 1872 by the British.

East of the Garos are found the Lalungs, now residing on the northern slope of the Jaintia hills and slowly advancing eastwards towards the Mikir country. They are in the process of Hinduisation and are inclined to drop their tribal language for Assamese. Of the 61,059 Lalungs only 7,824 still speak their tribal language.

East of the Lalungs are the Hill Kacharis or Damasias, once the dominant people in the north Cachar hills (north-east of the Jaintia hills). They are a strong and vigorous race, the women too are tall and sturdy. Their complexion is dark brown. They have thick lips, large noses with broad nostrils, and prominent cheek-bones. Their chin is small and pointed. They, as well as the Plain Kacharis, who have spread to West Bengal, Goalpara and other parts of Assam, and call themselves partly Koch partly Mech, are almost completely Hinduised. They were once a powerful and ruling people in their country. But after a rule of several centuries their power was broken by party dissensions, the invading Burmese, and the British who in the last century finally annexed their country.

The Mikirs, east of the Kacharis, inhabit mainly the hills named after them, but they have also spread to other parts of the country. They have mixed considerably with the Assamese of the plains, and speak Mikir only at home and Assamese with outsiders. They have adopted many customs of the Hindus. Due to racial mixture, the Mikirs are not as robust as the tribes who have kept their racial integrity. Their complexion is light-brown, their facial hair is scanty. They are fairly tall in stature, though slim. In spite of their inclination to intermarriage with the plains people, the Mikirs have largely retained their tribal homogeneity. They took no part in the internecine feuds of the other tribes, but kept aloof and concentrated on their own pursuits. They earn their livelihood by agriculture, hunting and fishing.

The bulk of the population of Tripura also seems to belong to the Bodo Group. But there are altogether nineteen different tribes in Tripura, and the Meitheis, who belong to the Kuki Chin race, have now more or less absorbed all the other tribes. The population of Tripura has increased much in recent years through immigration from Bangladesh.

South of the Cachar hills, east of Tripura, is the habitat of the Kuki, Lushai (Mizo) and Chin tribes. From the similarity of their dialects it is clear that all three tribal groups belong to a common racial stock; their original homes are probably the Chin hills in Burma.

In 1961 the Kuki tribes, with 37 sub-tribes, numbered 19,037 individuals. Since the Hmars (8,741) are also Kukis, their number is still higher. All these tribes are getting assimilated by the Lushais (Mizos).

The Mizos, since 1972 living in the Union Territory of Mizoram, formerly known as Lushai Hills, came into their present homeland in the 18th century. From A.D. 1400 to 1700 they inhabited the Chin Hills in Burma. The Mizos (214,721) consist of the following sub-sections: Lushai, Ralte, Khiangte, Chawnghu, Hmar and Paite. They are of Mongoloid stock, like their neighbours. They became notorious for their rebellion in 1966 when they wanted to secede from India. Now a compromise has been arranged, and they have become a union territory called Mizoram. The Mizo District is governed by a District Council under which are the village councils elected by all the adults in the community. In former times each village was practically a separate state ruled by a chief.

The Lakhers (or Maras) inhabit the southernmost region of Mizoram. In 1961 they numbered 8,791. As far as material culture and language is concerned, the Lakhers must be classed with the Kuki tribes. But it is possible that originally they were Nagas who became Kukis through their close association with the latter. Physically the Lakhers are taller and darker than the Lushais; otherwise they have the same Mongoloid traits. In pre-British times they used to raid the Chittagong hill tracts and carry off slaves. It was only in 1924 that they were fully subjugated by the British.

Another tribe in the south Lushai hills is that of the Pawis or Chins (4,587). Though the Pawis are very similar in race and culture to the Lushais their relations in the past were not cordial. The Pawis still continue to have social contacts with the Chins in Burma.

In the Chittagong hill tracts, in the border area of Bangladesh, India and Burma, lives another Chin tribe called Bawm-Zo. Their number is about 5,000 in forty-five villages (thirty-nine of which are now Christian). The Bawm-Zo immigrated into their present territory in the 18th century. They attacked and overpowered at first the original settlers, but were then themselves much harassed by the Lushais, living in the north of their homeland. Finally they had to give way and settle on the eastern slopes of the Chittagong hills (in present Bangladesh). Now they live in peace with the Lushais, but they still feel hostile towards the tribes living in the valley.

The Meitheis (330,545), the inhabitants of Manipur State, belong to the Kuki tribes. Manipur was originally occupied by several different tribes, such as the Kumuls, Luangs, Moirangs and Meitheis. Of all these the Meitheis became dominant and finally absorbed the other tribes. Though the Meitheis claim to be of Hindu descent, it can be proved by their linguistic and physical affinities that they belong to the Kuki or Naga tribes. They are well-known for their wholesale adoption of the Hindu religion and admission into the Kshatriya caste.

The following ethnic group to be discussed now is that of the Naga tribes (327,216 in 1961). They, too, are natives of north-east Tibet. But they seem to have reached their present habitats coming from the southern direction. A migration from the north to the south must have preceded, or they came by a circuitous route via Burma. But it is well evidenced that they entered Assam from the south and migrated northward, followed and pushed on by the Kuki-Lushai-Chin tribes. This migration is still continuing.

The Nagas appear to belong originally to that great race which long ago resided in south-west China. While its main body moved through Burma and Malaya to the Indonesian Islands, it sent a side-stream into the hills of Assam, such as that represented by the Naga tribes. But the Nagas occupied mainly the eastern parts of Assam and never ventured into the hills and lands in the west.

The Naga tribes represent a separate racial type with a sub-medium height, dolichocephalic to mesocephalic head form (76 to 81), with a flat (euryprosopic) face, mesorrhine nose, high cheek-bones, and the epicanthic fold (slit-eyes) which is, however, not universal. Body hair is as scanty and head hair as straight as in the Mongoloid races generally. Their skin colour is a brownish yellow. But in regard to pigmentation and stature, there is geat differentiation not only between the various tribes, but even within a given tribe. On the other hand, this differentiation may be influenced by the altitude and climate of their habitats, as also by their diet.

The Nagas are at present divided into the Angami (including Kezhama), Ao, Sema, Lhota, Konyak, Chang, Rengma and Tungkhul Nagas. There are also Naga tribes in Burma.

After seven hundred years of Bodo rule in the west of Assam, however, the country was again invaded in about A.D. 1550, this time from north-eastern Bengal. The invaders, who established themselves for over two hundred years in Cooch Bihar, were the Koches whom Dalton regards as the most north-eastern branch of the Bhuiyas, a Dravida-speaking tribe.

In spite of their mixture with Indo-Tibetan neighbours the physical traits of the Koches still distinguish them somewhat from the Indo-Tibetans: they have a flat, but rather angular, face; black eyes with the epicanthic fold; black and straight but sometimes curly hair; a short and fiat nose, prominent cheek-bones, thick and protuberant lips, a retreating forehead, and a very dark skin colour. They are now a caste into which all converts of Hinduism are admitted. In Goalpara the term Koch has been abandoned for the more honourable title Rajbansi—'men of royal blood'.

The Koches, who had established a dynasty in Cooch Bihar, were driven from power after two hundred years, in the west by the Muslims and in the east by the Ahoms.

The Chuia or Kachari dynasty, however, continued to hold southern Assam, Sadiya and a part of Nowgong until the middle of the thirteenth century when they had to yield to hordes of Shans or Thais, who invaded Assam from the south through Burma. The Shans were subsequently called Ahoms (249,434 in 1961) when they became the rulers of the whole country and gave their name to the State (Ahom-Assam).

Their history is well known because they preserved complete records of the fate that befell them in Assam. They had entered Assam in 1228 in consequence of a dynastic dispute, and settled in the north-east corner of the state. By 1500 they had subjugated the Chutiyas, and forty years later the Kacharis or Bodos. They suffered a severe defeat at the hands of the Koches, but recovered, and even repelled several times an invasion by the Muslims.

Their decline set in with the conversion of their chief to Hinduism and his adoption of the language and customs of the local population. A large portion of the Ahoms refused to follow the chief; some rebelled. To quell the rebellion the chief called in the Burmese who came and absorbed the whole kingdom, until the British took possession.

Lastly, another wave of Shan tribes arrived from Burma.

About 1760 they crossed the Patkai from Burma in small bodies and settled east of Sadiya, on the Brahmaputra. Among these Shans are the Kamjangs of Sadiya, the Khamtis (4,793), Turungs, Noras and Phakials (on the Dihang river). Of these the Khamtis and Noras are really Ahoms who had remained in Burma when the Ahoms had first entered Assam. But in 1760 they were pressed by the Singphos (literally, 'men') to cross over to Assam and they came with the permission of the king of the Ahoms. Unlike the early Shan immigrants, these tribes retained the culture, religion and costume of their forefathers.

Finally some Singphos even entered Assam in 1793 and settled together with the Shan tribes in the same corner of the Brahmaputra valley. The Singphos are a section of the great Kachen race of Burma and repudiate all connection with the Shans. In fact, their language is more akin to that of the Tibeto-Burmans. The Singphos had in pre-British times brought many Assamese into slavery. One British officer, it is reported, released no less than 5,000 slaves. At present they number 1,982 in India.

Down south there is another group of tribes, the Chakmas (135,508) of Tripura, and the Halam, Noatia and Mog tribes of the Arakan-Yoma hills. They are a short and rather dark race, of a brachycephalic Mongoloid type, probably of Burmese origin. The Chakmas profess to be Buddhists, though in the present generation they have come into contact with a rather crude form of Hinduism through eastern Bengalis. They speak a dialect belonging to the Burma branch of the Assam-Burmese languages. While in Risley's time they lived by shifting cultivation, they are now plough cultivators or field labourers. The Riangs (38,556), living in the same area, are believed to have reached their present habitat from across the Chittagong hill tracts. Around A.D. 1500 they were engaged by the then rulers of Tripura State to fight against the Muslim invaders from the plains of Bengal.

General Characteristics of the Tribes

CULTIVATION

In their majority the hill tribes of this easternmost region of India practise shifting cultivation which is called *jhum* there. A patch of land is cleared of tree and bush with axe and fire the soil is loosened with the hoe, and the seeds of various grains and vegetables are then either broadspread or dibbled in among the ashes with the digging stick. A crop is rarely harvested for more than two or three years in succession. Then the cultivated plot is left fallow for as long a time as possible. The shortest interval is four years, but it may take eight or ten years till a cultivator returns to an old plot. Where land is scarce, especially in the plains, shifting cultivation has been largely abandoned and plough cultivation is the rule.

The oldest grain crops in Assam seem to have been millet, because the sowing of millet is still connected with severe taboos. Paddy cultivation started later, and maize is still a later and comparatively recent importation.

For sacrificial purposes the tribes of this eastern area keep a certain number of domestic *mithan* or *gayal* (Bos frontalis). Some of the Konyak and Chang Nagas keep buffaloes for the same purpose. These animals are kept in a semi-wild state and are difficult to handle and dangerous. Besides these animals, which are highly valued, the tribals keep some inferior breeds of cattle, also goats, pigs, poultry, dogs and cats.

Proceeding from the west to the east, we begin with the Rabhas. They have been converted completely to plough cultivation. Paddy is their main crop on irrigated land. But many Rabhas have been forced to work as field labourers as they have lost their lands to immigrant Bengali farmers. In the past they seem to have been hunters and fishermen.

Further east, north of the Brahmaputra, is the habitat of the Monpas, some 20,000 strong, in the Kameng Frontier Division. They are *jhum* cultivators, but also grow paddy on irrigated terraces which they manure with cow dung and oak-leaves. Some of them are only graziers and breed horses, yak and other livestock.

East of the Monpas are the Miris who practise shifting cultivation. They cultivate each patch for two consecutive years and then let it lie fallow for four or five years. Their crops are paddy, millet, maize, yams and sweet potatoes. The only cattle they keep is the *mithan*. But they rear pigs and poultry, and a few goats.

The Daflas, Hrussos (Akas) and Minyongs, too, practise shifting cultivation and grow paddy, maize and millet on their hilly plots. The Abors (or Adis) were in the past shifting cultivators. As a result of the attempts by the Government to replace shifting cultivation by settled plough cultivation, the earlier system of land ownership is no longer tenable. Formerly, land was owned by the community, the individual families having only the right to its use. Now the Adis own land individually. Their neighbours, the Sherdukpens, have a material culture which is a blend between the Tibetan pattern and that of the Adis.

The Mishmis, on the mountain ranges of the northern frontier of Assam, cultivate rice, millet, pulses, wheat, barley and mustard, but also fruit trees like orange, citron and peach. On the whole, they are a pastoral people, however, and the number of cattle (and wives) are a symbol of wealth to them. They are keen traders in Tibet and Assam, or were so at least in past years.

The Apa Tanis, also a Bodo tribe, numbering about 20,000, are crowded into seven compact villages situated in a swampy valley of twenty square miles. But it is a fertile tract, well irrigated, and the Apa Tanis are extremely skilful at paddy cultivation. They raise paddy in elaborate irrigated terraces on the fertile valley bottom, and millet on the higher slopes. They use the hoe, and no plough or animals for cultivation. With their hard work, strong sense of order and tidiness, and their love for beauty, they have created and maintained an oasis of stability within a world of semi-nomadic, improvident tribesmen.

South of the Brahmaputra, in the west of Assam, now in west Meghalaya, live the Garos who practise the *jhum* system in their hills, but also plough cultivation. Their main crop is paddy, but they also grow vegetables, cotton, pepper and pulses in the same clearing. Among them shifting cultivation is closely associated with their particular type of matrilocal marriage, because men acquire rights to cultivate in a particular village only by marrying a woman of the village. Wherever shifting cultivation is practised, the Garos do not allow the private ownership of the land. But the wet-rice cultivation, which makes private ownership of the land essential, disrupts also their marriage system in the long run. Moreover, it concentrates wealth in the hands of a few people who have the foresight to claim land for wet-rice cultivation. Thus, each economic change is a vital factor in the disintegration of matrilineal social networks, which in consequence tend to patriliny, breaking the cross-cousin system.

The Khasis, the close neighbours of the Garos, too, were originally *jhum* cultivators. This is also indicated by the fact that they use the plough only for the preparation of the paddy field. As draft animals they use bullocks. While paddy is grown in terraced and irrigated fields in the valleys, the other crops, such as millet and potatoes, are raised on the bare hillsides. Potato cultivation was introduced in 1830 and is now very popular. The Khasis are good farmers and are not averse to the cultivation of new crops if they promise a good profit.

The Jaintias or Pnars, on the other hand, are not shifting cultivators. They are terrace-builders. They cultivate wet-rice in well constructed and skilfully arranged terraces so that water can be conducted to their fields from great distances. The Pnars use the plough drawn by bullocks. Other crops, such as maize, millet, sweet potatoes, potatoes, etc., are grown in gardens near the village. The gardens are surrounded by earth-walls on which hedges are planted.

The Mikirs, east of the Pnars, are excellent cultivators in their own way and at the same time good traders for the sale of their crops. Their main crop is paddy. Wherever possible they prefer shifting cultivation. Though good breeders of buffaloes, they do not drink buffalo milk.

The Dimasas (Hill Kacharis) practise *jhum* cultivation on hilly ground, while on flat ground they grow paddy. To supplement their living, they rear silk-worms, spin cotton and weave cloth. This work is done by the women.

The Kukis are paddy cultivators. They prefer shifting cultivation. In former times their chiefs redistributed the fields after three years' cultivation. They build their houses in their fields. In Chittagong they cultivate wet and dry rice, sesame, tea, bananas, oranges and maize (of several varieties).

The Mizos were in the past passionate *jhum* cultivators. Each family received for each working man 2.5 acres of land for cultivation annually. The plots were worked for one year only, and then left fallow for several years. But through the destructive effects of shifting cultivation which has eroded their land and with the rapid increase of the population, the Mizos are now forced to change over to plough cultivation and to use more up-to-date implements and more productive methods of farming. Their main crop is paddy. But they also grow cotton, maize, tea, coffee, sugar-cane and tobacco, pineapples and other fruits. They eat all kinds of meat, but their favourites are pork, fowl and beef.

The Lakhers live mainly by agriculture, which in their case is shifting cultivation. The chief and the elders of a village community redistribute the fields every year. Paddy is harvested by pulling the stems out by the roots instead of cutting them with a sickle. Supplementary crops are millet, maize, beans and tobacco.

The Pawis, too, are *jhum* cultivators. But they grow little paddy. They prefer millet and maize.

The Riangs of Tripura State have taken to plough cultivation since the last seventy or eighty years; but they have not completely abandoned their traditional shifting cultivation. They grow cotton, maize and sesame on freshly cleared land, while mustard, tobacco, sugar-cane and pulses are cultivated in ploughed fields. Vegetables, jute and paddy are crops raised both by plough or shifting cultivation.

While the Naga tribes are generally *jhum* cultivators, the Angamis and Tangkhuls among them form an exception as they are experts in terrace construction and irrigation. The Tangkhul Nagas mainly cultivate in comparatively flat valleys, but the Angamis are masters in building terraces on the steepest hills, revetting their narrow terraces with skilful stone-work.

The country of the Angami and Tangkhul Nagas lies too high for the cultivation of *jhum* rice, nor do they have sufficient land for this type of cultivation. The villages of these tribes are surrounded by admirably constructed terraced rice-fields built up with stone retaining walls at different levels, and irrigated by skilfully designed channels, which distribute the water over each step in the series.

FAMILY AND CLAN

The family and clan organisation of the tribes in Assam and in Arunachal Pradesh is far from simple and uniform. It is even more varied than the different origins of the tribes would warrant, because the long isolation of the tribes in the inaccessible hill ridges and valleys has developed a strong individualism, and so almost every village develops its own social forms and customs.

Still, some common traits stand out and certain generalisations about the social and familial life of the Assamese tribes can be made. All the tribes of this area have a patriarchal and patrilineal social organisation, and this is true not only of the Bodo and Naga tribes, but also of the more recent immigrants, the Kuki-Chins, Shans and Burmese tribes. Only the Austro-Asiatic Khasis and Syntengs and the Garos belonging to the Bodo group are exceptions. They have a matriarchal social structure.

The Khasis, Syntengs and Garos

They have matrilineal, strictly exogamous clans which are supposed to descend from a mythical ancestress ('mother of the root') and are divided into sub-clans according to rank; the sub-clans are of the royal, the priestly or the commoners' rank.

The clans possess land in common; this land is jointly farmed by the clan members and all share in its products. The eldest brother of the female head of the main family has the right of supervision over the clan land. Private land is what a man or woman has acquired individually. The landed property of a woman is inherited by her youngest daughter or other female descendants, while the landed property of the man is inherited by his mother's family. Cultivation of the land is carried out by men and women.

Of all ancestral spirits—a strong ancestor cult is in evidence in connection with a megalith culture—the female ancestress of the clan receives the greatest veneration. But the first clan ancestor and the brother of the clan mother are also respected. The priest is assisted by a priestess who is either his mother, sister or niece. He is only the delegate of the priestess. Sometimes a high-priestess is chosen as the head of the Khasi State. She rules through her son or nephew as her delegate. The office of high-priestess is inherited by her eldest daughter, eldest granddaughter or next eldest sister. The female head of a joint-family is responsible for the family sacrifice to the deceased. But the sacrifice is performed by the mother's brother.

The joint-family, sub-clan and clan have a cemetery of their own. A man can only be buried in the grave of his maternal group. Here again the importance of the matrilineal kinship group is emphasised. The bones left after cremation are carefully treated by female relatives. The burial of the bones in a pot is done first in the stone tomb of the smaller kinship group, finally in the stone ossuary of the clan.

The Khasis and Syntengs live in joint-families. Each joint-family inhabits a house with three rooms.

Marriage is matrilocal: the new family forms an economic unit with that of the wife's mother. But after the birth of one or two children the couple may take a separate house which, however, is built in the courtyard of the wife's mother; in this case the family does not anymore depend on the wife's mother. This is called a neolocal marriage.

The Khasis, however, have no institutionalised cross-cousin marriage. The Syntengs, who call themselves Pnar, practise the visit marriage custom. The husband remains in his own family and only visits his wife. He is not obliged to give any economic assistance to his wife and the children. The children live with the mother, in whose family her eldest brother exercises absolute authority. He plays an important role in many socio-religious ceremonies. But all the brothers living together pool their income for the maintenance of the family. Marriages are arranged by the matrilineal kinsmen. The owner of the family property is the youngest daughter who has to support the children of her elder sisters in case of death. The property of a deceased male is transferred to his widow (unless she remarries) or to his youngest daughter. If there are no daughters, his property is divided among his sons in equal shares. The Syntengs have matrilineal septs.

Monogamy, probably a consequence of the high social position of the woman, is predominant; polygyny and polyandry are absent.

The origin of the mother-right which the Khasis and Syntengs practise is still unexplained. It is possible that they brought it from south China or Indochina where mother-right is widespread among the tribes. The Munda tribes of north-eastern central India, at least linguistically related to the Khasis and Syntengs, have no traces of a former mother-right. But they may have left their original home in the Far East before mother-right was introduced there. It is not likely, in view of the well developed and complicated system of mother-right, that the Khasis and Syntengs have developed it locally and recently.

The Garos, though racially a Bodo tribe, also practise matriarchal descent and matrilocal residence. They obviously borrowed this system from the Khasis. They are divided into various geographical divisions (*jal*) which often differ in language, though little in race and custom. The whole tribe is futher divided into two main exogamous matri-phratries (*chachi*). Each main matri-phratry is sub-divided into many sub-sections (*mahari*), which again are divided into various local lineage groups. Structurally the two matri-phratries are really moieties, but in practice exogamous marriages can take place between two particular local lineage groups though they belong to the same matri-phratry. In this arrangement the usual form is a cross-cousin marriage.

Inheritance is in the female line and property passes either to the youngest or eldest daughter. In practice the property passes through the female heir to her husband who is thus compelled also to marry his mother-in-law if she is still alive.

Divorce is easily obtained among these tribes. The Khasis and Syntengs separate so frequently that the children often do not know their fathers. The ceremonial of divorce is short and cheap. The Garos only demand a repayment of the bride-price. The bad effects on the children usually resulting from divorce are largely absent in matriarchal societies as the children always remain with the mother and her family.

The Bodo Group

With the exception of the Garos, the Bodo tribes are patrilineally organised. They are divided into exogamous clans. Offenders against the incest rules are punished; usually they receive a severe beating. The Bodo tribes observe tribal and often village endogamy.

Boys and girls are generally free in the choice of their marriage partners though they must ask the approval of their parents before the wedding can take place. No marriage is celebrated without the payment of bride-wealth which consists of animals and agricultural products. The bride-price is paid in the form of gifts. To avoid the payment of the bride-price, sisters may be exchanged. But this can only be done if the girls agree to such marriages.

Pre-marital sex relations are freely tolerated, either in the dormitories wherever they exist, or in the homes of the girls. Such sex relations are considered a manner of courting. However, if a girl becomes pregnant, these sex relations cease and she is married off, not always to the father of the first child.

Polygyny is permitted, but rare. A man may take a second wife if the first one proves barren. But most marriages remain monogamous.

Divorce is easy for both husband and wife though it is generally disapproved by the community. Remarriage is not difficult. In case of divorce, sons go with the father, daughters with the mother.

Extra-marital sex relations are the usual reason for divorce. A man caught in adultery may be beaten severely and fined while the woman is often merely scolded.

The independent set-up of a young couple is often postponed until the birth of several children. A wife enjoys an almost equal social position in the family; she is only excluded from the attendance of a *mithan* sacrifice. Economically the women are equally important; most of the agricultural work, in addition to all the work at home, is done by the women.

Children are much wanted. But they receive no formal education. They are gradually and informally instructed and introduced into their future duties, and also into the tribal ways and customs.

The Akas, for instance, generally thought to belong to the Abor-Miri race, are divided into exogamous clans with cross-cousin marriage and patrilocal residence. Marriage is either ceremonial or by elopement; in either case a bride-price must be paid which must include at least one *mithan*. A man may take a second wife, but only with the consent of the first one. The Akas show great respect towards their women. One son is chosen as heir and most of the family property goes to him at his father's death. The other sons receive portions on marriage, the eldest son, if not chosen as the heir, receiving a larger portion than the others. The Akas use terms for father and mother which are not applied to other relatives, but they have no special terms for siblings. They are included in the classificatory groups which cover the whole clan.

The Daflas have joint families, each one living in a single large house. No religious ceremonies are included in their formal marriage ritual. Divorce is easy and apparently frequent. Widows may remarry and need not take a spouse from the first husband's lineage, as is usual in other tribes.

The Apa Tanis, neighbours of the Daflas and Miris, resemble the latter in their economic life and means of livelihood, but they differ from them in the prohibition of cross-cousin marriage.

The Galongs, neighbours of the Abors in the Siang division of Arunachal Pradesh, are divided into endogamous sub-sections consisting of exogamous clans. The members of a clan feel the obligation of helping each other economically.

Dormitories are absent; the sex urge of the unmarried is satisfied by polyandry. Cross-cousin marriage is the usual procedure. No marriage can take place without a bride-price.

The Idus, a sub-section of the Mishmis, in the Dibang valley, lack any centralised organisation, and are divided into a number of localised patrilineal exogamous clans. Marriage is contracted through the medium of bride-wealth and is paid in buffaloes. The wife takes up residence with her husband. Cross-cousin and parallel cousin marriages are considered immoral and unnatural.

The Mikirs, another Bodo tribe, are peculiar among their kind in these parts as they build their homesteads close to their fields in widely dispersed settlements; they do not live in closed villages as other Bodo tribes.

The Kukis in the Kachar hills are sub-divided into eight social grades, which intermarry with each other and with other tribes. The clans, however, are exogamous and patrilineal.

They demand a high bride-price—from three to ten *mithans*. These have to be paid to the bride's father, and other gifts have to be made to her other relatives. Inheritance is in the male line, the youngest son being the main heir.

Another Kuki tribe is that of the Lakhers, though they also have Naga affinities. They claim kinship with the tiger and regard the python as an object of great reverence and more or less taboo. They have a kind of individual totems, believing in the existence of a tutelary deity or spirit in animal form for every person.

They have six groups divided into clans. But the tribal unit is the village rather than the clan, and clan exogamy is not strictly observed. Only four clans seem to have a totemic origin.

The Manipuri tribes also have patrilineal, exogamous clans, named after common ancestors. Traces of totemism among these tribes are rare. They observe, however, a number of food taboos.

The Mizos are divided into clans. Some of them have the tiger as their totem. If a tiger had to be killed because of its attacks on domestic cattle, all men hunted it together and attacked it simultaneously, so that the tiger would not know who had killed it.

The totem of the Pawis is the goat. No Pawi may kill a goat and eat its flesh. A goat may not even be taken into the house.

In the past, the Mizos treated their womenfolk very harshly. Women often got a beating from their husbands, had to do most of the work in house and field, and were not allowed to keep any possessions. Divorce was easy and a frequent occurrence. The Mizos practise the rule of ultimogeniture, while among the Pawis the eldest son is the main heir.

The Chakmas have a rather strict family system. Marriages are arranged by the parents. Free mixing of boys and girls is not permitted. A man may divorce his wife, but the wife has no such right. The eldest son inherits all property left by the father.

The Naga Tribes

Though the social organisation of the Naga tribes is full of local and tribal peculiarities, all the tribes have at least a few traits in common. Descent is generally in the male line, while relationships in the female line are ignored. Thus, most Naga tribes, with the exception of perhaps the Angamis, have no objection to cross-cousin marriages; they even prefer them.

Levirate, the marriage of widow to the next eldest brother of her deceased husband, is a general custom. Sex relations with such a prospective wife are not taken seriously even in his lifetime, provided that he gives his consent and is absent for some time. This form of fraternal polyandry was permissible at least in some villages of the Rengma Nagas.

Exogamy is observed always within the kinship group, often also within the whole clan, more rarely it includes a number of related clans, a phratry. The more conservative tribes observe phratry exogamy, while the progressive tribes practise merely kinship exogamy.

All Naga tribes show traces of an original dual organisation which may even have existed in the form of a three-phratries' system. Thus the Angami Nagas have two phratries (*kelhu*) one of which is again sub-divided. But already around 1900 phratry exogamy was relaxed into clan exogamy and about 1920 only lineage exogamy was observed. The Angami Nagas have no trace of totemism.

The Lhota Nagas have a similar system of three nominally exogamous phratries; in practice, however, they observe only clan exogamy.

Phratry exogamy is more strictly observed by the Ao Nagas; their kinship system is very intricate, as instead of two they have three marriage classes. They have totemism; in fact, of all the Naga tribes the Ao Nagas have the strongest totemism. Some clans believe in their descent from certain animals which thereby became their totems. The totems are, however, not always taboo.

According to Fürer-Haimendorf, traces of a dual organisation can also be detected among the Konyak Nagas. They too have three phratries like the Aos, but their social gradation of the phratries is more marked than among the Aos. The Rengma Nagas have six phratries with exogamous clans.

All tribes claim an eponymous ancestor for their clans; in rare cases the clan name is taken from a place—the village from which they originally came.

It seems that the Naga clans were originally totemic, but in many cases totemism has decayed. Some clans, however, seem to observe the clan taboos more faithfully than others, especially the tiger clan. It is of course possible that totemism was not indigenous among the Naga tribes at all, and was adopted by only a few clans from neighbouring totemic tribes.

The former existence of a dual organisation is often reflected in stories of descent from two brothers: among the Konyak Nagas even the typical rivalry between the moieties could be observed.

The Sema Nagas, when founding a new village, always take members of the two clans along, so that the younger generation has no difficulty in getting marriage partners. Some clans have food restrictions which are obviously of totemic origin.

While all the Naga tribes are organised according to the

male line, traces of mother-right are not entirely absent, especially among the Sema Nagas. But that may be due to influence from the matriarchal Khasis and Garos.

POLITICAL ORGANISATION

The village and its constitution presents many interesting points of divergence among the wilder tribes of Assam and Arunachal Pradesh. While most of the tribes are divided into exogamous clans, which are partly totemic, others live in village communities without a clan system, each under its ruler, independent of the rest of the villages. The villages are closely stockaded and built in a good strategic position for defence. Other tribes acknowledge the sway of a local chieftain extending over several such villages.

(1) Thus the Khasis and Syntengs, closely allied to one another, are divided into four clans; the royal, priestly, minister and plebeian clans. The chiefs are always taken from the royal or priestly clan; clanship is inherited in the female line.

There is a definite order of precedence in public and state affairs among the clans, but no social gulf exists with regard to intermarriage. Social position is indicated less by the shape and material of the house (though the chiefs' houses are usually larger) than by the pattern and colours of the clothes worn.

The dignity of a chief is inherited by the eldest son of the eldest sister, after his death by his eldest brother or by the maternal grand-nephew. If male heirs are absent, the eldest sister (or eldest sister's daughter) has the right to succession. The queen, in turn, is then succeeded by her eldest son or another male relative.

Politically, the Khasi area was in the past divided into twenty-five Khasi states which were independent. Though headed by a chief (*siem*), administration was on democratic lines. A Khasi chief had no powers over land or forests. He could not impose taxes or promulgate new laws or any policy without the Darbar's consent. Such a Darbar was an open-door assembly in which all the male adults of the state took part. Attendance was compulsory.

(2) The tribal organisation of the Bodo group seems to be in the process of dissolution. Only the communities in the hills

are still able to retain their old tribal customs and laws, while in the valleys the Bodos are in the habit of replacing them for Hindu rules and regulations. Tribal discipline with regard to clan laws has weakened. Though they still inherit their old clan names in the male line, and even know the name of their totems, marriages are no longer regulated in accordance with the ancient exogamous laws, and totem taboos have been given up completely.

Not only is the identity of the clans generally lost, but even tribal membership is dropped, and with conversion to Hinduism the Bodos often drop their tribal names and assume those of a fully Hinduised caste. They also give up their tribal language in favour of Assamese. Thus many Bodos though only half-converted to Hinduism prefer to be called Rabhas and from then onwards consider themselves superior to the Bodos.

However, they still take Bodo girls in marriage though they refuse their daughters to the Bodos. The latter retaliate by performing purificatory ceremonies when marrying their daughters to Rabhas. The Rabhas, though they celebrate their feasts in the Hindu fashion and employ Brahmins for their rituals, still consider themselves a people set apart from the Bengalis.

The Garos, one of the Bodo tribes, are much sub-divided. They have four main clans, each of which has numerous exogamous sections. Their political structure is democratic. In fact, the Garos have no chiefs. A headman is only a nominal head: important affairs are decided by village councils consisting of elders or heads of families, including the headmen.

The Mikirs have a threefold village administration, the lowest office of which is filled by the Achom Asar, usually an old, influential man well versed in Mikir customs. He is appointed by a Habe, the next higher authority, the headman of a village, whose jurisdiction does not go beyond the limits of the village. But he settles all disputes within his village. The Habe is, in turn, appointed by a Pinpo, in the past appointed by the Jaintia ruler as his representative for the administration of the Mikir hills. There are now nine houses of Pinpos, and their office is hereditary. Each Pinpo is selected from the clan to which his predecessor belonged. Over all the Pinpos is the Karbi Recho, a Mikir king, but he rules only through the Pinpos.

A small Bodo tribe, akin to the Garos, is called Hajong. A part of the tribe has descended from the Garo hills into the Surma valley. This descent into the valley resulted in the formation of two sections, one, the upper, remaining true to its tribal ways of life, while the lower valley section became Hinduised and abandoned even its tribal dialect for a corrupt form of Bengali.

Of the Bodo tribes on the southern slopes of the Himalayas the Abors have a chief and a council in every village. All affairs of the community are discussed in the *morang* (village hall). Even the type of daily work is discussed first in the *morang* and a resolution must be passed before work can begin. The village boys act as messengers and run through the village lanes making the council decisions known to everyone. But the authority of their headmen and tribal councils is gradually getting lost, as the Abors can now appeal to the superior courts. Their bachelors' dormitory is also losing its importance and is turning into a mere club-house.

The villages of the Akas are governed by councils presided over by headmen chosen by the people. But the two largest villages have influential *ranis* (queens) descended from the old ruling family. The Akas are a warlike community, and in addition to their general title, which is not used by them and the meaning of which is unknown, they have two sub-divisions, each of which is known to the Assamese by a title implying 'plunder'.

The Galong community is ruled by a village council presided over by a headman who acquired his position by wealth and personal influence. In the past the Galongs were a warlike race, blood-revenge and plunder being the purposes of their raids. Prisoners became slaves.

The Daflas, another Bodo tribe, live in small unstable villages which are loose aggregations of long-houses and in the past were constantly involved in feuds, murders, kidnappings and the theft of cattle. They still are a happy-go-lucky, swashbuckling people, occasionally infringing on their hard-working agrarian neighbours, the Apa Tanis.

These Apa Tanis have a complex and highly organised social structure based on the division into two endogamous classes, the *mite* or nobility, and the *mura* or serfs; each class being sub-divided into exogamous clans.

The Murungs in former Tippera State which is now called Comilla in Bangladesh were originally also Bodos, since their chiefs intermarried with the Kacharis, but now they claim to be superior to the Bodos. Their chief calls himself a Rajput, and the nobles pose as Rajbansis. The tribe is much sub-divided, some clans holding a position far above others who are labourers and primitive cultivators in the interior. But all clans have retained their original Bodo language.

The formerly dominant tribe of the Chutiyas repudiates today the connection with the Bodos though their common Bodo language seems to indicate such a connection. In former times the Chutiyas ruled the north-eastern region of Assam and gradually extended their dominion southwards as far as Sibsagar and Nowgong. But in 1500 they were subjugated by the Ahoms. Some time previous to this date they were Hinduised in part and later assimiliated by the Ahoms.

Last to lose their tribal identity were the Deoris. Their more Mongoloid appearance seems to indicate that they have kept themselves free from racial intermixture with the Ahoms and the other Bodo tribes. One of their social peculiarities is the habit of lodging a whole family under one roof, enlarging the building as the numbers increase, until sometimes more than a hundred persons live under a common roof.

(3) The political organisation of the Naga tribes is marked by great diversity. Some of the Naga tribes are subject to chiefs who rule almost autocratically, while other tribes form democratic village communities in which the headman has only a nominal authority. On the whole it can be stated that the Naga tribes are organised on democratic lines; only two tribes, the Konyaks and the Semas, having autocratic chiefs.

Most of the Naga tribes have bachelors' halls which are the real centres of social and political life, though less so among the Angami and Sema Nagas. Usually each clan has its own *morung*, as these youth dormitories are called in Assamese. The unmarried men sleep there, and strangers are accommodated in it. All public affairs of the clan are transacted in it.

Thus in the northern district the Konyaks are subject to a chief who is sacrosanct and tabooed, and rules often several villages with much authority. He is regarded as the repository of tribal fortune, virtue, or its life-principle. In some villages he is, or was, so heavily tabooed that he was not permitted to touch the ground, and on a journey had to be carried, and leaves and branches were spread wherever he sat down. But his very sanctity prevented him from exercising his powers and, if he was not a strong character, he frequently left the government to his relatives.

Of the Naga tribes the Angamis reside in unusually large villages, some containing as many as 800 houses. The villages are set upon hills, and carefully stockaded and guarded against eventual attacks.

The basic unit of the tribe is not, however, the village, but a sub-division of the population thus concentrated, called *khel* or *tepfu,* which is exogamous and said to be derived from a single ancestor. Faction fights between these bodies are frequent and used to be bloody, as outside help was called in to take part.

The large size of their villages is probably the result of their adoption, apparently from the Manipuris, of the system of permament cultivation by irrigated channels, carried with extraordinary skill and labour round the slopes of the hills.

The Ao Nagas live in villages which, though nominally governed by a headman, are in practice independent democratic units. The constitution of an Ao village community is intricate; it consists of elders representing various clans and kinship groups governing for fixed, though fluctuating, periods.

Entrance into the Ao dormitory was given to the boys periodically every three years, while those age grades that were allowed to leave the *morung* and to marry entered the lowest grades of the village council.

A regular custom among them was the enslavement of members of the neighbouring tribes, now more or less suppressed. The victims were treated well, except when paid over as fine or ransom to another village, when they were usually sacrificed.

The Sema village, under the adjacent tribe, has a hereditary headman or chief, endowed with considerable authority and privileges. But he can retain his ruling power only if he is able to persuade his younger brothers and sons to leave the native village and settle with their retainers elsewhere. If they remain in the village they can claim share in his authority which of course soon reduces his political power considerably. The Sema Nagas have no *morung*. The front part of the chief's house is usually the place where public affairs are discussed.

The Lhota Nagas are, contrary to the Semas who are ferocious and warlike, a quiet and industrious people, and adhere to the old method of cultivation on burned patches of jungle.

The Kuki-Chin group in the Kachar hills, on the other hand, with the exception of the Rangkols, are all organised under the rule of hereditary chiefs. They are very clannish, and evince great solidarity with their chiefs and fellow clansmen. The Rangkols used to elect a headman for each village and allow him to manage its affairs.

The Meitheis became dominant over all the other tribes in Manipur. They provided the king who ruled autocratically. Treason against him was considered the most heinous crime. Manipur is now ruled democratically.

Among the Mizos, the chief, the priest and the blacksmith, in that order, were the three most important people in the village. In return for the services which the chief, the priest and the blacksmith rendered to the community, the villagers built their houses for them and supplied them with food. Mizos had a strong community sense. They did a good deal of work in common. The unmarried boys lived in a youth dormitory and could be called by the chief in a case of emergency for work as well as for the defence of the village.

In the past, the administration of the land was vested in the hands of the chief. In the annual distribution of the land for cultivation, the chiefs gave the first option for the selection of a *jhum* site to privileged families such as those of their own kin, or others who paid a fee of cash or paddy in addition to the usual tribute to the chiefs. After these families had selected their plots, the others could choose the land they wanted for cultivation. At present, the village councils decide in open meetings on the date of the land distribution. The heads of the families draw numbers in a lottery. Whoever draws No. 1, is the first to choose the best site; then follow the others according to the numbers they have drawn. The amount of land given is in correspondence with the size of the family.

Each village is well stockaded, like the villages of the Nagas, but the Mizo village is laid out differently, the streets radiating from a square in the centre, in front of the chief's house.

The Singphos, on the Burmese border, live in small villages, several of which are subject to one common chief. But his authority is rather weak. Until recent times, the Singphos lived in a semi-independent state of their own, in which slavery was an important institution. In the past, the British policy of liberating the slaves led to several Singpho risings, the last of which was suppressed in 1843.

The Lushais, of the same race as the Thados or Kukis, live in villages headed by entirely independent chiefs. These have certain duties towards their fellow villagers, and in return receive a certain share of each man's crops. The only remedy against a too despotic headman is flight and transferment of one's allegiance to another village headman.

Each village is well stockaded, like those of the Nagas, but it is laid out differently, the streets radiating from a square in the centre, in front of the house of the chief.

Among the Singphos on the Burmese border, the system of slavery was in former times an important institution. The British policy of liberating the slaves led to several Singpho risings, the last of which was suppressed in 1843.

The political and social structure of the tribes in Assam shows extreme variety and proves the strong individualism and spirit of independence of these tribes. No wonder that the modern Indian Government finds it difficult to curb their turbulence and to subject them to discipline and order.

RELIGION

As in many other aspects of life, the tribes in Assam display much variety in their religious beliefs and practices. But a few general features are common to most tribes. They shall be described here.

The Supreme Being

Most tribes in Assam believe in one deity superior to the rest, but as this high-god is passively benevolent he is generally of little importance in cult and daily life. More prominent are the minor deities and spirits who are near and always demanding propitiation through sacrifices and gifts or else they take revenge. Still, the tribes entertain a strong belief in the existence of a supreme being; his supremacy over the other gods and spirits in the world is undeniable.

(1) Of the Austro-Asiatic tribes the Khasis have a supreme god whom they call U Blei Nongthaw (god, the creator). This deity is however often conceived in female form. Another informant called the supreme god U Pyrtat whose sword is lightning. The Khasis believe that U Blei Nongthaw was in early times in close contact with men. But men became jealous, and U Blei Nongthaw retreated into inaccessible distance. For the Khasis, religion is the way to find the way back to the supreme god.

U Blei Nongthaw created heaven and mother earth. Mother earth had five children, the sun (female), the moon (male), the water, the air, and the fire. Out of these came all living beings on earth.

(2) All Bodo tribes believe in a creator god who is worshipped through a more or less formal cult.

The Garos call their creator god Tatara-Rabunga, while the Rabhas call him Ma-Bai. He created the earth out of a pre-existing watery plain in which darkness ruled. The work of creation was carried out by a minor deity and delegate of the supreme god. His name was Nestu-Nopantu.

The Mikirs have a god whom they call the 'Great God'. But he is now a mere household god. He receives a sacrifice every third year. The sacrificial victim is a pig. A feast with rice beer and wine is prepared on the occasion of the sacrifice.

The Abors and Galongs also believe in a supreme god whom they call the 'All-Loving'. But their knowledge about this supreme god is very hazy.

Dalton maintains that the Mishmis entertained no belief in a supreme god, though they admitted that there must have been a creator. But they believed that he had died long ago, as all living beings have to die.

The Daflas acknowledge, but do not worship, a supreme being. They state that they know nothing about him.

The Kacharis call their supreme god Alow Raja; this is probably Alhou, the supreme god of the Sema Nagas.

(3) All Naga tribes believe in a supreme god though he is for them often a remote deity to whom no sacrifices are due.

The Ao Nagas, for instance, call the supreme god Lungkijinga (deity of the stone house). They believe that he lives high up in the sky; therefore they also call him 'Spirit of the Air Room'. He sits on his stone house as on a throne. He dispenses the fates of human beings in the form of leaves. But he does little more. Only occasionally does he command the other deities to punish some men or to leave others in peace.

The Ao Nagas perform no official sacrifices in his honour except occasionally through a shaman. Sometimes Lungkijinga is also called 'Creator' (Tiaba), and held responsible for the creation of man; but the opinions about this function of god are vague.

Though Lungkijinga is now the high-god of the Ao Nagas, there is reason for the assumption that in fact he is the former high-god of the Konyak Nagas. For, the Ao Nagas have still another high-god who fits better into their whole culture. This other god is called Lichaba or 'creator of the world', or—literally —'he who walks over the earth'. The Ao Nagas believe that Lichaba created the earth and flattened the Brahmaputra valley. He is the acknowledged lord of the world, master over rain and storm. He prevents earth-slides, and can command famines and epidemics. In old times he used to visit the Ao villages; now he appears to them only in dreams.

This high-god receives rich offerings which are presented by the village priests. Usually the meat of pigs and fowls is offered to him. The sacrificial feasts are celebrated at the time of the ripening of the field fruits.

The Konyak Nagas call the supreme being Gawang. He is the lord of the sky. He is conceived as a definitely personal being though no Konyak can say exactly how he looks. He lives somewhere in the sky. Long ago he made the firmament, the earth and man. But they do not know how he made man. Gawang bestows wealth or poverty on the Konyaks according to his will. He can see and hear everything that goes on in the world and he punishes evil-doers and those breaking the taboo rules. The punishment is given during the lifetime of the culprit. The Konyaks pray to Gawang and offer him the first fruits of the hunt and the harvest.

The Lhota Nagas seem to have no clear idea about the existence of a high-god or creator.

The Sema Nagas, on the other hand, have a definite idea of a high-god whom they call Alhou (creator). His attributes are omniscience, omnipotence and omnipresence. His full name is Timilhour—creator of men. But he interferes little with the affairs of mortals, though he distributes good and evil, wealth and poverty among men. Since he is benevolent and does not do any harm to men, the Semas care little about his worship. Alhou's habitation is the sky, or the whole space between heaven and earth. He shares his habitation with the heavenly spirits, Kungumi.

The Rengma Nagas call their high-god Songinyu. His voice is the thunder. He has power over the heavenly bodies.

The Angami Nagas call their supreme god Kepenopfu (birth-spirit). He is sometimes addressed as the creator, but more as the creator of living things than the creator of the universe. It is not clear whether he is masculine or feminine, he appears at times as the first man and guardian of the kingdom of the dead; at other times as the primeval mother of men and as the wife of a being with moon-mythological features.

Kepenopfu dwells in heaven to which place the good souls also go. He casts the thunderbolt from heaven–found on earth as neolithic stone-axes. This high-god is a strange combination of a sky-god and a mother-goddess. About the cult of this god little is known. He is probably an otiose deity. He has some moral significance, because only the souls of the good are allowed to stay in heaven.

The Nagas of Manipur have a common belief that the world was created by a deity which causes earthquakes. But beyond that little is known of their religion.

(4) The Kabuis believe in a supreme and benevolent deity, the creator of all things. Man, however, was created by another deity, though on the command of the high-god.

The Tangkhuls believe that the supreme god is the judge of the evil-doers. He is addressed in prayer in times of need and sickness. Man was created by his son.

All Lushai-Kuki tribes venerate a sky-god Pathian or Pathen, which means 'father'. He is the creator of all things, benevolent and all-powerful; he lives in heaven and has little contact with human beings. But he accepts the sacrifice of pigs and fowls during certain agrarian feasts.

The Thados attribute to Pathen, their creator god, the power of controlling the evil spirits. Most of their sacrifices are addressed to him. Pathen is master over the rain; when angry with a man he kills him by lightning. He reminds the Thados of his existence by thunder.

The Lakhers or Maras call their supreme god Khazangpa. He resides in heaven. He is the creator and master of the world and he has full power over men whom he treats according to their merits. Khazangpa meant 'father of all things', i.e., of life. His second name is Pachhapa, 'the old man', or 'the source', i.e., of life. He possesses strong anthropomorphic features, for in their opinion he has a wife and children and takes nourishment

The most important sacrifices which the Lakhers perform are addressed to him. In a song the officiating priest asks for health, wealth, rich crops and success in hunting.

Other Chin tribes, like the Hakas and southern Chins, believe in a high-god living in heaven. They call him Kozin. The Siyins and all northern Chin tribes do not seem to believe in a supreme god. But more careful investigation about their religious beliefs will be necessary in order to be sure of it.

The religious conceptions of the Kachin tribes reveal a strange incongruence: Karai Kasang, their supreme god, appears late in the myth about the world's origin and plays no important part in it. But nobody doubts that he is the maker and master of the world. His other names are 'all-knowing', 'the one who is above in the clouds', 'the one supreme'. Karai Kasang cannot age or die, he has neither wife nor children. Without his permission no evil spirit can harm a human being. In case of misfortune individuals and whole villages address him in prayer when the spirits prove powerless. But sacrifices in his honour are rare and never of a bloody nature. Offerings of rice, eggs and beer are made; occasionally live chickens and buffaloes are let loose in his honour.

Karai Kasang is probably the god of the ruling class which immigrated from the north (inner Asia) and subjugated an earlier people. Karai Kasang recreates, perfects and beautifies a world created by a mother goddess.

The Minor Deities and Spirits

While most tribes of Assam have some conception of a personal divine being creating the world and directing its destinies, they also believe in a great variety of minor deities and spirits, demons and ghosts who people the world, the earth as well as the world above and the nether-world. They are nearer to man than the supreme god who is generally conceived as a distant divinity, less concerned with the fate of man and leaving the world to the mercy or malice of these superhuman spiritual beings.

Tribal religion is often believed to be the outcome of man's fear of the spirits, and religious rites are performed and offerings made to appease them and thus to avert the disasters which these deities and spirits are intent on inflicting on mankind.

This is not quite correct. Not only the supreme god, but also many deities and spirits are believed to be benevolent and helpful to men once they have been won over through prayer and sacrifice. And as the needs of the tribes are great and manifold, they have created a great number of such spirits to look after each particular need and to respond to prayer and sacrifice by human beings. And since men are emotionally more strongly affected by the troubles and difficulties of life, they are naturally more occupied with the veneration and appeasement of the deities and spirits than with the worship of the supreme god. They threaten them and, on the other hand, promise them assistance and relief in their immediate and urgent needs.

Thus the Rabhas, though now largely Hinduised, make offerings to the heavenly bodies, the sun, the moon and the stars, in particular the constellation of the Great Bear. They also venerate the spirits of the woods, hills and rivers, and every year, when they collect their first crops, they offer some of the first fruits to them as well as to their ancestors.

The Koches and Kacharis too venerate a great variety of deities and spirits residing in the world beyond or on earth. The elemental gods are usually worshipped outside the village, often on the bank of a river, the village gods at their shrine in the village or on the outskirts of it, and the household gods in the main room of the house.

The Khasis, besides venerating a host of gods, are said to have a secret snake cult. They occasionally offer a human sacrifice to the snake kept in the house.

The Garos too have numerous minor deities and nature spirits—a protector of the crops, a god of fertility, a god of strength, a goddess of wealth. The sun, moon and the stars are spirits, placed in the sky for regulating the seasons. Thunder, lightning, rain, wind, earthquakes have their controlling spirits.

All of them demand the sacrifice of birds and other animals and the offering of fruits and grain.

The Akas are spirit worshippers. They believe in the existence of good and evil spirits who may harm them if not properly and regularly propitiated.

The Lhota Nagas believe in a great number of heavenly spirits (*potso*) who live in a world beyond this earth. But beyond the heavenly realm there is another, higher one, and beyond this still another, higher world. Only the *potsos* of the second world concern themselves with the fate of human beings, appear to men and permit shamans to hear them. They must be venerated by prayer and sacrifice.

The Sema Nagas also believe in heavenly spirits whom they call *kungumi*. They are similar to the *potsos* of the Lhotas. The Semas also believe in spirits of the earth—*teghami*. The most prominent among these is Litsaba or Kichimiya, the spirit of fertility who gives a good harvest. In return he demands rich offerings, or else he comes as a strong whirlwind and causes much damage to the crops. He is probably identical with the Lichaba of the Ao Nagas.

The Mizos were in the past firm believers in spirits and thought that every tree, hill and stone was inhabited by them. They believed that all these were evil, and that every calamity which befell them—illness, death, drought, storms, winds, floods, failure of crops or accidents—was the work of these spirits. They were ignorant of material causes. They lived in terrible fear, afraid to anger the spirits. They constantly tried to propitiate them with sacrifices and offerings, and to avert their anger by the observance of many taboos and by wearing certain charms. Much of this fear has disappeared since the Mizos have become Christians.

The tribes of Assam usually have a professional clan of priests, but often the performer of the ceremonies is a medicine-man, either elected or hereditary, belonging to the tribe or clan. Occasionally, especially in the western hills, the village headman acts as the priest for the village community.

Eschatology

Belief in some sort of a future life exists in all tribes and is taken for granted as an unarguable fact of common knowledge. Some tribes believe that the spirits of the deceased members of the tribe may return to their former dwelling places. The disposal of the dead, however, varies much from tribe to tribe.

Thus the Khasis burn their dead with elaborate rites. The spirits of those whose funeral rites were properly performed go to the house or garden of the supreme god. The others are turned into animals, birds or insects, and wander about on the earth; the spirits of the wicked go to a place of punishment. The Khasis have different types of stone monuments to commemorate their dead ancestors. Two other forms of stone structure are merely for sitting purposes.

The Bodo tribes bury their dead.

The Garos believe that a demon guards the entrance to the realm of the dead. The souls of the deceased anxious to gain admission have to bribe him with brass rings and have to pretend that they had been married to a thousand women (to prove their erotic prowess).

Among the Naga tribes the realm of the dead is generally located in the nether-world. But the belief is not absent among some tribes that at least some of the deceased may reach heaven. Generally they also hold that the souls of the dead have to overcome great obstacles on their way to their final destination. The surviving relatives and friends can assist them effectively in these trials.

The Angami Nagas claim that the path to the realm of the supreme god is guarded by a spirit with whom the souls of the dead have to fight. If conquered they are forever excluded from heaven and must wander about between heaven and earth. This guardian spirit is often identified with the ancestors of the human race and is the mythical husband of the supreme goddess. He has lunar-mythological features—a long beard, he hides during the day, etc.

But they also assert that only those who have celebrated certain merit feasts and after that have never eaten impure food go to the supreme god in heaven, while the others go to the nether-world where they pass through further existences first as butterflies, then as other insects; after the seventh incarnation follows complete annihilation.

The belief in transformation into insects is, however, not restricted to the Angami Nagas; it is found among almost all Naga tribes, and also among the Khasis, Garos and Lushais.

This belief is, moreover, well known in countries beyond Assam, and is found in south-east and east Asia, and in Oceania and was held even in ancient Europe.

The Sema Nagas assert that the Wakha mountain is the last station before entering the nether-world. This nether-world is either in the sky or under the earth. Some Semas believe that good people go towards the East, the wicked ones towards the West, the direction of the setting sun.

The Rengma Nagas hold that the nether-world is divided into six identical worlds, one on top of the other.

The Tangkhuls locate the realm of the dead in a heaven which is dominated by a god who judges the dead on their arrival according to their merits.

The Ao Nagas place a spear in the grave. With it the dead must hit a tree in front of the house in which the king of the dead dwells. Only honest people can pass the test. These the king of the dead invites into his house, and later sends them to the village of the dead. Thieves miss the tree; they go by a side-path straight to the village of the dead. Life there is similar to life on earth, but without sexual enjoyment. After a while the deceased die a second time and go to a dim place where they slowly fade away.

The Lhota Nagas believe that a spirit guards the path to the realm of the dead; he tries to catch the dead just arriving and to kill them.

The Kabui Kukis believe that the dead dwell under the earth.

The Lushais, Kukis and Lakhers believe in a land of the blessed and a land of the dead; the great majority of the dead go to the latter place.

The Lushais also state that the ancestor of the human race shoots at the dead on their arrival. Whomever he hits cannot enter the dwelling place of the dead. But he is unable to hit those who have succeeded in killing a man and in celebrating merit feasts; nor those who have enjoyed three virgins or seven women.

For others, life after death means a continuous wandering about of the spirits without ever finding a resting place.

The Bawm-Zo, a neighbouring Chin tribe, already in Bangladesh, believe on the other hand that life after death is eternal, and that the actions of each individual during his present life will decide his fate after death.

Head-hunting

The custom of head-hunting prevailed in the past among many tribes of Assam, particularly among the Nagas. The head-hunting cult is based on a belief in a regular cycle of life which is a material essence abstracted from one owner and carried off to benefit the village and family of the successful taker of the head. Others believe that their object in capturing the head of an enemy is to bring into subjection the spirit of the dead person which is believed to accompany his skull to the home of the killer. Hence, with a perfectly logical grasp of the situation, the skull of a stranger is preferred, because the spirit does not know its way in a strange land and is, therefore, less likely to wander. An additional reason for head-hunting is that the head of an enemy is a trophy which gives a social prestige to the killer.

The Khasis, when they had taken heads from their enemies, used to fix them to the top of wooden shafts round which an altar was erected. The shafts crowned with the heads were then planted outside the village near a public road.

The Khasis believed in the past in fortune-bringing snakes, the *thlens*. These *thlens* were attached to different families. They had to be fed human blood. A human being had to be killed periodically, and the hair, the fingertips and a little blood were offered to the snake. Many families were known or suspected of being keepers of such snakes.

The Garos, who live in the neighbourhood of the Khasis, were also head-hunters and, previous to the year 1872–3 when they were subjugated by the British, they often made head-hunting raids in the plains north and south of their hills. When a raid was successful and a number of people were killed, their heads were carried off as trophies. Apart from the killing for sheer fun and bravado, human sacrifices were found necessary also at the death of a chief of a village or clan.

But head-hunting was more popular among the Naga tribes. It is said that in the past they shrank from no treachery in securing their eagerly desired trophies. Any head counted, be it that of a man, woman or child. A head taken entitled the killer to wear certain ornaments according to the custom of the tribe or village. Most heads were taken not in fair fight, but stealthily. A common method was for a man to lurk near the water-place of a hostile village and kill the first woman or child who came to draw water. Occasionally expeditions were made on a larger scale, several villages combining for the sake of making a large bag. If the village was found emptied of the adult population who were working in the fields, an attack could be made and as many children and old people as could be killed within a reasonable time would be murdered. A retreat was effected before the men of the attacked village could have time to receive the news and return from their fields.

The desire for heads was especially strong among the younger generation. This was mainly the fault of the women who taunted the men and refused to marry them unless they raided a village and took some heads.

The head-taking and ruthless disregard of life which characterised the Nagas greatly checked the social intercourse of the tribes. Every tribe, almost every village, was at war with its neighbour, and no Naga dared leave the territory of his tribe without the probability of losing his life.

It seems that some British administrators and ethnographers of the Nagas took a rather lenient view of this custom of head-hunting. Men like J.P. Mills and J.H. Hutton found excuses for head-hunting raids because they gave zest to the life of the tribals and were regarded as a kind of sport.*

But among the Angami Nagas, according to J. H. Hutton [(1921), pp. 156 ff.], heads were taken not only because warriors were vain and wanted to prove their manliness, but also because the killing of a human being was conducive to the prosperity of the community or of the crops. He tells of the case of a boy purchased from another tribe being flayed and his flesh divided. Each man who received a piece put it in his corn basket to avert evil and ensure a plentiful harvest. This reminds us of the *meriah* sacrifice of the Khonds in Orissa.

It was also believed that the ghost of a headless man was not admitted to paradise. It had to serve the man who was in the possession of its head. A man who had taken a head was entitled to wear special emblems, a hornbill, lines of cowrie shells, armlets, etc.

*But it can hardly be considered sporting if, for instance, the Semas used to entertain guests and to slay them when they were off their guard and take their heads. Moreover, they were notorious for their cruelty while engaged in killing.

Heads taken by the Lhota, Rengma and Sema Nagas were usually hung up in a tree near the edge of the village. The Ao and Konyak Nagas hung the heads in their houses. Effigies of human heads, carved of wood or small gourds and painted, are still hung up in Naga meeting houses.

The Mizos, too, were head-hunters. For a long time, the Mizos hunted for heads only in other Mizo villages. But later, when the need for iron and guns was felt more keenly, the Mizos often went from their hills down into the plains of Assam and Bengal, and raids were made on other tribes. With the spoils, they also brought heads home. Human heads would help young men to get wives. Girls admired a great warrior. Human heads also helped a Mizo to get entrance into the Village of the Dead.

Conversions to Christianity

Contrary to common opinion that the Christian missions concentrate mainly on tribals and low-castes it must be stated that Christian missions were started among the tribals only in the second half of the 19th century. Though Christians arrived in India already in the early centuries A.D. and settled on the west coast, they did not propagate their faith. Conversion work started after the arrival of the Portuguese. But they, too, showed little inclination for the conversion of tribals and the low-castes; their intention was to convert influential people and through them the rest of the population.

In Assam, Protestant missionaries were the first to contact the tribals. The first tribals to become Christians were two Khasis who were converted in 1812–13 by an Indian evangelist connected with William Carey. A mission was established among the Khasis in 1833, but had to be closed down five years later. It was reopened in 1841 by Welsh Calvinistic Presbyterians; after some initial setbacks, it flourished.

In Nagaland, the first Christian missionary effort was made in 1840. But at that time the Nagas associated the Europeans with the British soldiers who were carrying out punitive actions in retaliation for Naga raids. The first missionaries did not get a good reception. Moreover, their health was shattered in the rough and mountainous country. The missionaries had to withdraw. But a few years later missionaries befriended some Naga traders, and in 1851 the first Naga, of the Ao tribe, was baptised. Later, a dedicated medical missionary, Dr. S. W. Rivenburg (1886–1923), became the real founder of the Christian Church among the Nagas. He worked mainly among the Angami Nagas. Through the Angami converts, other Naga tribes like the Rengma Zeliang and Lhota Nagas were contacted.

In 1863 American Baptists opened a mission in the Garo hills. In 1883 they started a mission in Kohima.

Catholic missionaries arrived in north-eastern India only at the end of the nineteenth century and began their conversion work among the Khasis. Work among the Nagas started only in 1951, and in Manipur in 1956.

Mission work among the Mizos (Lushais) was started in 1894-5 by Welsh missionaries and by British Baptists. They were successful: of the 214,721 Mizos in the Lushai hills 208,165 are Christians. The Protestant missionaries found a good response also in the Khasi and Jaintia hills: Of the 356,155 Khasis today 168,311 or 52.87 per cent are Christians. The Garos responded less favourably to the Christian message: Of 258,122 Garos 97,924 or 37.94 per cent are Christians. Of the Kukis about one-third (exactly 34.78 per cent) are Christians. They were converted by American Baptists. Only a few Mikirs have become Christians.

Since 1954 no foreign missionaries, with very few exceptions, were allowed to work in Nagaland and in Arunachal Pradesh. But the Baptist Nagas no longer require any foreign missionaries; they are self-supporting and, in spite of the heavy pressure of the administration, they themselves continue the work of conversion.

The Christian Church has rendered three major services to the tribals of Assam: She has liberated them from the fear of evil spirits and from the evils of head-hunting and continuous warfare and blood-revenge; she has established centres of education and given extensive medical service at a time when no Government or other private agency bothered about the tribals.

The conversion of some tribes in Assam to Christianity has been regarded by some critics as a serious detribalising and denationalising factor. However, the Indian Government is at present taking all the necessary measures to counteract any such disruptive forces.

BIBLIOGRAPHY

Bareja, J. D.: *Across the Golden Heights of Assam and NEFA*. Shillong, 1961.
Barkataki, S.: *Assam*. New Delhi, 1969.
————: *Tribes of Assam*. New Delhi, 1969.
Besseignet, P.: *Tribesmen of the Chittagong Hill Tracts*. Dacca, 1958.
Bower, U.G.: *Naga Path*. London, 1950.
Burling, R.: *Rengranggri: Family and Kinship in a Garo Village*. Philadelphia, 1963.
————: *Hill Farms and Paddy Fields*. New Jersey, 1965.
Cooper, T. T.: *The Mishmi Hills*. London, 1873.
Dalton, E. T.: *Descriptive Ethnology of Bengal*. Calcutta, 1872, 1960.
Das, A. K. & M. K. Raha: *The Rabhas of West Bengal*. Calcutta, 1967.
Dunbar, G.: *Other Men's Lives*. London, 1938.
Dutta, P.: *The Tangsas*. Shillong, 1969.
Elwin, V.: *India's North-East Frontier*. Oxford University Press, 1959.
————: *A Philosophy for NEFA*. Shillong, 1961.
————: *Myths of the North-East Frontier of India*. Shillong, 1968.
Endle, S.: *The Kacharies*. London, 1938.
Fürer-Haimendorf, C. von: *The Naked Nagas*. Calcutta, 1946.
————: *Himalayan Barbary*. London, 1955.
————: *The Apa Tani and their Neighbours*. London, 1962.
Gait, E.: *A History of Assam*. Calcutta, 1826.
Gurdon, P. R. T.: *The Khasis*. London, 1907.
Hodson, T. C.: *The Meitheis of Manipur*. London, 1908.
————: *The Naga Tribes of Manipur*. London, 1912.
Hutton, J. H.: *The Angami Nagas*. London, 1921.
————: *The Sema Nagas*. London, 1921.
Mills, J. P.: *The Lhota Nagas*. London, 1922.
————: *The Ao Nagas*. London, 1926.
————: *The Rengma Nagas*. London, 1937.
Parry, N. E.: *The Lakhers*. London, 1932.
Playfair, A.: *The Garos*. London, 1909.
Shakespeare, J.: *The Lushai Kuki Clans*. London, 1912.
Shaw, W.: *Notes on the Thadou-Kukis*. J. A. S. of Bengal, Vol. 24, 1928, pp. 1–175.
Shukla, B. K.: *The Daflas of the Subansiri Region*. Shillong, 1959.
Sinha, K.: *Meghalaya*. Delhi, 1970.
Sm th, W. C.: *The Ao Naga Tribes of Assam*. London, 1925.
Stack, E. and Lyall: *The Mikirs*. London, 1908.
Stevenson, H. N. C.: *The Economies of the Central Chin Tribes*. Bombay, 1943.
Wood, R.: *The Hill Tribes of Assam*. J.B.B. of R.A.S. 1953, Vol. 28, pp. 187–214.

CHAPTER VII

The Tribes in South India

THERE IS good evidence to prove that south India was populated by human groups in very early times, aleady in the early Palaeolithic period.* It is possible that various jungle tribes of south India living there at present are descendants of the Palaeolithic man. Most of the tribes, except those with admixtures from different races, belong to the Proto-Australoid race. Some anthropologists suspect Negrito blood in some tribes, others deny this. Their complexion is dark; they are of medium height, with rather long arms. They have dolichocephalic heads, with pronounced orbital ridges and prognathous chins. The root of the nose is often deep-set. They have flat noses with flaring nostrils, thick mucous lips, and dark curly or wavy hair. The hair on the face and body is scanty. They are usually lean, but strong and can endure great fatigue in their search for food.

All of them have lost their original language and now speak local (Dravidian) dialects, though often with an unusual accent.

In course of time more and more peoples immigrated into India, and in the first millennium B. C. neolithic agriculturists either arrived from outside or evolved from the indigenous hunters and food collectors. But perhaps already in the first half of the first millennium B.C., a population of a superior culture and power grew up in south India, perhaps inspired or led by invaders from outside. They built the huge stone monuments or megaliths, possessed and used iron, and employed advanced farming methods.

Their numbers must have increased rapidly and they felt that

*Cf. Chapter I; the so-called 'Madras Industry' of the Early Stone Age.

land was getting scarce, for they never built their megaliths on arable land. They obviously dispossessed some indigenous peoples of their land, for we find Dravida-speaking tribes at present far in the north of their former habitats. They enslaved the rest of the peoples who had already learned to till the soil and thus were not prepared to abandon their land. The superior people treated the indigenous tribes as their subjects, even as serfs and slaves, and claimed as their tribute the greater and better portion of the fruits of their labour, leaving them only a bare minimum of material subsistence. This is the situation which we find at the beginning of the historical period, no doubt the result of a long development.

The forest tribes, on the other hand, who as hunters and collectors of jungle produce led a nomadic life and were thus less attached to the soil, were able to evade the domination of the superior people. They escaped to the inaccessible hills and jungles into which the ruling people were unable or unwilling to follow. In these regions of no man's land they remained the unquestioned masters of the wilds for many centuries, even though after some time their superiors had at least nominally taken possession also of these areas. For many generations the tribes were allowed to live their ancient independent life as hunters and food collectors undisturbed, paying perhaps a nominal annual tribute to the rulers living in the plains wherever such a tribute was demanded.

These tribes were rather small in numbers because they were only relicts of larger communities that had been enslaved while they themselves had escaped, or because they became separated in the forests and hills of south India, and in course of time developed into different tribal societies. Moreover, their hunting and collecting mode of life forced them to live in small groups or they would have starved.

Gradually the population in the plains increased and more and more jungle was cut down by the cultivators and converted into farm land. The jungle tribes retreated still further or by necessity turned into shifting cultivators when hunting and collecting could no more provide them with sufficient food or because they found this type of food to their liking.

But the conquest of the jungle progressed inexorably. When the British colonisers united India for the first time completely and extended their administration over the whole land they included in it also the evasive jungle tribes. It was the British who first became aware of the great riches that lay hidden in the jungles and they began to exploit them. Timber was cut and exported, forest products were collected on commercial lines and sold with great gain, and tea, coffee and rubber plantations were started on a big scale. Tram-lines and motor roads were built into the so long inaccessible jungle and the forest tribes soon found themselves disturbed by new invaders who claimed these jungles for themselves and began to exploit them. As a concession the British permitted the tribes to continue to live and collect in the forests, but the latter were forced often enough to cut timber, collect jungle produce and work in the new plantations.

The economy of the nomadic tribes in south India was entirely based on the accumulative method of gathering food and hunting. Tilling the soil, animal breeding or any handicrafts were originally unknown to them. The fertile jungle tracts yielded them plenty of nourishing food consisting of roots and tubers, fruits, vegetables and honey, and small and big game. The tribes thus enjoyed a healthy diversified diet, and the activities required to satisfy their needs of sustenance and of clothing and shelter made their life many-sided and interesting. The tribes were self-sufficient, healthy and carefree.

The food-gathering and hunting tribes were sparing in the use of the products nature offered them as also in hunting of wild animals. They seldom collected more than they needed for a day or two; the only thing they perhaps stored up was honey as a treasured luxury. When the food supply was exhausted in one area they moved on to another one, but always in their own territory. Trespassing was strictly forbidden.

But some decades ago the situation changed radically. The demand increased for most of the products which so far only the nomadic tribes had collected for their own sustenance or to barter them for knives and billyhooks, pots and clothes, ornaments and occasionally liquor, tobacco and other stimulants. The Government now took control of the jungle and leased plots of the forest to contractors who naturally tried, in the short time of their lease, to make as much gain from the allotted area as possible. In some places the contractors made an arrangement with the tribals. They were allowed to collect jungle produce but they had to sell it to their specific contractor at a price fixed by him. The tribals were thus denied the benefit of selling their goods to the highest bidder, but on the other hand the contractor could not force them to collect for him if the price was too low. Since they did not depend on the sale of jungle produce for their livelihood they could thus force the contractor to pay them a fair price.

The contractors however contrived to create new artificial needs in the tribals. They introduced and encouraged the tribals, through free gifts, to become addicted to alcohol, opium and tobacco; they insisted that to be respectable and civilised the tribals had to dress properly; they appealed to the vanity of the tribals and sold them ornaments and other luxuries. All this required money for which the tribals had to work. And wherever the tribes refused to be tempted, labourers from outside were brought in who not only deprived the tribals of their livelihood and depleted the forests, but also played havoc with the tribal sex mores and social safeguards. This practically resulted in a breakdown of tribal morality and social structure; particularly effective in this destructive process was probably the introduction of matriarchal social elements, accompanied by polyandry and the visit marriage custom prevalent among some of the Hindu castes of south India. Today many of the hill tribes have adopted elements of this matriarchal system, and in some tribes it has led to practical promiscuity in sex behaviour and a breakdown of family life.

The vices of civilisation have thus been introduced as welcome helpmates in the drive for increased production. They certainly have been very destructive towards the economic, social and moral structures of the south Indian hill tribes. Unfortunately, the accompanying benefits of civilisation—better and more effective tools and implements, medicine, education and industrial enterprises—have not been made equally available to the tribals. The contact of the tribes in south India with modern civilisation has been largely detrimental to them.

On the other hand, there is an imperative need for making the great resources of the south Indian forests available to the whole nation. No doubt, for the good of the whole nation, wide tracts of the jungle can no longer be exclusively reserved for the tribes in order to support them in their traditional quest for food, as hunters and food-gatherers. The Indian Government is probably justified in forcing them, if they are not willing, to adjust themselves to modern ways of living and earning their livelihood. The leisurely pace of former times has gone and the present overpopulated state of India makes it necessary for the small and evasive communities in the hills and forests of south India to change and adapt themselves to new and more effective ways of earning a living.

Of course, the Government and private social workers and charitable institutions and associations should do their best to make this transition for the tribals possible and to assist them in overcoming their handicaps and formidable difficulties. As the number of tribals in south India is relatively small, this should be possible with good will and a sincere interest in the welfare of these people.

We must not ignore the fact that the transition from a nomadic gathering and hunting life to a sedentary, regular, dull and often dependent life is difficult. It requires a fundamental change of mentality and, if forced on a tribe without ideological preparation and sufficient time for adjustment, it might create great mental anguish and lead to a loss of zest for life. In the past the foodgathering tribes achieved this change from nomadism into a sedentary cultivating form of life through an intermediary stage—that of shifting cultivation. Shifting cultivators are only tied down to working on a plot of land for a part of the year, for the rest of the year they can continue their free life in the jungle. And even their field plots are changed so often—every two or three years.

At present the foodgathering tribes have to change over to other work practically without any transitional period. This is hard on them and no wonder they often fail to get adjusted in the new situation.

The foodgathering and hunting tribes in south India are the following: Allar, Aranadar (44), Chingathar (c. 300), Irular (91,289), Kadar (1,250), Kader (c. 300), in the Wynaad, Karavashis or Hill Pulayar (2,982), Kattunayakar (10,449), Kochuvelar (c. 1,500), Koragar (6,936), Kurumbar (1,173), Kuruvikkar, Kudubis, Chenchus (a small part of the 17,866 Chenchus), Advichinchar (169), Malakarrar, Mala Malasar (2,982), Mala

Pandaram (816), Mala Panickkar, Mudugar or Muduvans (5,188), Nayadis (17,735), Urali Kurumar Uralis (2,597), Sholagar (6,138), Vettuvar, and others.

The aborigines of the Andaman Islands are also mere food-gatherers and hunters. They are divided into the following tribes: Jarawas, Chariar or Chari, Kora Tabo or Bo, Yere, Kede, Bea, Balawa, Bojigiyah, Juwai, Kol, Onge and Sentilenese. Their numbers are small, but no exact figures can be given.

The Moger (5,396), Paravar (3,786), Bagatas, Valar, and Arayar are more or less pure fishermen. The Kavundar, Idayar, Todas and Lamanas are pastoral tribes.

The following tribes are partly foodgatherers and hunters, and partly field and plantation labourers: Adiyar (5,699), Eravallar (518), Kalanadis, Kanikkar (11,254), Malasar (2,095), Mala Vedar (722), Mala Vettuvar, Malayariar (14,082), Malayar, Maratis (14,847), Thachanadar, and partly the Kotas (841).

The Karimpalar, Kurichchiyar (11,854), Malayalar, Erukulas, Kaikadis, Jungle Kurubas (partly) and others are or were in the past shifting cultivators. The Kudiyas, Kundu Vadiar, Mala Aryar, Mannar, Mavilar, Muthuvar, Palliyar, Pathiyar, Ulladar, Uridavan Gowdalu, and Vishvar are more advanced cultivators or farm labourers.

The Social Structure of the South Indian Tribes

MARRIAGE AND FAMILY

No uniform family pattern can be discerned among the primitive tribes of southern India; most of the tribes have been strongly influenced by their neighbours who are more advanced in culture. Parents are generally anxious to have their children married as early as possible. By an early marriage the eventuality of scandals is removed, young couples are supposed to fend for themselves and to be thus no longer a burden on their parents, and aging elders like to see grandchildren growing up. Though there is great freedom in the marriage regulations of the tribes in south India, most tribes hold to the conviction that some form of marriage is essential for the survival of the tribe, for the rearing of children and for happiness in a future life because in most tribes the obsequies of the dead have to be performed by the sons.

While in Tamilnadu most tribes are patrilineal, in Kerala some tribes are patrilineal, others matrilineal. Thus the Kadar, Paliyar, Mala-Pulayar and Hill Pandaram are patrilineal while other tribes are fully or partially matrilineal, no doubt influenced by the Nayar and other castes of Kerala who are matrilineal. The Vishavar, for instance, make the sister's son the heir—never a woman; among the Cheenganni Vedar the sons inherit two-thirds of the property, the sister's sons one-third. Among the Cheru Vedar the sons inherit half, the sister's sons the other half of the property. The same is true of the Ulladar and Kannikar, while the Muduvar and Thanta Pulayar make the sister's sons heirs of the whole property. This shows that in certain tribes a compromise between the patrilineal and matrilineal systems was achieved.

In acquiring marriage partners the south Indian tribes follow various means and ways: among some tribes the marriage is arranged by the parents or elders; so it is among the Kadar, Kannikar, Mala-Pandaram, Ulladar, Vishavar, Uralis and Thanta-Pulayar.

Probationary marriage or marriage by trial is not usual among these tribes since most marriages can easily be dissolved in any case when the mates find that they do not suit each other.

In Kerala marriage by capture is common among the Mannar and Badagas, and frequent among the Muduvar. Even now the first meeting of a couple in this tribe takes place in the jungle. Legends, songs and traditions current in other tribes prove that marriage by capture was in the past common also among the Koragar, Irular, Mala-Pandaram, Mala Vedar, Kattunayakar, Bulla and Urali Kurumar, and the Malakkarar.

Marriage by elopement is a common form of marriage among the Kadar, Mannar, Uralis and Sholagar. In the latter tribe the couples that elope usually return after three days, when they are considered married. This marriage form is often resorted to by members of other tribes, too, when the usual negotiations have failed, or when the parents object to the union or when the bride-price demanded cannot be paid by the elders. Among the Adiyar a woman dissatisfied with her husband elopes with another man. The elders who find them a couple of days later chastise them, but allow them to live together. Such cases of desertion and elopement are frequent.

Marriage by intrusion (when the woman forces herself on a man, usually a bachelor) is found among the Chenchus. It is sufficient if a man allows a girl who has entered his hut to stay a single might to consider them a pair.

Marriage by service is often practised. The service may last from one to six months, and is rendered either to the father, uncle or even the widowed mother of the prospective bride. Among the Palliyar, Paniyar, and Urali Kurumar the service consists normally in a daily delivery of fuel; among the Mannar and Malayar the bridegroom may live in the hut of the bride's parents during his time of service. The Jen Kurumbar in the Nilgiris celebrate the engagement of their children before puberty. The groom works for his future wife till she reaches puberty. Then the couple start their own household. No special wedding rite is performed.

But at present marriage by purchase is the most popular form. The bride-price has to be paid either to the father or the maternal uncle of the bride. Some groups permit the payment of the bride-price in instalments. Sometimes presents given to the bride or her parents before or at the wedding are considered equivalent to a bride-price. Some tribes, like the Kadar, demand a dowry, which means that the father of the bride has to pay it. Among the Aranadar and Allar, for instance, the payment of the bride-price is repeated annually. The Kalanadis and Vishavar, however, do not demand any bride-price or dowry.

The payment of a bride-price can be avoided by an exchange of sisters. The Uralis of Kerala, for instance, always demand a girl in exchange; a boy who cannot give a sister or cousin in exchange has no chance of getting married, while on the other hand a boy with several sisters can marry as many wives as he has sisters. The Uralis do not accept payment of money as a substitute for a girl. Such an exchange of sisters is usual also among the Vishavar, Mala-Vedar, Mala-Pandaram, Irular, Kurichchiyar, Ulladar, Maratis, Kudiyas and other tribes.

In choosing their mates, many tribes in south India have a preference for their cross-cousins; this is the established rule among the Hill Pandaram, Kannikar, Kundu Vadiyar, Kurichchiyar, Kalanadis, Nayadis, Vishavar and Muduvar; it is also found among the Veddas of Ceylon. It is always the marriage between the children of a brother and a sister. Cross-cousin marriage is further preferred by the Ulladar (with the daughter of a boy's maternal uncle), the Kuruvar (who allow marriage only with the daughter of the maternal uncle), the Mala Arayar (who allow marriage also with the daughter of a father's sister), the Mala Vedar, Mala Pulayar, Palliyar, Mannar and Kadar. The Mulla Kurumar, however, prohibit cross-cousin marriages, as do also the Eravallar, Adiyar, Kattunayakar and Maratis. They prefer a wife from an unrelated family. Among the Mala Kuruvar, Mala Panickkar and Ulladar, marriage with the paternal aunt's daughter is prohibited. It appears that tribes which possess landed property favour cross-cousin marriages; they strengthen the family ties and prevent the loss of a field. For, if the property is inherited by a daughter or nephew, it only remains in the family if the daughter marries a cousin, or a nephew the daughter of a land-owner.

Some of the tribes also practise levirate, that is, the younger brother marries the wife of his deceased elder brother. This custom is found among the Veddas, Ulladar, Kannikar, Kadar, Mannar and Mala Pulayar. Among the latter the elder brother may even marry the widow of his younger brother; the same is permitted among the Palliyar. Levirate is prohibited among the Adiyar, Muduvar and Mala Vedar. Among the Vishavar a man must support the widow of his elder brother, but he does not marry her. In the past, when a girl had reached maturity and a suitable husband could not easily be found, the husband of her elder sister was allowed to have sex relations with her. Later, she could leave him and marry somebody else. But in any polygynous marriage the second wife is preferably the sister of the first one. This is called sororate. It is common among the Kannikar, Kadar, Mala Kuduvar, Mala Pulayar and Uralis. Among the Palliyar, a man who wants to take a second wife can only marry the sister of his first wife. The Chingathar and Kalanadis who practise sororate forbid levirate.

No uniformity exists with regard to the numerical pattern of marriage. Some tribes, like the Kadar, Vishavar and Nayadis, practise compulsory monogamy, at least so long as the marriage lasts. Another wife can only be taken after the first one has been divorced. Other tribes permit polygyny, or polyandry, or both. Generally, when an excessive number of women is found in a settlement, polygyny is practised; but it is also practised if the fact of having several wives helps a man to live in greater comfort and to acquire greater wealth. This may be the case when remunerative employment can be found in estates and plantations. Polygynous marriages are permitted by the Muduvar who give a superior rank to the first wife. It is in practice among the Adiyar, Aranadar, Chingathar, Vishavar, Uralis, Mala Kuruvar and Mala Pulayar, and prevalent among the Ulladar and Mala Vedar. Among the Muduvar and Uralis the co-wives have separate huts, while in other tribes the co-wives live together in the same hut. On the other hand, the Muduvar of the Cardamon hills are purely monogamous, while the Kannikar and Mala Pandarams allow at least some exceptions from the rule of monogamy; if a man has more than one wife, the second wife is usually the sister of the first one. As said before, an Urali boy can marry as many wives as he has sisters for exchange. The Mala Arayar, Palliyar and Mannar permit polygyny if the first wife proves barren; in such a case, the Palliyar permit marriage with a sister of the first wife.

Polyandry is found in a settlement if there is a scarcity of females. The Irular practise polyandry; a woman can freely choose her lovers. It is permitted among the Muduvar of the plateau; but they forbid fraternal polyandry. Among the Ulladar fraternal polyandry is rare, as also among the Uralis and Mannar, Karavar and Mala Malasar. The Palliyar practise fraternal polyandry, the younger brothers sharing the wife of the elder one. The Malayarar and Mala Pandaram occasionally practise fraternal polyandry, the husbands being brothers or cousins. Fraternal polyandry is common among the Koragar, Mavilar and Aranadar. But the latter conceal it carefully. They also allow a visitor to enjoy their wives. Polyandry is forbidden among the Adiyar and Chingathar. In former times the Todas were known for their polyandry (not restricted to the younger brothers of the husband) and female infanticide. Both customs are probably responsible for their dwindling numbers. The evidence on the practice of polyandry is not easily collected as the tribes are very reticent about it; they are aware of the fact that polyandry is considered immoral by the vast majority of the Hindu castes [cf. Peter of Greece and Denmark (1963), p. 176].

Some groups among the Uralis, Kattunayakar, Koragar and others may combine polyandry with polygyny. The same can be found among the Todas of the Nilgiris. This practically results in promiscuity. Until recent times the Allar, for instance, permitted sexual promiscuity and even pre-puberty cohabitation for all members of the tribe. But recently some restrictions were set up with the introduction of a bride-price.

All these tribes permit a divorce to both the husband and the wife; the Nayadis, however, permit a divorce only when the wife has committed adultery. It consequently appears that the family system of the aboriginal tribes of south India is neither strong nor stable. It is difficult to say whether this kind of family system has been so from the very beginning; or whether it is due to the paucity of members in a group, or to the disorganisation of tribal life as a result of the influx of outsiders into their living space.

Despite this general looseness of family ties it is found that at least some tribes are strict and do not permit adultery. The Eravallar, for instance, at one time punished women caught in adultery, and even misbehaving unmarried girls, with death. Now they only ostracise them. Such women are forced to join an untouchable caste. The Vishavar did not tolerate adultery in the past and punished it severely. At present they are very lenient towards such offenders. Among the Malayar, at least in the past, a marriage was indissoluble, except in the case of a wife committing adultery. She was punished by a severe flogging and sent home to her parents. But she could remarry afterwards. The Malasar even now insist on conjugal fidelity. They observe social taboos which prohibit conversation between an uncle and his adult nieces, a man and his mother-in-law and the wife of his elder brother. But they permit divorce, polygyny and occasionally even (fraternal) polyandry.

This general looseness of family ties is in conformity with the fact that almost all these tribes permit, or at least tolerate, pre-marital sex relations. However, such relations usually end with the pregnancy of the girl. So it is, for instance, among the Vishavar and Malakudis among whom pre-nuptial chastity is rare. The Muduvar, who strictly forbid pre-marital sex relations and impose a severe punishment on offenders of this rule, are again an exception. They have a bachelor hall for the unmarried boys and a sleeping house for the girls where they are kept under strict supervision. The Uralis at least fine a boy when they discover him cohabiting with a girl and force him to marry her.

A marriage can be contracted either before or after reaching puberty. Child marriage is the rule among the Thachanadar, some groups of the Kannikar, Uralis and Vishavar. Among the Thachanadar a child-wife is expected to have sex relations with her adult husband immediately after the wedding. Among other tribes, cohabitation usually begins after reaching puberty though the wedding ceremony may be performed earlier. Some tribes have the pseudo-marriage (*kettukalyanam*) as practised by the higher castes. The actual marriage is then performed later. There are some tribes, like the Allar, Malasar and Mala Malasar, which usually have the wedding performed after the bride reaches puberty, but in exceptional cases also permit marriages before puberty. The Adiyar do not permit pre-puberty marriages.

KINSHIP GROUPS

Most south Indian tribes practise tribal endogamy, though in rare cases they do accept marriage partners from tribes or castes who are of a higher social rank. Thus the Kadar allow their women to have sex relations with the estate labourers of the plains. Aranadars may marry Chettis, Malayariar, Ambalavasis, Vellathies and Tiyar women. Mala Arayars accept Nayars and Arayars (Mukkuvar) as marriage partners. Still, such cases are exceptions.

The tribes usually also practise a kind of territorial endogamy; sections of the tribe within a certain area intermarry as a rule. However, there are tribes, such as the Mala Pandarams and Mala Malasar, for instance, who prefer to take marriage partners from distant groups. The Mala Pulayar have three endogamous territorial sections.

The rules of exogamy vary widely; not even kinship exogamy is observed by all tribes. Besides, the principles on which a kinship organisation is established also vary considerably. Thus the Malayar, for instance, marry only among themselves and recognise no rules of exogamy. And it is alleged that the Allar even allow marriages between father and daughter. The Aranadar of Calicut District are said to allow it too. But in the latter case it may not have been a real marriage but just the deflowering of a girl by her own father. This was the practice among the Aranadar until recently. Old reports allege that among the Kudiyas and Vishavar (Malakudis) a widowed mother could become the wife of her eldest son. Brother and sister marriages are reported to happen even now among the Allar and Palliyar, for instance.

But many tribes practise clan exogamy. They are divided into clans or septs which originally might have been totemic in part. Descent is reckoned either in the male or in the female line.

It is doubtful whether the Kadar had totemism. They have at present no clan organisation or totemism, but they still observe certain food taboos which might be of totemic origin. They are not allowed to eat the meat of certain animals (buffalo, tiger, bear, elephant, white monkey) and the fruits of some trees. The Kannikar in south Travancore trace the origin of their clans to the finding of a dead elephant or to the killing of a deer. Other clan names of theirs are taken from localities. Descent is in the female line. The Chenchus too have exogamous septs which, however, do not seem to be of totemic origin. Nor do the Chenchus observe any totemic food taboos. The Iruligar of Mysore have patrilineal septs which are named after family gods, trees or inanimate objects. This points at a former totemism. The Sholigar of Mysore have four endogamous sections and five exogamous clans showing traces of totemism.

The Todas of the Nilgiris are divided into five clans, one of which is superior to the other four and supplies the priests. These clans are divided into two endogamous sections. Each clan owns a number of villages, is named after its chief and has its own clan god. Descent is patrilineal. The clan system of the Todas is consequently territorial.

The Kotas, on the other hand, have no clans, but also follow a territorial system. They inhabit seven villages, each of which is an exogamous unit. The Uralis, again, have clans; the members of each clan have a strong feeling of solidarity, so much so that they raise subscriptions among the clan members to help pay a fine imposed on any one of them. The Urali Kurumar are definitely totemic. They have many sub-sections which are endogamous, but each sub-section has exogamous septs which are totemic. The members of a sept believe that they are actually descended from the totem—they feel related to it and treat it with respect. They are not permitted to kill and eat their totem, and may not even touch it nor any part of it, and sometimes may not even look at it.

The Malayar and Mannar, too, have a clan system. The Malayar clans are named after forest tracts which they inhabit after distinguished ancestors. It is, therefore, a territorial system. One section of the clan follows the male line, another section the female line. The Mannar have clans named after the place of habitation. They, too, follow the female line, obviously imitating the local superior castes observing the matrilineal system. The sister's son inherits a deceased person's property, but he gets possession of it only two years after his uncle's death. In one settlement, sons and nephews share equally; other sections still have patriliny. Thus the tribe has not completely changed over to matriliny; it is in a stage of transition.

The Malayar, inhabitants of the Cannanore and Tellicherry Districts, do not observe any rule of exogamy, probably because of their small numbers. But they have a tradition that in the past they had even a dual and quadruple tribal division. They observe matriliny today.

The Kattunayakar worship trees, rocks, hills, snakes and other animals, and even claim origin from them. This would suggest originally a totemic social organisation. But nothing certain can be stated about their original social structure, as at present they do not observe any clan rules and regulations, and have even forgotten their clan names, if they ever had any.

The Koragar, on the other hand, are divided into four exogamous septs which they call *bali*.

This survey of the kinship systems of the south Indian tribes would suggest that the tribes followed originally various systems—the local group system, a clan system with or without totemism, or a territorial and even a village system. But the tribes also frequently changed over from one system to another. Sometimes they changed their system incompletely, mixing parts of one system with parts of the other. The result is a bewildering confusion, one tribe differring in its kinship structure from the other. The reasons for this confusion may be several. One reason probably is that some of the tribes have declined so much in numbers as to make the laws of exogamy illusory. They have to marry close relatives since no other mates are available.

Sometimes a tribe is still relatively numerous, but the single groups are dispersed so much over a wide area that they lose contact with each other. In such cases too intermarriage within a small group becomes necessary. Other tribes have changed their original kinship system because they were subjected to the influence of superior castes whose social organisation they felt obliged to adopt. This becomes the more striking and confusing when an originally patrilineal and patriarchal society adopts matrilineal and matriarchal traits.

Political Organisation

Most of the tribes of south India live in small groups dispersed in the jungles or on the outskirts of the villages of the cultivators. Usually they live a life of their own and try to avoid all interference from outsiders, be they Government officials, police, social workers, or block development officers. They want nothing more than to be left alone and to pursue their traditional way of life as they learnt it from their forefathers.

Few of them are ambitious and want to get on in life and to improve their economic or social conditions. Those who do, have long since separated and have been assimilated in the villages of the plains. They pretend to be 'civilised', which in most cases is equivalent with being 'Hinduised', and give themselves superior airs looking down on their wild fellow tribesmen.

In a few of the nomadic tribes there is no such institution as a headman of a settlement. The heads of the single families simply come together and settle the affairs of the group whenever problems arise and decisions have to be taken.

Other tribes have the institution of headmen who may be elected as such and can be deposed when they become unable to carry out their duties or for some reason or other lose the authority or respect of the community which so far they have enjoyed.

In other tribes the office of a headman is hereditary and often connected with a certain family or clan. In more developed tribes the headman may even be assisted by other office-bearers to whom specific duties are assigned and whose offices are also hereditary.

Thus in Kerala the Allar and Aranadar have no headmen. Affairs of the community are discussed at a gathering of elders whose decision is then binding. Those who disagree simply leave the group and join another one. While social disputes and even cases of marital infidelity, etc., are usually settled amicably, sometimes serious quarrels may result over the just distribution of a kill in a hunt.

The Chingathar of Cannanore District, too, do not seem to have a headman. But they have a priest who performs the ceremonies at their spirit dance. This priest may play the role of a headman as well. Members of a family are supposed to obey the senior male member.

The same is true of the Eravallar. The institution of a headman that existed in their early society has disappeared, and in their settlements it is now the much respected priest who performs the duties of a headman as well. Among the Kadar, too, the hereditary institution of the headman (*muppan*) has ceased to exist. In former times, when their tribe was more numerous, they had headmen who possessed a stick as the symbol of their office. This stick had a silver band with the insignia of the ruler of the Cochin State. At present the tribe, or better, the various groups of the tribe, are ruled by a committee of elders which decides all disputes, settles divorces, and allows deserted women to remarry.

The Kochuvelar, too, have priests who act occasionally as headmen. The Koragar do not seem to have headmen. Nothing is known of a headman among the Mala Vedar, a very primitive tribe of hunters and foodgatherers. Even where he exists he has not much to say except to preside over some ceremonies at a birth or marriage.

Among the Mala Vettuvar the office of the headman is not hereditary for he is usually appointed by the landlord for whom the group works. The headman enjoys certain rights and privileges, but at present he receives little attention and commands only slight obedience. The Malayadiyar do not seem to have headmen in their settlements. The Mathas do have a headman but he is seldom obeyed or treated with respect. The only privilege he enjoys is an invitation to a wedding or a funeral feast. On assuming his office he is supposed to marry the widow of the late headman whatever her age. The community does not contribute to his maintenance. Among the Nayadis also the headman has little power and he can command only scarce respect. But the assembly of elderly men and women which gathers to settle disputes and discuss tribal affairs is important. He is, however, consulted before a marriage is finalised and he plays a part in funeral ceremonies. The Paniyar do not seem to have headmen.

Among the Kurumar only some groups have a headman. Their social problems are usually discussed and decided at a tribal meeting consisting of elders. The headman presides over it if he is present. There is no definite rule regarding the choice of a headman. His office is either elective or hereditary but, once elected, a man is headman for life. Personal qualities and abilities are the basis of his authority.

The Vishavar, too, have a headman whose office is hereditary, but his authority is negligible.

But not all tribes in Kerala have such a slightly developed institution of headmanship. The headman among the Adiyar is typical of these tribes. His office is hereditary; if a son is unsuitable for the office, a nephew may inherit it. The headman has a special title which is shared even by his wife. But he is not an autocratic ruler; he only presides over the meetings of the elders at which affairs of the community are discussed. His sanction is required, however, for any important undertaking, a marriage or divorce, and he presides at funeral ceremonies.

The Irular have a senior headman and a junior headman. They have respect for them, obey them and invite them to weddings and funeral feasts. The Irular choose their headman by common consent. Among the Kalanadis the headman plays the same role, and he might even be their priest. Each family is supposed to make a contribution towards the maintenance of the headman and his family.

Among the Kannikar the headman was in the past an important and influential person entitled to the contributions of the community of which he was the head. But in present times his status has declined considerably.

The Karavar respect and obey their headman and his wife. He has an assistant and an executive officer. His office is hereditary. In the past the community had to cultivate his fields and maintain his hut, but today no contributions are made. The headman is often also the priest of the community.

The Kattunayakar, too, respect and obey their headman; nothing can happen in a settlement without his approval. In the past he had civil and criminal jurisdiction over his community. He is often the priest and shaman of the settlement and acts as their oracle.

Among the Kudiyar the headman is still an important person though not as much as in the past. He is at the same time their priest who functions at weddings and funerals and other ceremonies. Disputes are settled by a council of four or five elders. The headman plays the same role among the Kundu Vedar.

The Kurichchiyar have two headmen, a senior and a junior one. The symbol of his office is a knife with a silver handle. He is chosed by divination. He receives no contributions from the community.

The Kurumban headman has an assistant and an executive officer, at least he had them in the past. His office is hereditary. But today he is little respected and obeyed.

The Mala Arayar have a headman who can nominate his successor, but his choice is subject to the approval of the forest officer. The former's status has declined considerably.

Among the Malakkarar the headman is still an important person. The community makes small contributions to him. He is informed about everything that happens in the settlement. Often he is also the priest. His office is hereditary and is inherited by his nephew.

Among the Mala Kuruvar the headman is so important that a member of the settlement who disobeys him is outcasted. The Mala Kuruvar have even a council of headmen. But in a settlement decisions are taken in a meeting of elders over which the headman presides.

The Mala Malasar have, as a headman, a person with outstanding abilities; courage, knowledge of the forest and a talent for hunting are the requisite qualities of a headman. He must be present at all important functions in the settlement.

The headman of the Mala Pandarams and his wife are treated with respect. His office is hereditary. In former times the community contributed to his maintenance, now they help occasionally. He is often priest, and shaman occasionally for which services he is paid. The same is true of the headman among the Malasar. Among the Malayar, the headman was selected by the Raja of Kottayam, hence his important status. The Malayar, too, respect their headman and obey him. Among the Mannar the headman has an assistant, and is entitled to a cot to sleep on. The members of his settlement thatch his hut annually, as also the hut of his assistant. The Maratis perform the same service for their headman.

The Mavilar call their headman 'lion' (*simhan*). They respect him and his wife and let him preside over the meetings of elders. The headman of the Mudugar has two assistants, but his authority is little. They can decide their affairs without his presence. The headman of the Mulla Kurumar wears a silver bangle on his right arm as a sign of his office. He is much respected. For all affairs in the settlement his approval is required. The Muthuwans also respect and obey their headman. But the community does not pay any contributions to him. His office is inherited by a nephew. The same is true of the Palliyar and Pathiyar headmen. The latter is still supported by his community, not the former.

The Thachanadar have two headmen in every settlement. The senior one settles secular affairs, while the junior one is the priest and shaman, and fixes the date and time of weddings. He performs offerings to the female deities, while the senior headman makes offerings to the male gods. No contributions are made to them as headmen; but they are paid for their priestly services.

Among the Ulladar the headman has not only to perform his secular duties, he must also be an accomplished shaman and competent to exorcise the spirits of disease. His wife, too, should be good in these arts. The headman of the Uralis, too, should be competent in magic and incantations.

The Religion of the South Indian Tribes

The tribes of south India practise a religion which, to some extent, can be characterised as animistic. Most tribes venerate the forces of nature and find their gods on the hills and in the forests of their habitat. They venerate tiger and snake gods, and also the sun and the moon. They have a strong veneration for their ancestors. But their religion has been more or less strongly influenced by the religion of the Hindu peoples who live around them. The degree of Hinduisation is perhaps less noticeable among the foodgathering tribes, but has made more progress among the tribes which are shifting cultivators. It is much advanced among the field and plantation labourers and those cultivators who live in close contact with the Hindu castes.

FOREST AND HILL GODS

Many tribes of south India venerate hill gods whom they locate on the crests and tops of hills. Thus, the popular god of the Adiyar, agricultural labourers, is Mala Deivom, god of the hills.

The Mala Arayar worship five hills which, in their opinion, possess superhuman powers. Five stones, symbols of the hill gods, are installed in a shed or in the open. The shed is purified and the stones are given a bath. Raw rice grains, sandal-paste and leaves of the basil plant (*tulsi*) are offered on a plantain leaf, while five coconuts are offered on another leaf. Then a fowl is sacrificed and the coconuts broken. A dinner is served. A little rice is placed on twenty-one leaves and offered to the ancestors.

The Palliyar and Mannar consider the crests of hills as their gods and believe that these hills are haunted by spirits. They used to preserve a portion of the primeval forest and dedicate it to the forest spirits.

The Uralis, on the other hand, believe that the hills are inhabited by evil spirits.

The Mala Kuruvar believe that their hills are inhabited by spirits and they sacrifice to them before making a clearing and again after sowing.

The Muduvar venerate Kottamala Swami, Vadaganatha Swami and other gods and believe that they reside on hill crests.

The most popular deities of the Kattunayakar are Masti and Mala Deivom, the god of the hills. The Mala Panikkar also have as their favourite deity Mala Deivom, the hill god.

The Mala Pandarams believe in a powerful god who resides on certain very steep and inaccessible mountain tops. They call this god Malagal (mountain) or Mala Devam (hill god). The name of the god's mountain is Daivamivikum Medu, which translated literally means: the mountain on which god is sitting. The Mala Pandarams are convinced that they are able to observe certain movements on the peak which for them prove the existence of God.

The head of each family has to offer sacrifice on a hill-top opposite the holy mountain. He places some meat on a banana leaf, together with roots and vegetables. Then he sprinkles some toddy on the offerings. Facing the holy mountain he joins his hands and prays that the god may give him food, cure him, protect him, or give him a child. He bows down in obeisance. Then a dinner is prepared and the whole family has a meal.

The Urali Kurumar have a female deity, Betta Chikamma, the mother of the hills, who is very popular among them and receives offerings when they have disturbing dreams warning them of impending epidemics. She is given an offering and it is expected that she then protects them against all evils.

The Malakkarar can often be observed bowing to hills or even prostrating themselves in front of trees and rocks.

The Irular worship three gods whom they believe to inhabit the Mallesvaram peak in the Attapady area. They avoid climbing the hill.

A characteristic feature of Ullathan religion is the worship of spirits residing on certain hill peaks. They make offerings to these spirits on Tuesdays and Fridays. The offerings consist of fruits, beaten rice, milk, sugar and molasses. While offering prayers, the priest often falls into a trance, breaks coconuts, and all join in the acclamations. The hill spirit speaks through the priest and promises them his protection. All bow down in worship. The Ullathans are convinced that they can be saved from dangers and troubles in the jungle only through the assistance extended by the spirits of the hills. After this sacrifice they are no longer afraid of wild animals in the forests.

The Allar are known to revere various kinds of plants, trees, rocks, hillocks and streams in the jungle. The Eravallar are said to do the same.

The Mudugar, too, are at times seen standing in silent veneration at the foot of large trees or rocks in the forest.

The Chenchus of Andhra venerate a jungle goodess, Garelamaisama, whom they consider a powerful sylvan deity. She receives offerings of parts of the animals killed in a hunt and of first fruits. Garelamaisama controls the wild animals in the jungle and drives them on the path of the hunter. When a Chenchu goes hunting, when he brings down an animal, and when he returns home with the kill he prays to Garelamaisama.

Some of these tribes also worship the tiger. Thus the Irular treat the tiger as their visible god and worship his footprints. In former times the Allar did the same. But the tiger has now become extinct in the region which they inhabit, thus the new generation has given up venerating the tiger.

The Nayadis also believe in gods and spirits who reside in the hills and forests. They watch over them and protect them against the attacks of wild animals, provided the Nayadis make them offerings. All accidents are attributed to their disfavour, and even rain and thunder are believed to be caused by them.

The Nayadis have a god of the hunt, Parakutty, who assists them on their hunting expeditions, leads the game to them, and protects them against the attacks of wild animals. The god is represented by a crude stone raised on a platform under a tree. Once a year at night a priest performs an offering to the god; boiled rice, toddy and fruits are offered. After that they partake of a dinner and then go home.

The Eravallens also believe that spirits reside in rocks, trees or hill-tops. They have influence over particular families or villages and must be appeased by gifts of food to satiate their hunger. The Eravallens propitiate the sylvan deities both before the construction and before the occupation of their dwellings.

The Kadar have two hill gods, Malavay and Malankuratti. They are brother and sister. They were the two first beings on the earth and they had come from the interior of the earth. They were the creators of the first Kadar man and woman. They also created the mountains. The pair also taught the Kadar to wear clothes, how to use fire and how to cook food.

SUN AND MOON

Many of the south Indian tribes venerate the sun and the moon. The Kanikkar, for instance, believe that the sun is the creator of all things. The sun is a female diety, while the moon is a male god. The spots in the moon represent a hare. The Kanikkar worship the sun on Fridays. Early at sunrise they place a lighted lamp in front of the hut, and also beaten and fried rice, and fruits. They pray that God may accept their offerings. Then they take the offerings and make a meal of them.

The Mala Pandaram too hold that the sun and moon are deities, but they are of minor importance.

Elderly Kadar still venerate the rising sun, but the younger generation has given up this rite. The Kattunayakar worship the sun and also the moon.

The Koragar admit that they worshipped the sun in the past. Now the present generation prefers to worship the Hindu gods.

The Mala Malasar, too, bow in adoration before the rising sun. The Uralis recognise the sun as the creator of all souls. They offer a short prayer to the sun. They consider the sun as a male god. Sun worship is a part of their religion. They conceive the moon as the mother of all.

The Thanta Pulayar worship the sun. The Muduvar worship the morning and evening sun. The sun is greeted by raising folded hands up to the face.

The Mala Arayar believe that the sun and the moon are the children of one goddess.

ANCESTOR WORSHIP

Almost all the tribes venerate and worship their ancestors.

Thus the Adiyar worship the spirits of their ancestors and believe that those who have led a good life are reborn as human beings. The same belief is held by the Eravallar.

Among the Mala Vedar the worship of the ancestors is their principal form of religion. It is performed in a solemn form.

The Kadar believe that their ancestors and the dead are their best protectors in danger and come to their assistance when they are in misery and difficulties. Before they go out on a honey-collecting expedition they make an offering to their ancestors. They also invoke their ancestors when they go out to hunt or to collect jungle produce. They believe that the ancestors help them to find abundant food and protect them against wild animals.

The Kadar believe that the ancestors occasionally appear to them in dreams. At every offering the ancestors get their share. They are also invited to witness wedding ceremonies. The Mala Vettuvar worship their ancestors as domestic gods.

Among the Mulla Kuruvar also, the worship of the ancestors seems to be most popular. The Ullathans have many ceremonies for the propitiation of their ancestors and ask them for protection against epidemics and the attacks of wild animals.

The Urali Kurumar examine the dead to find out who was good and who bad. The spirit of a good person is venerated, that of a bad person is feared as an evil spirit and must be propitiated by offerings.

The Karimpalar, Koragar and Kurichchiyar, on the other hand, do not seem to venerate their ancestors and, if they do, they do so with little zeal.

The Mala Arayar of central Travancore also venerate their ancestors. On the death of a member of the family, they make a small stone box and, after the funeral, place a small silver or brass image in it. If the family is poor, an oblong stone is enough. The spirit of the dead is suppose to pass into the figure. Offerings of milk, rice, toddy and clarified butter are made. These offerings are repeated on the anniversary days. Then the stone cover is lifted off and quickly replaced. The box is not touched at any other time.

PRIESTHOOD AND SHAMANISM

Some of the south Indian tribes do not seem to have a well organised priesthood. Nor do they regularly perform sacrifices. Offerings are made and sacrifices performed by the head of the family. Sometimes the village headman acts as a priest as well.

The majority of the tribes, however, have professional priests. The priest is distinguished from the exorciser or shaman, though he may also act in these capacities. The exorciser uses white or black magic. First he must divine the nature of the sickness or misfortune that has befallen his client. Then he must find out the particular deity or spirit who has caused the sickness. Finally, he must discover the kind and number of offerings which are required for a cure.

If the sickness or the misfortune was caused by black magic or witchcraft, he has to counteract it by white magic or exorcism. The divination can be accomplished either by natural means or by shamanism. South Indian shamanism means possession of the person by a spirit or deity. The shaman falls into a trance and loses his consciousness partly or completely. The people believe that a spirit or deity has taken possession of him and speaks through him. The trance is brought about through prolonged singing and drumming in a monotonous rhythm, by turning the head quickly round for quite some time, and by the liberal use of liquor and drugs.

Some of the so-called sorcerers are accused of being members of the famous Oti cult which is alleged to have its origin from among the lowcaste Parayans. The members of this secret cult are supposed to be indulging in black magic. They are believed to be able to turn themselves into animals (bulls, dogs, cats, even elephants). Those who want to join the cult must pass severe tests before they are admitted.

No doubt, most of the dreadful stories told about the machinations of the members of this cult are simply products of human imagination motivated by a certain amount of ill-will towards the low-caste and tribal people. If the tribes and low-castes were such powerful sorcerers they would not be so desperately poor and degraded.

Similar stories are current about the sorcery of the Kurumbar. It is interesting that they are supposed to work their magic in much the same manner as the aboriginal Australians: 'A man was first rendered unconscious by magical manipulation with plant lead and incantation. They then ripped open his abdomen, extracted the entrails which they cooked and ate, filled the cavity with dirt and stones, then closed it so that no scar showed. On awakening the victim remembered nothing of what had happened to him, but within eighteen days he would sicken and die' [S.G. Mandelbaum (1957), p. 294]. There is no doubt that much of the sinister reputation the Kurumbas have as sorcerers is unfounded and exaggerated.

But the Kurumbas are still the professional exorcisers for the Todas and Badagas. Whenever a Toda or Badaga gets sick, or believes that he has been bewitched or that his children have been affected by the evil eye, the Kurumba exorciser is called and requested to ply his magic arts and to remove the curse. The Kurumba recites his magic incantations. But when he fails to effect a cure, he may be blamed and severely punished by his clients. In the past many murders were committed by the Todas and Badagas in revenge because they believed that the Kurumba exorcisers failed intentionally to cure the patient.

The Kurumbas are paid an annual fee by the Badagas for their magic services, and they receive a donation whenever a Badaga dies or a child is born.

But the Todas also have their own sorcerers and exorcisers, and they too are consulted by the Badagas.

The Uralis frequently take refuge in exorcism for the cure of any ailment. They have their own magicians. Among them an aspirant for the vocation has first to leave his community and wander in solitude for some months in the jungle. After this preparation he may fall into a trance. He believes that his forefathers appear to him in the shape of young women who teach him the magic arts. When he has learned his lessons he returns as a full-fledged exorciser to his community.

HINDU INFLUENCE

It appears that the tribals of south India have no clear and definite concept of a so-called high-god, a god above all the other gods and spirits—benevolent, just, the creator, the lord of life and death. Wherever such a deity appears he bears a Hindu name and his characteristics are also that of the Hindu supreme god, Vishnu, Shiva, or one of their incarnations. It seems, therefore, that the tribals have above all borrowed the form of the high-god from Hinduism, but along with him also a host of other gods, especially of female deities.

The name which this high-god bears is either Parama Shiva, Parameshwar, Suriya-Ilura, Malavay (hill-ruler), Ayappan or Ayanar, and Sasta or Sastan, with consort. The latter is conceived as a sylvan deity and often identified with Shiva. He has a companion, Karuppaswami.

The Mannar, for instance, worship Sasta and his satellite Karuppaswami at three different places. The Vishavar venerate Sasta under the name of Mattingal at Mad, a waterfall sacred to the god. Votaries break coconuts when passing the waterfall and pray for prosperity and protection against illness. The Malayalar worship Sasta by offerings in January. Paddy is collected by all men of a settlement and given to the priest who prepares a dinner which all attend. The Kanikkar worship Sasta for the prevention of evil and for material prosperity.

Sasta is conceived as a mountain god, riding on a horse or

elephant and fighting with the spirits. He is a hunting god; whoever meets him in the jungle must die.

The majority of the Irular worship Vishnu under the name of Rangaswami. But they also venerate Shiva. The favourite god of the settled Kadar is Ayappan. In the Wynaad the Kadar worship Shiva as Malakari, his manifestation as a hunter. Other members of the tribe worship Vishnu.

The favourite deity of the Kurumbar is Sanchali Karuppan, a form of Shiva. The Malakkarar, on the other hand, worship Malavedan, a personification of Krishna as a hunter. The Mala Pandarams occasionally make offerings to the god Ayappan. He and Karuppaswami are their favourite gods. The Malayalar, too, are regular worshippers of Shiva as high-god. But they also venerate Ayappan. The Mulla Kurumar worship Kariappan and Iyyappan.

The Kanikkar worship a high-god by the name of Padacha Thampuran. He is the creator of all. Every morning on waking up the Kanikkar invoke his name and the names of other gods to ward off evil spirits.

The Mudugar worship the god Shiva in the Malleswaram peak, rising steeply from the Attapady valley. On Shivaratri they once a year climb the mountain top. The week before, they must live a chaste life, offer prayers to Shiva and take a bath. On the feast day they cross the river and climb the mountain, taking along fruits, coconuts, sacred food, incense, and bamboo tubes for carrying water. All the way they invoke the gods. A few yards from the top there is a spring in which they bathe. At sunset they light their torches, fast and pray throughout the night. The next morning they bathe again, fill the bamboo containers with water and climb down the hill. They cross the river and proceed to Shiva's temple. They sprinkle the holy water over the people and worship in the temple.

The Kurichchiyar prefer the worship of Shiva under his manifestation as a hunter; they call him Muttappan. They worship him in the form of a heap of stones in various jungle places.

The Muthuvans worship as their high-god, the god Subramania. In each hamlet is a thatched shed created for the god. It is at some distance from their settlements. On a bamboo mat in the shed they place a cane and a bundle of peacock feathers, the emblem of the god Subramania.

The supreme god is often represented in a crude stone slab. His worshippers sing his praises and make offerings of rice boiled in milk, of sugar, plantains and fruits. Other tribes prefer bloody sacrifices, of goats, sheep and cocks.

Besides the main god, the tribals worship with preference mother goddesses who often appear as the consorts of Shiva or Vishnu. No doubt, this is a strong indication of Hindu influence. Sometimes even the high-god is conceived as a goddess.

Prominent among the famale deities is Kali or Bhadrakali (Kali with many arms). She is also called Bhagavati, the wife of Shiva. The tribes also worship the goddesses of disease, the 'Seven Sisters' or 'Seven Mothers' (*ammas*). They are also called Kannimar. Mariamma, the goddess of cholera and small-pox, gets special veneration. She is worshipped all over south India. The sacrifices to these female deities are always bloody animal sacrifices. The spilling of blood is an important part of the ritual.

A Description of the Various Tribes

From the economic point of view the tribes of south India can be divided into (*a*) foodgatherers and hunters; (*b*) shifting cultivators supplementing their livelihood either by hunting and food collecting, or by field and plantation labour; (*c*) dependent farmers with the plough, either as tenants or labourers; and (*d*) independent plough cultivators. These four sections can of course be made only in a broad sense, as few tribes belong exclusively to one section; often there is a conservative section and a more progressive section in a tribe, or groups which have become separated geographically have also, in terms of culture, developed differently. Broadly speaking, it can also be said that the economically more advanced tribes have adopted more of Hindu culture and religion. But by doing this they have not always risen in social rank. The permanent field labourers commonly rank the lowest in social status, the mere foodgatherers come next, and then the shifting cultivators who occasionally work as labourers. Highest in the social rank are the independent farmers. There are also some shepherd tribes.

FOODGATHERERS AND HUNTERS

A very primitive foodgathering and hunting tribe is that of the Palliyar (3,134 in 1961) in Tamilnadu, Kerala and Mysore states, mainly in the Periyar hills. They prefer the higher altitudes of the mountains. They live principally by collecting jungle produce, by snaring and trapping wild animals and birds, and catching fish in the rivers. They own no personal property except the scanty clothing they wear, a cooking pot, a digging stick and a bill-hook or an axe. They do not even keep dogs. They depend largely on wild honey and on the sale of wax from its combs. To get the honey a man is usually let down over a cliff, by a rope of twisted creepers, to dislodge the beehives with his digging stick.

The Palliyar live in scattered communities in the forest. Often they spend the night on platforms up the trees, in caves or under rocks, or build themselves grass huts.

They speak Tamil with a peculiar intonation. Most Palliyars cannot count beyond the numbers of their fingers and toes. When a member of their community dies, they do not bury him. They simply leave the body and move away. They avoid the spot for some months. But recently they have started to bury their dead, in order not to lose the plot of land where they had been staying. Some of the Palliyar have a good knowledge of medicinal herbs. Like many of the thoroughly wild tribes of the forest the Palliyar, too, are feared as powerful sorcerers by the people of the plains.

Another such tribe, on the Nilgiris, is that of the Sholagar (6,138 in 1961). In 1807 Buchanan described them thus: 'They speak a bad or old dialect of Kannada, have scarcely any clothing, sleep round a fire on a few plantain leaves using the same to cover themselves. They live chiefly on summits of mountains which the tigers do not frequent. Their huts are most wretched—bamboo bent and both ends stuck in to form an arch and covered with plantain leaves.'

Some of the Sholagar today are a little more accomplished and wear a loincloth and maybe even a coat. But they still collect forest produce and honey, and occasionally get employment as farm servants and cattle grazers with the plainsmen.

There are various foodgathering and hunting tribes in the

hills and jungles of Kerala. Perhaps the most primitive of the south Indian forest tribes is that of the Kadar (1,244 in 1961) belonging to the former Cochin State and to Coimbatore. In this tribe the Proto-Australoid element is definitely dominant. The Kadar may even have some Negrito racial strain. While some groups of the Kadar have remained mere foodgatherers and hunters, other groups have been strongly influenced by contact with timber coolies and with the contractors who exploit the minor forest products. A section of the tribe has even settled down to cultivation of a primitive type.

The food collectors and hunters among the Kadar file or chip their incisor teeth to a point. They bury their dead, but observe no period of taboo after a death has occurred in the family and erect no memorial. Their family life has been destroyed by the forest labourers who, having left their families behind in the plains, often forcibly cohabit with Kadar women.

The Arunadar are the most primitive of all the hill tribes north of the Palghat gap. They are a small black race, short of stature, with thick bushy hair and flat noses. They are considered the lowest among even the untouchables. They pollute all others within a hundred yards. They use bows and arrows principally for shooting monkeys. They are not at all particular as to what they eat and devour snakes and vermin and eat putrid flesh of various animals without harm to their stomachs. They extract oil from the python and use it as a cure against leprosy.

Mainly engaged in food collecting, they also find employment in felling trees in the Nilambur forests. They also cultivate fields for the Mohammedans. They wear scanty clothing and even plantain leaves when hard up. Their chief habitat is the Ernad taluq near Nilambur, hence their name Eranadar or Arunadar. The Census of India returns 44 Arunadar, but A.A.D. Luiz [(1962), p. 39], thinks that their number is about six hundred. In 1941 their number was given as 489.

A similar tribe that is considered very polluting is that of the Koragar (6,936 in 1961). They live mainly in the northern parts of Mysore State, but are found also in Kerala. Not so long ago the Koragar had to carry pots around their necks in which to spit as they were not allowed to spit on the ground. They were bought and sold as slaves, forbidden to use anything new, compelled to live in leaf huts, and forced to cook in broken pots.

They were a jungle tribe in the past, later they took to basket-making and at present earn their livelihood in the villages of the plains as scavengers or work on their own small fields on which they raise vegetables, *ragi,* etc. They eat almost anything, also carrion.

While they are treated as low and polluting by the people of the plains, they in their turn treat the Chakkiliyar and Mala Vettuvar as untouchables. There is no caste or tribe in India that does not consider other castes or tribes still lower and more despicable.

Another Kerala tribe living in extreme primitivity is that of the Mala Pandarams (816 in 1961) in the former Travancore State near Lake Periyar. In physical appearance the Mala Pandarams are of short stature (154.26 cm average), with a light yellowish skin (due probably to defective nourishment), brownish eyes, wavy black hair, a steep forehead, a small flat nose, and a receding chin. The whole appearance is infantile.

The Mala Pandarams still live in the hunting and collecting stage. The principal implement is the digging stick with a point hardened in fire. Nowadays they also use an iron bill-hook. For hunting they use bows and arrows, blow pipes and spears. They have no domestic animals except dogs which they keep for hunting. Exclusively engaged in hunting and food collecting, they need about two square miles of forest per head to support themselves. In recent times their food problems have become acute as a result of the deforestation and the inundation of their hunting grounds due to the erection of new dams. They are nomadic within a limited area, and their dwellings are either rock shelters or flimsy huts of leaves.

Unlike most of their neighbours they are not matrilineal, but reckon descent from the father. The Mala Pandaram tribe may soon be extinct since there is a shortage of women. But in spite of the shortage of women the Mala Pandarams do not permit polyandry.

As they consider a woman in childbirth impure they leave her alone during her confinement and for about thirty days afterwards. Her husband cooks and looks after her. A woman is impure for ten days during her menstruation. She must stay away from her family during this time.

In former times a mother had to sacrifice her first-born child to Malagal, the mountian god. She had to expose her baby in the forest on a banana leaf to fall prey to the wild beasts of the jungle. At present, the baby is exposed but, after a short time, taken back by the mother.

The Mala Pandarams bury their dead wherever they have died and then the whole group leaves the place and moves elsewhere. In the past the old and sick people who could not move when they had to change residence were simply killed.

They do not kill wild cattle and avoid the bear and the tiger, nor do they kill monkeys. For, they believe that monkeys were originally human beings who had been driven into the forest and forced to stay on trees. The tiger is for them an accursed animal, for god has given him the order to kill evil persons in punishment for their crimes. Thus they do not defend themselves when attacked by a tiger nor do they rescue a person attacked.

Very similar to the Mala Pandarams are the Allar of Palghat District in Kerala. Their number is about 350. They too are exclusively foodgatherers and hunters. They change their habitats rather frequently, but within a restricted area. They stay overnight in caves, pits, in the hollow of trees and under overhanging rocks. For longer halts they build themselves flimsy huts or wind-screens. For protection against wild animals they always sleep around a fire. Their equipment consists of an axe, a chopper, a digging fork, nets, snares and traps. They cook in earthen pots which they occasionally make themselves. They hunt with dogs and take good care of them. They never sell or give away a dog. They consider monkey flesh a delicacy. For barter they sell honey and wax, bamboo or charcoal which they burn in pits. They have no bows and arrows nor spears. Unlike the Mala Pandarams, they are not much concerned about ritual pollution through menstruation or child-birth. They are patrilineal.

The Kattunayakar (10,375 in 1961) in Kerala and Tamilnadu states believe that they are the progeny of a high-caste chief and his tribal wife, or the descendants of the ancient Pallavas who were defeated by the Cholas in the seventh century A.D. and had to flee into the forest. Whatever value these pretensions may have, they are today mainly foodgatherers and hunters, while some are employed by the Forest Department as elephant mahouts and forest guards. Recently they have started cultivation in the forest plantations. But in their whole appearance and cultural life they seem to be simply one of the indigenous hill tribes. They follow the patrilineal system. They bury their dead in niche graves.

Another tribe of collectors of forest produce, who occasionally do agricultural labour and wood-cutting on hire, are the Malasar or Malayar (2,095 in 1961). At present they reside mainly in Tamilnadu (Coimbatore District) while in the former Census Reports a considerable number of them were found in Kerala. They are rather unsteady in their habits and desert a place or estate on the slightest excuse.

Ehrenfels would prefer to class them as shifting cultivators, but he has only one group in view; the other groups are mainly nomadic foodgatherers.

The Malasar are divided into two sections, the Nattu and the Kongu Malasar. These two sections differ in their racial features, the Kongu Malasar being taller, darker, with a flatter nose and thicker lips. This may be due to a racial mixture with other tribes, possibly the Kadar and Irular. The Nattu Malasar have adopted the mother-right system, while the Kongu Malasar are patrilineal. Ehrenfels [*A Malayalar Mock Fight,* (Vienna, 1956), pp. 291–307] characterises this tribe as medium-sized, wavy-haired, light coloured and, generally, of a Mediterranean type. He groups them racially together with the shifting cultivators such as the Kuruchar, Muthuvar and Kanikkar, and not with the Proto-Australoid or Negritoid foodgatherers. But he has obviously only the Nattu Malasar in view, not their Kongu section. The Nattu Malasar are known for a ceremonial mock-fight, connected with the initiation of boys.

The Malasar live generally in huts built of bamboo and leaves high on clumps over which planks are spread to make a flooring. A single bamboo with knots serving as steps is used for access. Sometimes the huts are built on tree tops. This location is chosen as a precaution against wild animals. The Malasar have bows and arrows, a bill-hook and a staff as weapons. They do not bury their dead, but expose them in the jungle.

The Uralis (2,597) claim to be related to the Sholagar, though they do not intermarry with them. They earn their livelihood by the collection of jungle produce; some cultivate fields; others own and tend sheep and cattle. The food-collecting Uralis are known for building their huts fifty feet or so above the ground, and it is in such houses that the girls are kept separated when in their first menses, and the women in child-birth. No one helps a woman in labour; advice and instruction is shouted from a distance to the woman in trouble.

The Uralis are found chiefly in the Alleppey, Kottayam, Quilon and Trivandrum districts of Kerala. They are clever huntsmen, and passionately attached to their hunting dogs. They do not hunt elephants and wild buffaloes; even crossing the tracks of these animals is religiously avoided.

The Mala Vedans (722 in 1961) are inhabitants of the Kottayam and Quilon districts. The majority have now moved to rural areas. The Elijathi Vedans habitually eat rats, and the Cheegani Vedans crocodiles. For this reason probably the other sections do not inter-dine with these two. The primitive Vedans (hunters), as their name indicates, subsist exclusively on hunting. Some collect jungle produce. Today many work on farms and plantations for a pittance.

The Mala Vedans were in former times known for filing their front teeth to a sharp point. It was done when the boys were about eighteen and the girls ten years of age.

At present the Mala Vedans lead a most wretched existence on the outskirts of the Kerala villages, shunned by all, always on the verge of starvation. But they accept their fate with stoical patience and passive endurance; they prefer a free life to regular employment and steady work. Their present life is devoid of any higher cultural values. Their religious practice is confined to an occasional worship of their ancestors. They are not permitted to attend the religious ceremonies of the Hindu villagers.

The Ulladans (3,366 in 1961) are found all over Kerala; their hill sections live mainly in Quilon and Kottayam districts. They seem to be related to the Nayadis who are today a scheduled caste. Some Ulladans are engaged in cultivation or are farm labourers, but the majority are nomadic foodgatherers and hunters. They are good trappers and clever in making traps, snares and nooses. They eat anything, even carrion. Some specialise in catching rats which they eat. They are believed to be experts in black magic and in the Oti cult.

They build special huts for their women in childbirth. After the birth of her child the mother is not allowed to mix with the family for about a month. As they eat all kinds of food, even rats, they are regarded as unclean by the Hindu castes. In the past a Brahmin felt polluted if an Ulladan approached him within a distance of sixty-four feet.

Aboriginal tribes of the mere foodgathering stage as well as of shifting cultivation can also be found in eastern south India, in the regions of the Eastern Ghats and to the north of them.

One of these tribes is that of the Chenchus (17,814 in 1961). They inhabit chiefly the Nallamalas of Kurnool District in Andhra Pradesh. The greater part of them has now settled down in the plains villages, either as farmers or as farm labourers. But a number of Chenchus still lead a nomadic life, subsisting purely on the collection of vegetable foodstuff in the jungle and on hunting wild animals. They hunt with bows and arrows, and also set traps. They are accomplished fishermen. The Chenchus have a dark complexion and lean and wiry bodies; they are agile and enduring in the hunt.

They seem to be racially related to the Yanadis, another jungle tribe. Their number is much greater—205,381. They have prominent cheekbones, a pointed chin, scanty hair on the face and body, curly hair and a platyrrhine nose. They might have some Negrito blood. The main homelands of this tribe are the Nellore, Chittoor and Chingleput districts. Most of them have lost all jungle characteristics and live as domestic servants and even as scavengers in the villages of the plains. One sub-section manufactures charcoal. The jungle Yanadis are keen on fishing. They also catch cobras and have a great partiality for field rats. They collect honey and other jungle produce, and have a good knowledge of medicinal herbs.

Their sex life is rather loose and divorce is easy. Polygyny is widely practised, but not polyandry. Thefts and house-breaking are common crimes of the Yanadis. Their funeral rites and rites of worship resemble those of the Hindus. They worship the Hindu gods.

Another tribe of a similar type is that of the Yerukulas (128,024 in 1961). They are also called Koravas or Korachas. They have the reputation of being thieves and house-breakers.

SHIFTING CULTIVATORS AND FOOD COLLECTORS

The afore-described tribes are more or less pure hunters and foodgatherers, though some sections of them may have settled down in the cleared areas as farmers or may have found employment as labourers in the forest or on plantations. The next step in the evolution is shifting cultivation. In this primitive form of agriculture a jungle plot is burned down, cleared of the trunks and the seeds are sown, by means of a digging stick, into the soil fertilised by the ashes. After a few years the plot has to be changed and the cultivators shift to a new jungle plot. During the time when their crop grows the people find time enough to collect vegetable food in the nearby jungle and to hunt. Thus, shifting cultivation can be considered an intermediate step between mere nomadic collecting and hunting and the settled life of an agriculturist.

One such tribe, inhabiting the broken country to the east of the Nilgiris and elsewhere, is that of the Irular (82,077 in 1961). The Irular, also known as Iraligas, Illigarus and Kadu Pujaris, are perhaps related to the Yanadis, Uralis and Chenchus. Like the Kurumbar, they are divided into a section of the forest and one of the plains. The Irular of the plains are more or less Hinduised, live in villages and work on the land. The Hill Irular are engaged in forest and plantation work, grow paddy and other crops in the swamps and valley bottoms, and supplement their diet with bamboo seeds and edible roots which they collect in the jungle. Some of them are good cattle men. In former times the Irular practised shifting cultivation. This necessitated a frequent shifting of their settlements which they call *ur*, hence the name Urali or Irular.

The Irular bury their dead in a side niche of the rectangular grave which they dig.

The Mannar (3,610 in 1961), now living in the Cardamon hills, have the tradition that in the past they revolted against the king of Madurai and subsequently fled his country. Their chiefs still have ceremonial swords and canes which had been granted to their forefathers by the rulers. However, in their physical appearance they resemble the aboriginals among which group they are counted by the Government. Originally shifting cultivators, they had to give up this type of agriculture and are now either settled plough cultivators or field labourers. They occasionally supplement their diet by collecting forest produce in the jungle. They are experts in collecting honey and medicinal herbs. They practise matriarchy.

The Karimpalar (c. 6,000), inhabitants of the Cannanore and Calicut districts of Kerala State, were in the past mainly shifting (*ponum*) cultivators. Deforestation and the opening up of new plantations have largely stopped this type of cultivation. While some groups are now independent farmers, others make and sell charcoal or work in plantations.

The Malakkarans (c. 1,000) of Calicut District were foodgatherers and hunters in the past, but then became shifting cultivators. In recent years they have had to earn their livelihood also as farm labourers and watchmen. They still collect jungle produce to supplement their meagre income. They consider themselves a superior race and do not like to associate with other tribes. They reckon descent in the female line.

The Kanikkar (11,254 in 1961) in Kerala and Madras states are shifting cultivators, who have already taken to plough cultivation. But they also hunt wild animals. They have a bachelor hall in the settlement, which is prohibited to females, and live in huts on piles. They are matrilineal.

Another tribe in Kerala (north Malabar) is that of the Mala Kudis or Vishavans (1,239 in 1961). They live in the Western Ghats near the Mysore border. Their language is Tulu. They work as coolies in the estates or cultivate land on lease on which they grow paddy and tapioca. They are partly Hinduised and matrilineal. When the Mala Kudis bury a deceased member of their tribe they fix a bamboo tube or reed near the nose of the corpse so that the spirit of the deceased can breathe or escape. They shoot fish with a blow-gun. They have common halls for visitors.

In the past they lived for the most part in the jungle, beneath rocks, in caves, or in low huts, and shifted frequently from one place to another. In the season of the cardamom crop, they came down once a week to the plains with the produce.

The Malayalis (144,034 in 1961) live in the hills of Salem, north and south Arcot, and Tiruchirapally districts of Tamilnadu and in Cannanore District of Kerala. They are supposed to have belonged originally to the Tamil Vellala caste who retreated to the hilly tracts when Muslim rule became dominant in south India. Others claim that they are the descendants of unions of Vellala men with Vedan women. This would be more in keeping with their cultural level which is partly primitive.

The Malayalis are spread over a vast area and, therefore, divided into numerous sections. They practised shifting cultivation in the past, but are now settled agriculturists or plantation workers since land is scarce. In the hills they supplement their livelihood by hunting and food collecting. In Kerala they still do not use cattle for ploughing.

In Kerala they follow the matrilineal system. In one part of Tamilnadu they have, or had in the past, a peculiar form of marriage: A boy-child marries an adult girl with whom the boy's father cohabits. The children are considered to be those of the boy-child.

DEPENDENT LABOURERS AND FOOD COLLECTORS

Many food-collecting tribes of south India were forced by the dwindling resources of the forests to surrender their freedom and to seek work in the plains. It made them utterly dependent on the land-owners.

Such a tribe of low-paid agricultural labourers is that of the Adiyar who are mainly found in the Cannanore District of Kerala. In 1961 their number was 5,699. They claim that their ancestor was a Brahmin who lost caste because of his marriage to a non-Brahmin girl. However, Government regards the Adiyar as belonging to the 'scheduled tribes'. They are attached to certain landlords, and may have been slaves in the past. They are usually paid in kind for their work—two kilos of paddy for a man's work in a day, somewhat less for a woman's. The Adiyar are forced to supplement their meagre wages by collecting jungle produce and by hunting.

The Eravallens (518), also in Kerala, are in a similar situation. Originally a small forest tribe, they have now started to work as farm labourers. They are perhaps related to the Kadar, but they are more steady and remain longer at one place. Their language is Tamil which would suggest that they are immigrants from Tamilnadu. They are also engaged as tree cutters and forest guards in the jungle. They are patrilineal. In their customs they largely conform to the standards of lower Hindu castes of the region.

The Kalanadis (less than 400), inhabitants of Calicut District, are now also mainly agricultural labourers in the estates near their habitats. In former times they were famous for their fire-walking. They perform dances in which they represent various gods. They bury their dead in niche graves. Their headmen are, however, cremated.

The Mala Vettuvans (c. 3,500) are the forest section of the low caste of the Vettuvans (26,317) in the plains. They live in the Cannanore District of Kerala State. They were originally hunters, as their name indicates, but now they are mainly agricultural labourers. But wherever land is available they prefer to cultivate paddy and pepper on their own. The Mala Vettuvans have now given up their hunting and collecting in the jungle and earn their livelihood by basket making. They seem to have been matrilineal in the past, but now follow the patrilineal system.

The Mavilans of the Cannanore District in Kerala (7,225) were also obliged to abandon their carefree life in the jungle. A few of them are at present shifting cultivators, but more members of the tribe earn their living as labourers, basket makers, elephant drivers, and collectors of medicinal herbs and forest produce. Though wretchedly poor and not particular in the choice of their food, their touch is not polluting for Hindus. They follow the patrilineal system and there is no indication that they had been matrilineal in the past.

The Malakkuravas (246 in 1961) of the former Travancore State are primitive hunters and foodgatherers in the hills. They form the jungle section of the Kurava caste now settled in the plains. The Malakkuravas are the rest of those who had formerly lived in liberty as hunters and foodgatherers. But scarcity of food had since many years forced most of the Kurava tribe to seek work as agricultural labourers in the plains. They had been enslaved by the Hindu landowners and in the past had been sold along with the land. In 1855 slavery was abolished, but the economic and social conditions of the Kuravas have not improved much. In the past the Kuravas had to keep at a distance of 48 paces from a high-caste Hindu for fear of polluting him. This part of social degradation has gone, but their economic exploitation has remained.

TRIBES OF HIGHER SOCIAL STATUS

A tribe claiming aristocratic origin, though now much reduced economically, is that of the Kurumbas (11,419) in the Nilgiris and their vicinity, or the Kurumans (13,587), who are the Kurumbas but living on the western slopes of the mountains. The Kurumba section living in the plains is called Kuruba (9,246 in 1961). The general assumption is that after the downfall of the ancient Kurumba dynasties in the eighth century A.D., a part of the people escaped into the jungle where they have since remained after their defeat by the Cholas. It has also been suggested that their forefathers were the people who erected the dolmens and cairns found in great numbers in these regions.

The Kurumbas are spread over a wide area of south India and are found in Kerala (Wynaad), in Tamilnadu (Nilgiris) and in the adjoining Mysore hills. They are divided into a number of sub-divisions which, isolated from each other, have now adopted not only the languages spoken in their respective regions, but also the cultural peculiarities of the people among whom they live.

The fugitive Kurumbas lost much of their former culture and splendour in the wild surroundings of the forest and were reduced to a very poor state of economic life. In Kerala they apparently refused to adjust to their reduced condition, refused to do farm work and any other manual work and consequently could eke out a meagre existence only as hunters and collectors of jungle produce. In Tamilnadu and Mysore, however, where they took to farm work, the Kurumbas are today petty cultivators and field labourers, workers in the forest and on coffee, pepper and orange plantations. The Betta Kurumbas, one of their sub-sections, are expert woodmen and good mahouts. They make themselves useful in the capture of wild elephants (*keddah*). The Jen Kurumbas in the Nilgiris, who do not mix with the Betta Kurumbas, though they live in close proximity to them, are often plantation workers. They have youth dormitories, one for unmarried boys and another for the girls.

The Kurubas, the section living in the plains, are petty land-owners, herders of sheep, weavers of coarse blankets, and even stone-masons. They are comparatively better off than their fellow tribals in the hills. They are much more Hinduised than the Kurumbas. The Kurubas are said to erect temples which are dolmen-like and also monuments for the dead which closely resemble the old megalith tombs though they are much smaller. The Kurubas are said to have a peculiar form of sacrifice at a temple in north Arcot. They break coconuts on the head of the temple *pujari* (priest) and on the head of the sacred bull kept there.

Another similar tribe, of good social standing, is that of the Kurichchians (11,854 in 1961). They are found mainly in north Malabar, especially in the Wynaad. Their name may be Kanarese: *kuri*—hill, and *chian*—people. The Kurichchians, who claim

Nayar descent, are a community of relatively high social standing. Originally a hunting tribe, they also practise shifting cultivation today. Many of them seek work in the plantations as labourers. They are much exploited by the Mappilas who used to take their whole paddy harvest as interest for outstanding debts.

The Kurichchians are excellent hunters; they use well-trained dogs in the hunt. Good bowmen, they shoot fish with bows and arrows. They also use the blow gun.

They are matrilineal now, but seem to have been patrilineal and patrilocal in the past. Their marriage is still patrilocal.

They feel polluted if approached closely by a Paniyan, Adiyan, Kurumba or Pulayan, but they also affect great contempt for Brahmins. After a Brahmin has visited a Kurichchian house, the place where he has been sitting receives a coating with purifying cow-dung as soon as he has left.

Another such community is that of the Maratis (55,391 in 1961), one-third of whom live in Kerala and two-thirds in Mysore. As their name indicates, they come from Maharashtra, probably as soldiers who settled in Kerala and Mysore states. They claim Rajput origin, observe the caste rules of the higher Hindus, and are cultivators and field labourers. A few of them are petty traders. But it is said that in the past they practised shifting cultivation and collected jungle produce. They are counted among the scheduled tribes, but in fact they are no tribals.

The Muthuwans, too, enjoy a high social status though they live in the hills and are generally very poor. Their number was 5,188 in 1961. But it appears that in the Census enumeration two tribes have been confused. A. A. D. Luiz [(1962), p. 193] distinguishes between the Muthuwans and the Mudugar or Muduwar. The Muthuwans are probably the more progressive section of the tribe. They have the tradition that they escaped to the hills in the company of a Pandyan prince. This was probably in the fourteenth century or later. They claim to have come from Madurai. The name of the tribe is derived from the fact that they carried their children on their back when they climbed the Ghats, *mudugu* being the Tamil word for 'back'. The Muthuwan males even now carry their loads on their back, and the women, their babies.

The Muthuwans live at present in the high elevations of the Anamalai hills, while the Mudugar are found in the Palghat hills.

They cultivate small holdings of their own or taken on lease and disdain work on farms or plantations not their own. They also collect forest produce, rear goats and poultry for sale, distil lemon grass and hunt wherever possible.

The Muthuwans have youth dormitories for unmarried boys and girls. The latter are looked after by elderly women. This institution has the purpose of preserving pre-nuptial chastity which is highly valued by them.

The Mudugar, on the other hand, are still foodgatherers and hunters. They collect forest produce for sale or barter. They shun field work. Not only culturally but also racially they seem to differ from the Muthuwans. They are dark complexioned; they have flat noses, with wide nostrils and thick lips. The Muthuwans frequently have aquiline noses and thin lips. Nor are they so dark. The Mudugar use blow-pipes at hunting.

The Mala Panickkar (c. 1,000) are found in Calicut District. They claim that their forefathers were Nayars who had to take refuge in the hills. They are probably the progeny of Nayar soldiers who had served in the hill regions. The Mala Panickkar treat all communities lower than the Nayar as inferior. They follow the matrilineal system. But in about the last ten or fifteen years they have begun to change over to the patrilineal system.

The Mala Arayans (2,173 in 1961) in the Kottayam and Ernakulam districts of Kerala claim descent from a Brahmin or even an ancient sage—Rishi Gautama. They are farmers as well as food collectors. Among the farmers are many affluent families with fairly large land holdings, while the forest dwellers earn their livelihood either as collectors of forest produce or pepper growers. They are very poor and scarcely able to escape starvation. In the past they followed the matrilineal system, but recently they have adopted the patrilineal system. They are strict in observing the rules of pollution; women marrying into other communities are permanently outcasted unless they marry Nayars.

THE TODAS AND RELATED TRIBES

On the tableland of the Nilgiris where they have been isolated from early times some tribes are found who live in a kind of economic and social symbiosis; these are the Todas, the Kotas, and to some extent also the Badagas. The Todas and the Kotas seem to belong to the same ethnic stock; at present the Kotas are, however, of lower social status. On the other hand, they have proved more adaptable to new circumstances and are consequently more prosperous.

Anthropologists are still at a loss to explain the racial position of the Todas as well as their peculiar culture which centres around the buffalo. Prince Peter of Greece who recently did some research among the Todas made the suggestion based on a similarity of names that the Todas had cultural connections with the ancient Sumerians. This hypothesis is so far-fetched that it needs no refutation.

The Todas (879 in 1951, 716 in 1961) have developed into a peculiar pastoral community. Their whole economic and religious interest centres on the care and cult of their stock of buffaloes. Since their settlements are in the vicinity of a popular hill-station, the tribes have received much attention. W.H.R. Rivers [(1906)] has written a detailed monograph on the tribe. Ever since, numerous reports about the Todas have appeared in magazines and scientific journals.

In spite of the striking physical appearance of the Todas, the picturesque form of their houses and the peculiar mode of their life, this interest is perhaps not quite justified. It seems that their peculiarities are rather the result of the growth of a small community in isolation than the remnants of an old original culture surviving perhps from ancient times. Theirs is a case of extreme specialisation due to the concentration of a very small and socially exclusive community on the breeding of buffaloes.

An analysis of their language and culture proves that both do not differ essentially from those of the neighbouring tribes and peoples. The Toda language seems to be old Kanarese, with Tamil admixtures, while their invocations are more influenced by Malayalam, but without its Sanskritic additions. It is probable, therefore, that the Todas moved up to the seclusion of the tableland from the Malabar forests in the neighbourhood of the Wynaad or possibly from Coorg. The Todas then remained static or developed along their own line of evolution.

The whole basis of the Toda social structure seems to be directed towards the ceremonial purity of the sacred herds, the sacred dairy, the vessels and the milk, and of those whose duty it is to perform connected rituals. In the dairy, the sacred vessels are always kept in a separate room and the milk reaches them only by transfer to and fro of an intermediate vessel kept in another room. The dairyman who is also a priest is admitted to office only after an elaborate ordination, which in effect is a purification. By means of this rite, he is removed from the rank of ordinary men and elevated to a state of fitness for sacred office. His conduct is governed by regulations which, for instance, permit him to sleep in the village only at certain times, or forbid him to attend a funeral or to forfeit his office as a sacred dairyman.

The Todas sacrifice buffaloes periodically to their main god and at funeral feasts. They cremate their dead. The sacrificed buffaloes are given away; the Todas do not eat them.

The Kotas (1,250 in 1951, 922 in 1961) live in a kind of symbiosis with the Todas. They are smiths and musicians, living in seven villages interspersed among the Toda settlements and the many Badaga villages. But their main source of livelihood is agriculture. They speak a dialect of their own which, however, can be understood by the Todas.

They serve the Todas, Badagas and Kurumbas as smiths and musicians. They manufacture iron tools, wooden utensils, pots and other useful articles for them. They provide the music which is essential for many of the Toda and Badaga ceremonies. In partial payment they receive the carcasses of the cattle and buffaloes which have died a natural death or been killed in sacrifice. They in turn invite the Todas to their feasts and expect them to furnish refined butter for the rituals. On arrival they greet the Todas formally by bowing their heads down to the Todas's raised foot. At harvest time they set some grain aside for the Todas.

The Kotas are an industrious people though dirty in their habits and despised for their custom of eating carrion. They are not allowed to enter a Toda or Badaga dwelling. Their touch is polluting and a bath is required if a Toda or Badaga has touched them even inadvertently.

The Badagas (c. 300,000) live in the neighbourhood of the Todas and Kotas. They probably belong to a primitive race, but have been largely Hinduised. Their complexion also is lighter than that of the Todas and Kotas. The Badagas are an agricultural caste; their main occupation is at present potato-growing. They are prosperous and ambitious enough to buy up all the land suitable for potato cultivation. In the past they were notorious robbers.

They are a peaceful community now; though they may occasionally indulge in gambling and heavy drinking.

The Badagas seem to be immigrants from Kanara. They speak a dialect interspersed with Tamil and Hindi words. They venerate Shiva and worship a god called Rangaswami, but also the other deities of the Hindu pantheon in the manner common among the Hindu castes of south India.

It is interesting that for important religious ceremonies they employ Kurumbas. Before sowing begins, a Kurumba must yoke the bullocks, make three furrows, stop, kneel on the ground and say 'Dho, dho' three times while facing the east. Then he scatters the seed three times over the ground. At another agricultural ceremony called Devve a Kurumba heads the procession scattering fragments of *tud* bark and wood on the way. At a buffalo sacrifice it is the Kurumba who has to kill it with a spear and push the victim over a cliff. At the fire-walking ceremony which takes place before cultivation begins, the fire is lit by Badaga priests and a Kurumba.

But the Badagas entertain really close relations only with the Todas and Kotas. The three tribes are economically interdependent and peacefully share the same territory. However, each community has its own separate settlements, and there is no intermarrying or inter-dining among them. Each community has also its distinctive type of dress, house form, social organisation and religion. The three communities have lived together amicably in undisturbed relations because they have always kept a certain distance between one another.

The Andaman and Nicobar Islanders

One small group of primitive tribes remains still to be described—the tribes of the Andaman Islands and of the Nicobar Islands. The Andaman Islands, a group of 24 islands of various sizes, are, together with the Nicobar Islands, situated in the Bay of Bengal and form the tops of a mountain range submerged in the ocean in a curved north-south line leading from Rangoon to Sumatra. They cover an area of a little more than 2,500 square miles. In 1951 their total population was 18,981 (12,754 males and only 6,227 females). The density is only 7 per square mile, while it is 901 in Kerala and 284 in the whole of India. Only 973 of the population belong to the aboriginal people; the rest were early and later settlers, mostly from India.

The Andamans belong to India though they are 590 miles from Calcutta, only 120 miles from Burma and 340 miles from Sumatra. Situated in the tropical zone, the islands are largely covered with luxurious forests; but they are primitive and undeveloped and await settlers, hard-working and frugal pioneers, to people these islands and to turn them into fit and happy homelands for a content and prosperous population. The potentialities of the islands are great; but so far India has sorely neglected this maritime possession, in spite of overpopulation and the lack of land and employment in India.

The indigenous population of the Andaman Islands belongs to the most backward and peculiar of all the primitive peoples of the whole world. This is doubtless the result of their isolation which has kept the islanders apart from any racial and cultural mixtures. Isolation has also prevented any stimulation towards cultural progress; nor was there any necessity for it on the islands because nature was always bountiful in providing for all the bodily needs of the small population.

Racially the Andamanese belong to the Negrito group, a highly specialised race split off long ago from the Negro race. On the average they are below 1500 mm. in height, though otherwise well proportioned and graceful, with infantile features. They are dark-skinned, and have copper-coloured curly short hair growing in insulated tufts. They share this peculiarity with the Bushmen of South Africa who also belong to the Negrito race. Still another feature is common to both races: the women are often steatopygous, i.e., with a strong accumulation of fat on the buttocks. The Asiatic Negrito race is spread over a wide area of south-east Asia; it is found in Sumatra (Kubus), Malaya (Semangs and Sakais), in the Philippines (Aetas) and probably even in New Guinea (Tapiros). They lived long ago on Flores in the Sunda Islands of Indonesia, but have died out. Skeletons of this race were recently found.

The Andamanese came to their islands many centuries ago when the islands were probably still connected with Burma by land. Owing to their long isolation they are today one of the purest races of the world, with the least racial admixtures from outside. They also speak a language of their own which so far linguists have not been able to connect with any known language group.

Due to their existence on various isolated islands, the Andamanese, in spite of their small number, have split into several tribes* which have practically no contact with one another and do not intermarry. One group, the Jarawas, are implacably hostile and have so far rejected all friendly advances of the Indian settlers.

The necessity of marriage within a very small group has obviously resulted in the low fecundity of the Andamanese women, and the population is steadily decreasing. Another reason for the decrease is that the immigrants have brought new diseases to the islands against which the aboriginals have no resistance. Many succumb to tuberculosis and venereal diseases.

Economically, the Andaman islanders are very backward. They do not cultivate the soil, nor domesticate and breed any animals except the dog. They simply collect what a bountiful nature offers them in food, and do a little hunting and fishing. They thus still belong to the so-called foodgathering stage of culture.

Vegetable products growing wild, honey, the meat of pigs and turtle and fish are their staple food. They generally do not preserve any food; what they cannot eat themselves they share with friends and neighbours. They build canoes which they carve out of trees; they manufacture two kinds of bows, one of a peculiar flat S-like shape. The women are skilled basket makers. The art of pottery is unknown among them.

Their dress is of the scantiest; both men and women shave their heads with broken glass, and paint their bodies white. They have no sense of cleanliness.

The family life of the Andamanese is a happy one. Early marriage is the rule. Husband and wife are devoted to each other. Though divorce is permitted, many marriages are for life. While sex relations are permitted among the unmarried, this freedom ceases with marriage. Husband and wife are generally faithful to each other. They show great affection for their children. Unfortunately, births are rare and infantile mortality is high. This is probably the reason why children are often adopted by families without children and sometimes children change hands several

*These tribes are: the Chariar or Chari, Kora, Tabo or Bo, Yere, Kede, Bea, Balawa, Bojigiyab, Juwai, Jarawa, Kol, Onge and Sentinelese.

times. The elders instruct their children in all the activities essential for life. They even have so-called initiation ceremonies for both boys and girls; through these ceremonies the children pass from one age-group into the next higher one, and certain food taboos which they have to observe in the lower age groups are progressively lifted.

The religion of the Andamanese is not well known. At least one tribe, however, is known to have a supreme god who is called Puluga. The islanders say that though his appearance is like fire yet he is invisible. He was never born and is immortal. The world and all the objects in it, animate and inanimate, were made by him except the powers of evil. He has given man fire. He is omniscient while it is day, and he knows even the thoughts of the heart. Puluga is angered by the commission of certain sins, while to those in pain or distress he is full of pity. He is the judge from whom each soul receives sentence after death.

It appears, however, that this comparatively pure concept of god is not found among the tribes of the northern islands; there the high-god is confused with the monsoon-Puluga, meaning the 'rain-cloud'.

Besides Puluga, they believe in evil spirits residing either in the woods or in the sea. The sun is the wife of the moon, and the stars are their children. They feel much afraid during an eclipse of the sun or the moon.

They have a number of myths about the origin of the world, and of man and woman, their ancestors. They have even a belief in a deluge which cannot have come to them through missionaries, because they have never been visited by any.

On the whole, the Andamanese are a happy and carefree people, well adjusted to their environment which, however, has been seriously disturbed by the new settlers who are now taking over the islands.

In the Nicobar Islands there are two different races, the very primitive and reserved Shom Pens (71 in 1961) and the Nicobarese proper (13,903 in 1961). The origin of the Nicobarese as also of the Shom Pens is still controversial. Nor is it known when they settled on the islands. They have been isolated for centuries from outside cultural influences until modern times and thus developed a cultural identity of their own. In their racial appearance, ways of life, language, social organisation and economic pursuits they differ from the Andaman islanders as well as the people of Burma.

In general the Nicobarese have Mongoloid features though these are tempered by another racial strain. They are darker in complexion than the average Mongoloid, have less prominent cheek-bones, less straight hair, and more prominent noses. They are of medium height and strong build. They have scanty face and body hair. Their language seems to belong to the Austric or Mon-Khmer linguistic group. Six different dialects are in existence, as is natural when one considers the isolation of the various islands.

The Nicobarese live in large joint families which may include even distant relatives. Men and women enjoy equal rights. The joint family is controlled by its head, not always the eldest member of the family. He must be distinguished by age, character, intelligence, personality and leadership. A dying head of a family appoints his successor. If the new head proves himself incompetent, he is replaced by a worthier man. The members of a joint family, even if very numerous, usually eat together though they may live in separate huts. The Nicobarese are fond of children and the birth-rate is high.

Various such joint families form a village, controlled by a village headman. The headman enjoys wide powers and usually inherits his position from his father. If he is too autocratic or misbehaves he can be deposed by the community. He has one or two deputies or assistants who with other heads of the families form a village council.

Land is owned by the heads of the families. The Nicobarese practise shifting cultivation combined with garden and tree (coconut, areca) cultivation. Almost no cereals are grown. Their livestock consists of pigs which are very important and highly valued, poultry, cats and dogs. The Nicobarese supplement their livelihood by fishing. They build their own canoes, with outriggers. They are capable of making trips of forty to fifty miles on occasional visits to other islands. The Nicobarese are skilled artisans, housebuilders, carpenters, carvers and potters. They now wear readymade clothes purchased in the stores, while in former times the women wore grass skirts.

Their traditional religion was an animistic belief in many nature spirits of whom they lived in constant fear. They also had shamans and strongly believed in magic and witchcraft. Persons suspected of witchcraft were cruelly done to death by having all their bones broken. Now eighty per cent of the Nicobarese have been converted to Christianity (Church of India). The Christian faith was introduced by Indian missionaries from south India.

BIBLIOGRAPHY

Aiyappan, A.: *Social and Physical Anthropology of the Nayadis of Malabar*. Madras, 1937.

Dass, F. A. M.: *The Andaman Islands*. Bangalore, 1937.

Ehrenfels, U. R.: *Kadur of Cochin*. Madras, 1952.

Fürer-Haimendorf, C. von: *The Chenchu*. London, 1943.

Iyer, A. L. K.: *Cochin Tribes and Castes*. 2 vols., Madras, 1909–12.

————: *Travancore Tribes and Castes*. 2 vols., Trivandrum, 1937.

————: *Social History of Kerala*. Vol I: *The Pre-Dravidians*. Madras, 1968.

Luiz, A. A. D.: *Tribes of Kerala*. New Delhi, 1962.

Mathur, K. K.: *Nicobar Islands*. New Delhi, 1967.

Nanjundayya, H. V. and Iyer, A. L. K.: *Mysore Tribes and Castes*. 4 vols., Mysore, 1928–36.

Peter of Greece and Denmark: *A Study of Polyandry*. The Hague, 1963.

Radcliffe-Brown, A. R.: *The Andaman Islanders*. Cambridge, 1922.

Ragaviah, V.: *The Yanadis*. New Delhi, 1962.

Rivers, W. H. R.: *The Todas*. London, 1906.

Seligman, C. G. and B. Z.: *The Veddas*. Cambridge, 1911.

Spittel, R. L.: *Wild Ceylon*. Colombo, 1927.

————: *Vanished Trails*. Oxford University Press, 1950.

Subbarayan, V.: *Forgotten Sons of India*. Madras, 1948.

Thurston, E.: *The Castes and Tribes of South India*. 7 vols., Madras, 1909.

Whitehead, G.: *In the Nicobar Islands*. London, 1924.

CHAPTER VIII

Tribal Welfare in India

THE ABORIGINAL problem is very old. It was created by the first immigration of foreigners who invaded the homeland of the tribes and tried to displace them. Due to their superior culture they often succeeded. But there was plenty of empty space to which the tribals could escape and where they were left to lead their own life without interference. The first serious troubles started after the British occupation of India when the British administration began also to take control of the tribal areas. An unjust land settlement, moreover, gave non-tribals control over vast areas of tribal land. The result was a merciless exploitation of the tribals. When conditions became unbearable, the tribals staged uprisings against their exploiters which the British Government, in the name of peace and order, suppressed ruthlessly. Such uprisings took place in 1772 when the Mal Paharias rose, in 1831 with the mutiny of the Hos in Singbhum, with the Khond uprising in 1846, and the Santal rebellion in 1855. The British Indian Government was forced also to send punitive expeditions to Assam and Nagaland—in 1744 to the Jaintia hills, between 1850 and 1890 repeatedly to the Lushai hills, in 1878 to the Naga hills and in 1912 to the Abors.

The underlying causes were almost always the same: the deep dissatisfaction created among the tribal people as a result of exploitation by their culturally more advanced neighbours. The British Government finally decided on a policy of segregating the tribes into special areas where their lives and interests could be adequately protected. For this purpose on Act was passed in 1874 to specify tribal areas into 'Scheduled Districts'. These areas were reconstituted under Section 52A of the Government of India

Act of 1919, and finally in 1935 more stringent provisions for a special treatment of the tribal areas were incorporated by converting them into 'Totally and Partially Excluded Areas'. In the subsequent years and up to 1947 numerous Acts and Regulations were promulgated and various important reforms introduced [Cf. G. S. Ghurye (1959), pp. 70–97].

After independence, the Indian Constitution, adopted by the Constituent Assembly on 26 January 1950, visualised a policy of progressive acculturation of the tribal communities in India. Thus the former policy of their isolation and segregation was finally abandoned. To promote the desired integration of the tribals into the national life of India the Constitution provided special safeguards for the tribal population (along with the scheduled castes and other underprivileged communities) for a period of ten years. This period was extended in 1960.

These safeguards consisted of special facilities for the promotion of education among the tribals, such as scholarships, dispensations from school fees and special grants, reservation of seats in Government services and such elected bodies as the Parliament, State legislatures and Territorial Councils, and specified funds for organising tribal welfare in the States and Union Territories. The Constitution also provided for the preparation of schedules of those tribes and castes which were backward and thus eligible for these privileges. The tribes which were designated as 'scheduled' were listed in a Presidential Order of 1950 which was modified in 1956 by another Order. A second Presidential Order promulgated in 1950 listed certain areas which were considered backward and designated them as 'Scheduled and Tribal Areas'. Special efforts were to be made for their development.

A Tribal Welfare Department was instituted and launched in 1951. Its work was not intended to supplant, but rather to supplement, the general development programmes undertaken by the Government through such agencies as the National Extension Service and the Community Development Project.

The Five-Year Plans gave a great impetus to such welfare activities by making ample funds available for their implementation. Thus the First Five Year Plan provided Rs. 39 crores (390 millons) for tribal welfare, the Scond Plan allocated a total of Rs. 47 crores, and the Third Plan Rs. 61 crores for the same purpose.

For more concentrated welfare work foı the benefit of tribals the so-called 'Tribal Development Blocks' were created during the Second Five Year Plan. By the end of the Second Plan, 43 such Blocks were functioning. It was decided to start 450 new T.D. Blocks during the Third Five Year Plan, but by the end of 1964 only 163 new T.D. Blocks had been created. Welfare work in these Blocks could be greatly intensified and, in the judgement of the Commissioner for Tribal Welfare, bring gratifying results.

The welfare activities for the tribal people and their areas may be broadly divided into four categories, namely, educational, economic, health and housing, communications and other categories.

Education

Already during the period of the First Five Year Plan which provided Rs. 39 crores for meeting the special needs of the tribal population, a sum of Rs. 11 crores was allocated for the provision of educational facilities. By the end of the First Plan about 4,000 schools had been established in the tribal areas. (These included more than a thousand ashram schools, seva ashram schools, and about 650 sanskar kendras, balwadis, etc.). Attempts were made to impart education to the tribal youth in their regional languages, and primers were prepared in various tribal dialects. Emphasis was laid on vocational and technical training. Concessions were granted to tribal students in the form of free tuition, stipends, scholarships and the provision of books, hostel fees, stationery, and other equipment. In certain cases the aid extended to clothing and midday meals.

Economic Assistance

Various schemes to protect the economic interests of the tribal people have been started by all State Governments. A good deal of money has been spent on irrigation schemes, the reclamation of wasteland and its distribution among members of the scheduled tribes. In addition, facilities for the purchase of livestock, fertilisers, agricultural implements, better seeds, etc., were also provided. Some states have started demonstration farms for the training of tribal agriculturists in methods of scientific cultivation.

In some states small-scale experiments have been undertaken for evolving improved methods of shifting cultivation and for encouraging plough cultivation. In Assam, in particular, centres were set up where improved patterns of land utilisation could be demonstrated to the tribal people. These involved afforestation of hill-tops and slopes, the cultivation of new crops like coffee, cashew-nuts, etc., along the slopes, and soil conservation measures.

Cattle-breeding and poultry farming, as also pig-keeping, were encouraged among the tribal people. Certain states have also introduced cottage industries, subsidising them with loans, and opened training centres for handicrafts and small-scale industries.

In various states multipurpose cooperative societies for giving credit in cash and kind to the tribals have been established. A different type of cooperative society had to be created for the tribal forest labourers.

Legislation exists in almost all states to extend relief to indebted tribals. Measures for the abolition of debt bondage have been introduced in some states. Relief was granted by way of reduction on accumulated debts, and laws have been enacted for the protection of tribal landowners against any attempts at dispossessing them. Some states enacted tenancy laws to ensure security of land tenure to the tribals.

Medical Help and Hygiene

Vigorous measures were taken in most states to augment medical and public health facilities in the scheduled areas. One of the principal difficulties experienced in the tribal areas concerns the supply of clean drinking water. Already in the period of the First Plan, more than 10,000 wells were dug or repaired. In addition to the opening of 3,144 hospitals and dispensaries and mobile health units in the tribal areas, medical aid was given by way of free distribution of medicine, reservation of hospital beds, etc.

Other Welfare Schemes

Other welfare schemes included the grant of housing sites, free or at nominal cost, and assistance by way of loans, subsidies and grants-in-aid to local bodies for the construction of houses. Attention has been given to the improvement of the means of communications in tribal areas. In addition to their other road development programmes in the First Five Year Plan a sum of about Rs. 6.5 crores was spent on the construction of small approach roads, hill paths and bridges in the areas inhabited by the tribal people.

In order to gain a better knowledge of the aboriginals, their ways of thinking and living, their problems and difficulties, and to find better and more effective ways and means of helping them, research institutes were set up in various states for the study of the tribes and their environment. These research institutes were given the task of studying the following problems in particular: shifting cultivation, the relation of the new *panchayat* system to the former system of tribal justice and organisation, the incidence of diseases and epidemics, tribal dietary systems, sorcery and suicide, the desirability and practicability of replacing tribal drinking habits, the collection of literature on tribal culture heroes, local exploits, and moral values for the purpose of obtaining suitable material for primers and textbooks in the local languages.

This all too cursory description of the development programmes for the benefit of the tribal population of India, with their vast expenditures and comprehensive plans, proves convincingly that the Indian Government has taken effective steps to integrate the tribals into the national life and to extend to them all the benefits to which all citizens of India are entitled.

However, surveys of tribal welfare work, supported by statistics, show that the aborigines of India are not being integrated as effectively and completely into the national culture as intended by the Government and as warranted by the great number of workers engaged in tribal welfare work and the vast expenditures provided for this work. In fact, it has been alleged that the ample funds made available for tribal welfare work have not even been utilised fully. Thus five crores of the 19.83 crores provided in the First Five Year Plan were not utilised. In the Second Plan the shortfall was even more—ten crores. The non-use of financial provisions is particularly marked in the field of education. At the present rate of progress it will take at least fifty years more for the tribal people of India to catch up with the rest of the population as they are now. In the meanwhile, 'the rest' will progress further at an even faster rate during the next fifty years. Thus the gap between the tribals and the non-tribals will widen even more. This is a serious problem.

The reasons for the non-implementation of the various Government schemes for the benefit of the 'scheduled tribes' are many. The main reason which, however, is rarely mentioned in the report, is the fact that any tribal welfare work runs up against the vested interests of a powerful non-tribal population. Almost everywhere in India the tribal communities are surrounded by and live in more or less close symbiosis with non-tribals who supply certain indispensable commodities to them—but at a price. Sometimes the price which the tribals pay for these services is very high: economic exploitation, social degradation, and cultural subservience. Any cultural, social and economic improvement of the tribal peoples is consequently against the interests of these non-tribals dominating over and exploiting them. No wonder that they oppose, openly or secretly, any attempts at a large-scale tribal uplift. The authorities guiding the tribal welfare work are either not fully aware of this most powerful opposition to their programme or do not dare to expose it.

Another reason for the relative failure of the tribal welfare work is the relative haziness of the men directing the acculturation programme about the means and ways to achieve the integration of the tribals in the national life. Tribal welfare work has in practice turned out to be the endeavour of the welfare workers, political leaders and Government officials to 'uplift' the tribals and turn them into more prosperous, but drab, puritan and 'virtuous' Hindus. But the tribals do not find this ideal very attractive: it consists of too many prohibitions. They should not smoke, they should not drink, they should not eat meat, they should not dance, they should not enjoy sex. They should work all the time, and for whose benefit? It appears that the authorities in charge of tribal welfare work do not know the tribal mind sufficiently and feel, therefore, baffled by the tribals' passive resistance to welfare schemes planned with the best intentions and with a sincere desire to help.

Moreover, most of the social workers, the officials and political leaders who now so loudly profess that they have the welfare of the triblas at heart belong to the same class of people who in the past have been, and perhaps still are, their most ruthless and merciless exploiters and tyrants. Thus the tribals are wary of their advice, be it ever so sincere and well-intentioned, and offer passive, if not active, resistance to all welfare schemes set up by Government agencies. Their resistance may be stiffened by the tactless behaviour of some welfare workers who look down on the tribals with an air of superiority or ridicule their beliefs and customs.

It must also be admitted that not all workers employed in tribal welfare work are sincerely dedicated to their task. Many have taken on this job for want of a better and easier one. Nor are they always qualified for such work. Besides, living and working conditions in the tribal areas entail a lot of real hardships. It seems that the Tribal Welfare Department did not always take sufficient care that its personnel working in the tribal areas was properly housed and provided with special facilities for certain amenities in their unfamiliar, often unhealthy and isolated environment.

The Tribal Welfare Department has also largely failed to gain the goodwill of the tribal leaders and the willing cooperation of the tribal population for their uplift schemes. Too many of the workers employed are non-tribals, or detribalised individuals who often show an even greater intolerance and snobbery towards their tribal fellow than outsiders. The tribals have a pronounced self-respect and great love for freedom and independence and keenly resent any interference from outsiders.

The Commissioner for Scheduled Castes and Scheduled Tribes, in his report for 1958–59 [p. 135], lists additional reasons for the poor results of the welfare work planned and carried out by Government agencies.

An unfortunate fact is lack of coordination between the Tribal Welfare Department and other Government departments working in tribal areas. This often results in duplication of work and unnecessary and avoidable tensions and conflicts.

Frequently, the Tribal Welfare Programmes are ill-planned. Too many projects are taken up at the same time, and the planners are too impatient to wait for the results which mature slowly. There is a too frequent change of projects and policy, with the result that the officers and workers lose confidence and consistency, while the simple tribals get confused and demoralised. It would be more appropriate to take up only such projects for which funds and personnel are available and to complete them before taking up new ones. A list of priorities should be drawn up considering the needs of the various areas and the funds and personnel available for their implementation. The programmes should be arranged accordingly.

The Tribal Welfare and Development Programmes are frequently planned at too high a level and are too comprehensive. Directives are issued from the State Government headquarters without prior consultation with the local officers. Schemes are planned for the entire State without regard to the fact that local conditions vary much. Projects which suit conditions in one area are not necessarily feasible in other areas. It would be better to work out general lines of procedure, but leave the manner of achieving the targets to the local authorities.

Comparatively more effective welfare work is being done apparently by non-official agencies. Prominent among these are the Bharatiya Adim jati Sevak Sangh and various organisations affiliated to it, such as the Banwasi Seva Mandal, the Bhil Seva Mandal, etc. The Ramakrishna Mission is also doing some welfare work among the tribals. These organisations are liberally subsidised by the Government. They do a certain amount of good work, but their activities, too, are impaired by a lack of competent and idealisic workers, by lack of training and by misplaced zeal for rather conservative Hindu ideals of a puritanical type, such as vegetarianism and other food taboos, anti-alcoholism, and an intolerant attitude towards certain soical customs of the tribals, such as scanty dress, the enjoyment of dancing and great freedom in sex morals [NCAER (1963),pp. 83–7].

The welfare work carried out among tribal communities by Christian missionaries seems to have been much more successful and impressive. Especially in Chota Nagpur (Bihar) and in Assam it was organised on a grand scale. The missionaries do not seem to have had any scarcity of dedicated and highly trained personnel, and they were also able to gain the confidence and willing cooperation of the tribals. Their welfare work extended over all possible spheres of economic and educational uplift:* they have opened many schools and hostels, hospitals and dispensaries,

* In the Chota Nagpur area (Bihar) the Catholic missions alone managed in 1968 no less than 659 primary schools (with 73,483 pupils), 103 middle-schools, 40 high-schools, 2 colleges, 6 teachers' training schools, and 11 technical schools. They also supported and managed 16 orphanages, 8 hospitals, 40 dispensaries, 6 creches and 3 leper asylums. In the dispensaries 185,428 patients had been treated in 1968.

leper asylums, orphanages, and run almost the only cooperative banks that are functioning well.* The Christian missionaries have everywhere taken up the cause of the tribals and effectively helped them to get a better deal from the Government officials, landlords, contractors, money-lenders and merchants.

If purely humanitarian reasons were not strong enough for the Indian policy-makers to improve the lot of the tribals and to give them their full and equal rights as Indian citizens, the present political situation may finally force the authorities concerned to pay more attention to the needs of the tribals. The Chinese war has shown that the Indian boundaries towards Tibet are not at all safe if the tribals who inhabit the sub-Himalayan regions from Kashmir and Ladakh to Arunachal Pradesh are disaffected and not well integrated in the Indian nation. Compelling reasons of national security demand the utmost attention to the ambitions, demands and needs of the tribal population inhabiting the border regions. Only thus can any agitation and unrest stirred up by anti-national elements and foreign agencies be checked and a strong front created against any aggressors. The tribals, especially those in Assam, Nagaland and Arunachal Pradesh who are better educated and more alive to their own particular problems and ambitions and more articulate in their own demands, have become aware that they have a right to demand the preservation of their traditional culture and tribal identity. National integration should not demand from them complete assimilation by the majority community. A large degree of cultural and even political autonomy should be granted to these tribes if by it they can be pacified and kept attached to the Indian State. The political history of the last decades has also proved clearly that the large tribal pockets within the Indian sub-continent, especially in Bihar, Madhya Pradesh and Andhra Pradesh, can easily fall prey to the irresponsible agitation of communal and political parties and be roused to acts of violence. Again, the instability and liability of the tribal groups are simply symptoms of their deep dissatisfaction with their own economic, social and political conditions. Their legitimate aspirations must be fulfilled as quickly and as fully as possible.

*Cf. Report of the Commissioner for Scheduled Castes and Scheduled Tribes (1963–4), part 1, pp. 102–4.

On the other hand, it has also been alleged, and with good reasons, that the new dispensation of giving liberal assistance to the 'scheduled tribes' has caused much damage and degradation of their character. At least in Assam the tribal people had a strong spirit of self-help and self-reliance. They made and maintained village paths, constructed school, church and hospital buildings, wells, water tanks, playgrounds and did other works of public utility voluntarily without asking for any remuneration. These were community projects in the true sense of the word. The establishment of Development Blocks on a stereotyped all-India pattern without taking local conditions and the temper of the people into account and the liberal doling out of grants, loans and subsidies in the name of community development have now completely changed the picture. The people not only refuse to perform any of the tasks mentioned above without payment, but these doles have affected their attitudes to such an extent that they have stopped giving proper attention even to their paddy fields, knowing that, if the crops fail, free or at least subsidised rice would be made available by 'Government'. Extracting something out of 'Government' for nothing has in fact become a practice with them and it is looked upon as a creditable performance. These once sturdy, self-respecting and self-reliant people have thus been so demoralised and corrupted that they do not hesitate to resort to chicanery in order to obtain gifts which they look upon as graft for keeping them quiet and peaceable [S. Barkataki (1969), p. 14].

The Government of India must use all possible discretion to extend effective help to the tribals in such a manner that it does not demoralise them, but puts them on a sound basis for self help. Above all, a change of their mental attitude is required. They should no longer feel as strangers and separate communities in India but become fully integrated in the Indian nation as rightful citizens with equal rights and opportunities.

Index of Subjects

Aboriginal life, 74–6
Acculturation 50–3, 265, 288–97
Acrobats, 105, 115
Adamgarh, 2, 5, 7
Afghanistan, 9
Ahar, 15
Alpino-Dinaric race, 16
Ancestor worship, 154–5, 260–1
Andaman Islands, 132, 282, 283
Anglo-Indians, 36
Animal breeding, 50, 80, 81, 89–91
Animism, 63–5, 155, 229–30, 257–9
Anjira, 9
Anthropus crectus, 2
Arabs, 35
Art, 69–74
Artisans, 121–2, 159–60
Aryan languages, 28, 157
Aryans, 1, 18–20, 35
Australia, 27
Australopithecine, 2, 4
Austric languages, 36–7
Austro-Asiatic languages, 164

Baluchistan, 7, 11
Bamboo workers, 105, 118–19
Basket makers, 72, 97, 105, 119–21
Bene Israels, 36
Bengalis, 34, 201, 219
Bharatiya Adimjati Sevak Sangh, 295
Bhutan, 103, 199
Brahmin, 62, 131, 279
Brass smiths, 160
British, 48, 106, 122, 201, 205–6, 235
Buddhism, 81, 93, 96, 100
Burma, 197–8, 283
Burzahom, 9
Bushmen, 2, 283

Cane workers, 119, 199, 200
Caste, 60–3
Caucasus, 17
Chamar, 117
China, 10, 34, 197, 198
Cholas, 277
Christian missions, 69, 140, 143, 165, 235–6, 295–6
Criminal castes, 105, 122–3
Criminal tribes, 105, 122
Cultivators, 46–9, 135–7, 206–10, 272–5

Dance, 72–6
Dardic languages, 42
Denotified Caste, see: Criminal Castes
Diji, 9
Divination, 66–7
Divorce, 146, 213–14, 248, 284
Dom, 117, 118, 119, 129, 131
Dravidian languages, 18, 19, 28 42–3, 80, 174–5, 238
Drummers, 105

Earth-mother, 154
Economy, 135–9, 206–10, 238–43
Economic assistance for tribals, 290–1

Edith Shahr, 17
Education for tribals 139–40, 290
Ethics, 155–7, 230–2

Fishing, 201–2, 243
Foodgatherers, 44–6, 239–43

Ganges, 4, 7, 108, 110, 116–17, 125
Garo Hills, 11
Gondi, 31

Handicrafts, 50
Harappa, 9, 10, 11–14
Hastinapur, 19
Head-hunting, 233–6
High-god, 63–4, 153–4, 224–8
Hinduisation, 56, 60–3, 64, 67–8, 131–2, 140–1, 142–3, 146–7, 167, 256–7, 263–5
Hominisation, 2
Homo habilis, 4
Horse domestication, 21
Human sacrifice, 156, 229, 268–9
Huns, 35
Hunting, 102, 108, 120, 130, 138, 161, 168, 170, 192, 239, 243, 265, 266–7, 271, 276, 284

Indo-Aryan languages, 40
Indus Valley Civilisation, 9–14, 16
Industrialisation, 138
Iran, 17

Jat, 79, 106, 126, 129, 183
Jericho, 9
Jharkhand movement, 142
Jugglers, 105

Kalibangan, 9
Khandivli, 4
Khondi, 31
Kili Gaul Mohamed, 9
Kinship organisation, 146–8, 249–52
Knifegrinders, 105
Kolami, 31–2
Kurmi, 112
Kurukhi, 32

Ladakh, 87, 91
Land acquisition, 49–50
Langhanj, 8
Languages, Indian, 36–44
Levirate, 216–46
Literacy, 139–40
Lothal, 14

Madras Industry, 4, 238
Magic, 66–7, 155, 272
Malto, 32
Marriage, 144–7, 210–13, 243–9
Mat maker, 119–21
Matriarchy, 54–5, 210–13, 278
Matriliny, 54–5, 210–13, 244, 274
Medical help for tribals, 291
Megaliths, 16–18, 31–2, 198
Messianic movements, 143
Millstone makers, 105
Mimes, 105
Mithan, 207
Mohenjodaro, 11–14
Moghuls, 35
Moh-Khmer languages, 30, 33, 37, 163, 198
Mongoloids, 29, 33–5, 95
Munda languages, 36–7, 163–5
Mundari, 29, 109, 164
Mundigak, 9
Music, 72–3
Musicians, 105

Naga hills, 10, 27
Nagda, 15
Nahali language, 37
Naiki, 32
Narbada, 4, 6
Navda-toli, 15
Neanderthalers, 7
Negrito, 26, 33, 107, 129, 197, 283
Nepal, 95–103
Nevasa, 6
Nicobar Islands, 282, 285–7
Nomadic tribes, 105–33

Olduvai, 4
Ollari, 32
Ornaments, 70–1, 172

Oti cult, 262, 271

Painted Gray Ware, 19
Palaeolithic period, 1, 2
Parji, 32
Pathan, 20, 81–6
Pindari, 122
Pleistocene India, 3
Pluvial, 1
Poetry, 72
Political organisation, 58–60, 148–53, 218–24, 252–6
Politics, 141–2
Polyandry, 88, 91, 93, 100, 145, 247–8
Polytheism, 153–4
Prakrit, 41
Proto-Australoids, 27–33

Rajputs, 35, 96, 101, 106, 108, 111, 122, 123, 124, 129, 131, 168, 187–8
Ramapithecus, 2
Rana Ghundai, 9
Rebellions, tribal, 165, 288
Red and Blach Ware, 17
Religion, 63–9, 224–36, 256–63, 285–7
Robbery, 80, 85, 89, 117–18, 123–4, 127, 201, 203

Sakas, 35
Sanghao Cave, 6
Sanskrit, 41
Shamanism, 66–7, 155, 261–3
Shepherds, see: Animal breeding
Shifting cultivation, 45–7, 136–7, 206–10
Sind, 5, 7
Siah-damb, 9
Sikkim, 98, 102–4
Sino-Tibetan languages, 38–40
Siwalik hills, 2
Slavery, 87, 102, 206, 267
Soan, 3
Stone Age, 1, 4, 5
Sun worship, 170, 259–60

Telugu, 32
Thai-Chinese languages, 38
Theft, 109, 272
Thugs, 122
Tibet, 88, 204
Tibeto-Burman languages, 38, 94, 98, 99, 201
Totemism, 54–8, 169, 193, 215–17, 249–52
Tribe, definition of, 22–5
Tribal research centres, 139, 292
Tribal self-sufficiency, 23
Tripura, 199, 202, 206

Untouchability, 141, 267, 268
Uplift work, 138–9, 288–97

Vagrant castes, 114–16
Vargant tribes, 106–14

Walfare work for tribals, 139–40, 288–97
Witchcraft, 66, 155, 261–3, 287

Youth dormitory, 71, 94, 145–6, 222, 279

Index of Authors

Agrawal, D.P., 20
Aiyappan, A., 31, 76, 287
Allchin, B. and R., 3, 7, 10, 17, 20
Amir-Ali, H., 195
Anderson, K., 132
Archer, W.G., 195
Avery, J., 76
Ayyangar, A., 132

Baines, A., 76, 132, 185
Banerjee, N.R., 20
Bareja, J.D., 237
Barkataki, S., 76, 237
Basu, A., 12
Basu, P.C., 163
Bell, J., 158
Besseignet, P., 237
Bower, U.G., 237
Bhargava, B.S., 132
Bhowmick, P.K., 110, 132
Biswas, P.C., 195
Blunt, E.A.H., 132
Bonington, C.J., 132
Bose, N.K., 4, 6, 22, 76
Bowles, G.T., 163
Bradley-Birt, F.B., 195
Briggs G.W., 132
Burgmann, A., 30, 76
Burling, R., 237
Burrow, T., 20 , 76

Caldwell, R., 76
Chapekar, D.L.N., 195
Chatterjee, N.K., 20
Chatterji, S.K., 76
Clerk, J.D., 2, 20
Cooper, T.T., 237
Crooke, W., 132
Culshaw, W.J., 195

Dalton, E.T., 199, 205
Dani, A.H., 29, 163
Das, A.K., 132
Dass, F.A.M., 287
Datta, J.M., 11
Datta-Majumdar, N., 195
Dave, P.C., 195
De Terra, H., 3, 6, 21
Doshi, S.L., 195
Drew, Fr., 104
Dube, S.C., 158
Dunbar, G., 237
Dutta, P.C., 13, 21

Ehrenfels, U.R., 24, 287
Eickstedt, von E., 22, 26, 183, 186
Elwin, V., 76, 161, 176, 195, 237
Endle, S. 237
Enthoven, R.E., 195

Fairservis, W.A., 17
Ferreira, J.V., 58, 76
Fischer, E., 35
Forsyth, J., 195
Fuchs, S., 76, 128, 133, 157, 158, 195

Fürer-Haimendorf, von C., 17, 21, 195, 217, 237, 287

Gait, E., 237
Gaukovsky Yu. V., 104
Ghurye, G.S., 76, 196
Glatter, A., 195
Gordon, D.H., 21, 29, 31
Gorer, G., 104
Grierson, G.A., 76, 173, 195
Grigson, W.V., 195
Guha, B.S., 12, 16, 21, 22, 26, 27, 35, 77, 183
Gunthorpe, E.J., 133
Gupta, P., 13, 21
Gurdon, P.R.T., 237

Haddon, A.C., 163
Heine-Geldern, von R., 17, 20, 21, 30, 163
Hermanns, M., 98
Hevesy, von W., 30, 37
Hivale, S., 196
Hodson, T.C., 237
Hoffmann, J. and van Emelen, A., 77, 196
Hutton, J.H., 21, 27, 33, 77, 133, 197, 237

Iyer, A.L.K., 287

Joshi, R.V., 3, 7

Karan, P.P. and Jenkins, W.M., 104
Karve, I., 77, 196
Katiyar, T.S., 133
Khatri, A.P., 2, 21
Krishnaswamy, V.D.K., 3, 21
Kuiper, F.B.J., 37, 77

Lal, B.B., 3
Lawrence, W.R., 104, 133
Lokanathan, P.S., 196
Luiz, A.A.D., 287

MacBurney, C.B.M., 4, 21
Majumdar, D.N., 26, 133, 163
Malik, S.C., 2, 21
Marshall, J., 13
Mathur, K.K., 287
Mills, J.P., 237
Misra, S.C., 133

Naik, T.B., 23
Nanjundayya, H.V., 287
Nath, Y.V.S., 196

Orans, M., 196

Parry, N.E., 237
Patel, M.I., 77
Paterson, T.T., 3, 6, 21
Peter of Greece and Denmark, 287
Pfeffer, G., 133
Playfair, A., 237
Punekar, V.B., 196

Radcliffe-Brown, A.R., 287
Ragaviah, V., 287
Rahelia, S.P., 133
Randhawa, M.S., 104
Risley, H., 22, 77, 108, 169, 173, 183, 206
Rivers, W.H.R., 287
Robertson, G.S., 104
Roy, Sarat Chandra, 196
Russell, R.V. and Hiralal, 183, 196

Sankalia, H.D., 4, 7, 21
Sarkar, S.S., 26, 29, 77, 163
Save, K.J., 196
Schmidt, W., 30, 77
Seligman, C.G. and B.Z., 287
Sen, Dharani, 4, 21
Sengupta, S., 196
Shah, P.G., 133, 196
Shakespeare, J., 237
Shashi, S.C., 104
Shaw, W., 237
Sher Singh Sher, 125, 133
Spittel, R.L., 287
Shukla, B.K., 237
Sinha, K., 237
Smith, W.C., 237
Stack, E., 237

Subbarao, B., 21
Swinson, A., 104

Thomas, M.M. and Taylor, R.W., 77
Thompson, C.S., 30
Thurston, E., 287
Todd, K.R.V., 6
Turner, A.C., 133

Vakil, D.F., 133
Vidyarthi, L.P., 24, 77, 162, 196

Waterfield, H.G., 133
Weling, A.N., 196
Wheeler, M., 17
Whitehead, G., 287
Wood, R., 237

Zeuner, F.F., 4, 8, 21

Index of Tribes

Abor, 199, 200, 215, 220, 228
Adiyar, 243, 254, 257, 260, 275
Advichinchar, 242
Afghan, 83
Agaria, 159
Aheriya, 108
Ahir, 183
Ahom, 34, 205
Aka, 199, 214, 220
Allar, 242
Andamanese, 26, 40, 282–5
Andh, 182
Apa Tani, 199, 208, 215, 285
Arayar, 243, 255, 257, 285
Aranadar, 242, 250, 267
Asura, 164

Badaga, 279–82
Badi, 117
Bagata, 243
Bagdi, 112
Bahelia, 108
Bahurupiya, 116
Baiga, 153
Bajania, 116
Bajhangi, 102
Balti, 33, 90
Baluchi, 79–80
Band, 115
Banjara, 116
Bansphora, 119
Bantar, 120
Bargunda, 120–1
Basor, 119
Bauri, see: Bawariya
Bavuri, 107
Bawariya, 107–8
Bazigar, 117
Bediya, 112
Bhagat, see Band
Bhand, 116
Bhantu, 126–7
Bhar, 111
Bhatra (or Bhattra), 31, 178
Bhavaio, 116
Bhavod, 183
Bhil, 30, 61, 134, 186–8
Bhilala, 183
Bhotiya, 94–5
Bhuiya, 111, 169
Bhujel, 102
Bhula, see Bahelia
Bhumij, 167–8
Birjia, 162
Bodo, 34, 198, 199, 201, 215
Bondo, 174
Brahui, 180–1

Chak, 88
Chakma, 34, 206
Chapparband, 126
Chaupan, 89–90
Chenchu, 188, 242, 252, 272
Chepang, 100
Chero, 111, 168
Chingithar, 242, 246, 247, 253

Chitrali, 84
Chodri, 192

Dafali, 116
Dafla, 199, 207, 215, 220, 225
Damasia, 202
Dard, 20, 88
Dhanka, 189
Dharka, 110
Dhodia (or Dhundia), 190–1
Dhokra Kamar, 160
Dholi, 116
Dimasa, 209
Dosadh, 108
Dotiyal, 102
Dum, 20, 89, 118

Eravallar, 243, 253, 258, 275
Erukula (or Yerukula), 243, 272

Fakir coiner, 126

Gadaba, 31, 172
Gaddi, 91–2
Gadolya Lohar, 122
Galawan, 88
Galong, 199
Gamit (or Gamta), 189
Garo, 34, 199, 201, 208, 211–2, 213, 219, 225, 229, 231, 233, 236
Ghisara, 121
Gond, 31, 134, 158–9, 175–6
Gondhali, 116
Gopal, 118
Gujar, 34, 92, 183
Gurkha, 33, 95
Gurung, 33, 95

Habura, 125
Halba, 179–80
Hill Reddi, 181–2, 188
Ho, 29, 166, 198
Hrusso, see Aka

Idayar, 243
Irular, 242, 254, 273

Jatapu, 180–1
Juang, 160–1

Kabui, 227
Kabutara, 117
Kachari, 34, 199, 202, 225, 229
Kadar, 242, 259, 260, 267
Kader, 242
Kafir, 20, 86–7
Kaikadi, 32, 113, 243
Kalanadi, 243
Kamar, 158
Kamara, 102
Kanauras, see Kinner
Kanikkar, 243, 254, 275
Kanjar, 120
Karavashi, see: Mala Pulaya
Karimpalar, 243, 272
Katkari (or Kathodi), 192–3
Kattunayakar, 242, 255, 257, 269
Kavundar, 243
Khampa, 94
Kharia, 168
Kharwar, 167
Khasi, 31, 37, 197, 201, 209, 211, 212, 218, 225, 229, 233–4, 235
Khond (or Kondh) 31, 180–1
Khumra, 120, 121
Kinnara, see: Kinner
Kinner, 92–3
Koch, 205, 229
Kochuvelar, 242, 253
Kokna, 191
Kol, 167
Kolam, 31, 182
Kolgha (or Kolcha), 195
Kolhati, 117
Koli, 184
Konda Doar, 180
Kora, 162
Koragar, 242, 268
Korava, see Erukula
Korku, 37, 58, 98, 171–2
Korwa, 161
Kota, 243, 279, 281
Koya, 178–9
Kudubi, 242, 243, 255
Kuki, 202
Kundu Vadiar, 243

Kurichchiyar, 255, 277–8
Kuruba, 277
Kurukh, see Oraon
Kurumba, 22, 242, 256, 276–7, 282
Kuruvikkar, 242

Ladakhi, 35
Lahouli, 33, 93
Lakher, 203, 210, 228
Lalung, 34, 199, 201
Lamana, 243
Lasari, 79
Lepcha, 33, 102–3
Limbu, 33, 98
Lodha, 109–10
Lushai, 203, 209, 225, 227, 232, 236
Lyngnam, 198

Magar, 96–7
Mahali, 170–1
Mahtam, 109
Majhwar, 171
Mal-Paharia, 162
Mala, 123
Mala Arayar, 257, 261, 279
Mala Kudi, 274
Mala Malasar, 242, 255, 270
Mala Pandaram, 242–3, 255, 257, 268–9
Mala Panickkar, 243, 279
Mala Pulaya, 242
Mala Vedar, 243, 271
Mala Vettuvar, 243, 260, 275–6
Malayalar, 243, 274
Malakarrar, 242, 255, 258, 274
Malakkurava, 255, 276
Malchi, 81
Maler, 32, 112, 161–2
Mang-Garudi, 113
Mannar, 243, 257, 273
Mannewar, 31
Marati, 243, 278
Maria Gond, 31, 177
Mavilar, 243, 256, 276
Mazari, 79
Mech, 34, 199
Meithei 202, 203
Meo, 184–5
Miana, 136
Mikir, 199, 203, 215, 219
Mina, 183, 185–6
Minyong, 199, 200
Mirasi, 116
Miri, 34, 199, 200, 207
Mishmi, 199, 200
Mizo, see: Lushai
Mog, 34
Moger, 243
Moghiya, 199
Monpa, 199, 207
Mudugar, 243, 279
Muduvan (or Muthuvan), 199, 256, 257, 278–9
Munda, 28–9, 110, 111, 164–5, 198
Muria, 31, 177
Murmi, 32

Naga tribes, 34, 204
Nagarchi, 116
Nagesia, 175
Nahal, 63, 159
Naikda, 190
Nat, 117–18
Nayadi, 243, 259
Nayak, 190
Newar, 99
Nicobar Islanders, 31, 37, 198

Ojha, 159
Oraon, 32, 174–5

Padam, see: Abor
Pahira, 171
Palliyar, 243, 266
Pangwal, 93
Paravar, 243
Pardhan, 158
Pardhi, 112
Parhaiya, see: Pahira
Parja, 32
Pasi, 108
Pathan, 78, 81–3
Patelia, 187
Patlyar, 243
Patua, see: Juang
Pauri, 169

Pawi, 203
Pentia, 160
Poroja, 172, 181
Powindah, 84–5
Poya, see: Parji

Qalander, 116

Rabari, 183
Rabha, 34, 199, 201, 207
Rai, 98
Raj-bansi, 205
Rajwar, 110, 111
Riang, 206
Rind, 79
Rongpa, 33

Sahariya, 109
Saiqulgar, see: Shikligar
Sanaurhiya, 128–9
Sansi, 123–4
Santal, 28, 170
Sapera, 117
Savara, 113, 172–3
Shan, 205
Sherdukpen, 208
Sherpa, 99
Shikligar, 121
Sholaga, 243, 266
Singpho, 206
Sunwar, 97
Synteng, 33, 197, 211, 212

Takari, 121
Tamang, 96
Thachanadar, 243, 256
Thai, 34
Thakali, 97
Thakur, 194
Tharu, 99–100
Thori, 120
Tipperahs, 34
Toda, 243, 297-81
Turaiha, 117
Turi, 110, 169

Ulladar (or Ullathan), 243, 256, 258, 271
Urali, 257, 260, 260, 263, 271
Urali Kurmar, 243, 261
Uridaran Gowdalu, 243

Valar, 243
Vedda, 27, 246
Vettuvar, 243
Vishvar, 243, 254
Vitolia, 194

Waghri, 128–9
War, 197
Warli, 194

Yanadi, 272
Yolmo, 100